D0565191

Create a home page quickly with Adobe PageMill. **Page 64**

Discover the meaning of FLAs (Four Letter Acronyms) like ISDN and ADSL. **Page 128**

Find out what the heck all those ports are for. **Page 110**

Cheat and beat Nanosaur. **Page 27**

Create killer letterheads in AppleWorks/ClarisWorks. **Page 3**

Generate cool, customized certificates for any occasion. **Page 10**

Make a custom greeting card quickly and easily. **Page 13**

Learn Quicken tricks to help you with your finances. **Page 15**

Customize your Excite start page and make it truly useful. **Page 41**

Use the EdView Internet Safety Kit to keep your kids safe. **Page 60**

Manage a small busines with Quicken. **Page 85**

Learn everything you need to know about memory (RAM). **Page 131**

Control your computer using your voice. **Page 140**

Make your monitor look better. **Page 152**

Create and install your own desktop backgrounds and pictures. **Page 161**

Eliminate pesky extension and control panel conflicts. **Page 179**

iMac™!
(and iBook™)

I Didn't Know You Could Do That...™

Bob LeVitus

SYBEX®

San Francisco • Paris • Düsseldorf • Soest • London

Associate Publishers: Gary Masters, Roger Stewart
Contracts and Licensing Manager: Kristine O'Callaghan
Acquisitions & Developmental Editors: Tracy Brown, Ellen Dendy
Editor: Linda Recktenwald
Project Editors: Julie Sakaue, Chad Mack
Technical Editor: Rima Regas
Book Designers: Franz Baumhackl, Kate Kaminski
Graphic Illustrator: Tony Jonick
Electronic Publishing Specialist: Maureen Forys, Happenstance Type-O-Rama
Project Team Leader: Lisa Reardon
Proofreader: Nancy Riddiough
Indexer: Matthew Spence
Companion CD: Ginger Warner
Cover Designer: Daniel Ziegler
Cover and Chapter Photographs: PhotoDisc

SYBEX is a registered trademark of SYBEX Inc.

IDKYCDT and I Didn't Know You Could Do That… are trademarks of SYBEX Inc.

Screen reproductions produced with Collage Complete.
Collage Complete is a trademark of Inner Media Inc.

Digital imagery® copyright 1999 PhotoDisc, Inc.

TRADEMARKS: SYBEX has attempted throughout this book to distinguish proprietary trademarks from descriptive terms by following the capitalization style used by the manufacturer.

Library of Congress Card Number:
ISBN: 0-7821-2589-1

Manufactured in the United States of America

10 9 8 7 6 5 4 3 2

Software License Agreement: Terms and Conditions

Acknowledgments

First and foremost, thanks to my family and pets—Lisa, Allison, Jacob, Sadie, Rosie, Duncan, Jobe, and Longhorn—for putting up with lengthier-than-normal absences as I wrote this book. I love you, I missed you, and now that this book is done, I hope to be seeing more of you.

Thanks also to Deborah Shadovitz for templates and advice, and C.B. Mac-Manus for advice, shareware picks, and inspiration.

I'd be remiss if I didn't also thank my agent, Carole "Swifty" McClendon and Waterside Production, for another project completed. This is number 32 you know....

Thanks to everyone at SYBEX—Tracy Brown, Ellen Dendy, Julie Sakaue, Chad Mack, Linda Recktenwald, Rima Regas, Maureen Forys, Lisa Reardon, and Matthew Spence—for making the process nearly painless.

And last but not least, thanks to you for buying a copy.

Table of Contents

Introduction . . . . *xv*

GET THE MOST OUT OF STUFF YOU HAVE 1

1 Letterhead Just Like the Pros 3

2 In Living Color(ing Book) 7

3 Certified Certificates 10

4 Instant Card 13

5 Quicken: It's Not Just for Checkbook
Management Anymore 15

6 AOL: It's Not As Bad as You Think 22

7 Nanosaur Play Action Guide 27

8 Sounds Good to Me: Recording Sound with
Your iMac or iBook 30

9 Improve Scans and Digital Photos with
Kai's Photo Soap SE 34

YOUR iMAC OR iBOOK AND THE WEB 39

10 Your Dream Start Page 41

11 Seeing the Sites 46

12 Buy It on the Net 50

13 Getting the Most out of Sherlock 55

14 Safety First on the Internet: Using the EdView
Internet Safety Kit 60

15 Home Sweet Web Page with Adobe PageMill 64

16 Publish or Perish on the Web 71

17 Fixing Pix for E-mail 74

SOHO: THE SMALL OFFICE/HOME OFFICE iMAC OR iBOOK **79**

18 Just the Fax, Ma'am 80

19 Quicken Can Manage Your Business (Maybe) 85

20 Getting Along with the Aliens 90

21 Organize This 95

22 Windows on Your iMac or iBook 104

YOU CAN DO IT, BUT IT'LL COST YOU **109**

23 Ports in a Storm 110

24 Getting Your Stuff from an Old Mac to an iMac or iBook 118

25 Making Memories with Your iMac or iBook 121

26 Backup/Storage Solutions for Your iMac or iBook 125

27 ISDN, ADSL, and Cable Modems: Fast Alternatives to Your Built-in Modem 128

28 Memory Is Made of This 131

29 What to Do about Your Legacy Hardware 135

MORE COOL STUFF YOU CAN DO WITH AN iMAC OR iBOOK **139**

30 How to Talk to Your iMac or iBook 140

31 How to Get Your iMac or iBook to Talk to You 145

32 Turn Your iMac or iBook into a Virtual Sony PlayStation 146

33 How to Make Most CD-ROMs Run Significantly Faster 150

34 Tune Up Your Monitor 152

FUN AND SILLINESS **157**

35 Discovering iMac and iBook Easter Eggs 158

36 How to Create and Install Desktop Background Pictures. 161

37 Icon Mania: Make Your Own Icons 166

38 Making Music Come Out of Your iMac or iBook 170

THINGS TO KEEP YOUR iMAC OR iBOOK
RUNNING STRONG. **173**

39 When Bad Things Happen to Good iMacs or iBooks. 174

40 How to Resolve Those Vexing Extension and
   Control Panel Conflicts. 179

41 How to Keep Your iMac or iBook Running Strong 186

42 How to Survive Tech Support 191

43 Getting Organized with Your iMac or iBook 194

44 Back Up, Back Up, and Back Up! 200

SOFTWARE ON THE CD-ROM **207**

UTILITIES **211**

45 ACTION GoMac 212

46 ACTION Files. 215

47 Aladdin DropStuff. 218

48 Aladdin Expander (a.k.a. StuffIt Expander) 220

49 CatFinder 222

50 CMTools 224

51 Conflict Catcher 8 Demo 226

52 CopyPaste 229

53 Default Folder 232

54 Desktop Resetter 235

55 DiskTracker 236

56 Drag'nBack 239

57 EZNote 241

58 File Buddy 243

59 FinderPop 248

60 HelpLess 250

61 QuicKeys Demo 252

62 Snitch 255

63 T-Minus Ten 257

64 TechTool 259

65 TypeIt4Me 262

66 ZipIt 265

GRAPHICS **267**

67 GraphicConverter 268

68 Icon Tools 271

69 Kaleidoscope 273

70 Planet Earth 276

AUDIO AND SOUND **279**

71 Agent Audio 280

72 MacAMP Lite 283

73 SoundMachine 285

WEB AND ONLINE STUFF **287**

74 Banish AOL Involuntary Disconnects with
AlwaysONline 288

75 Downloads by the Batch: Now or Later with
Download Deputy 290

76 ircle Is "the" Chat Client for IRC 292

77 Clean Up Text with textSOAP 295

78 URL Manager Pro Lets You Manage Your URLs Better . . . 297

BUSINESS-LIKE THINGS **299**

79 Simple and Swift: Address Book 300

80 The Text Editor of Champions: BBEdit Lite 303

81 Consultant: Organize Your Life and Much More 307

82 Idea Keeper: The Idea Processor 313

83 ReminderPro: So You Never Forget Anything Again! 315

84 Tex-Edit Plus: More Than a Mere Text Editor 319

GAMES AND GAME DEMOS **325**

85 3D Klondike: Solitaire with a Sense of Humor 326

86 Alan's Euchre: Like Bridge with a Computerized
Partner and Opponents 329

87 Bubble Trouble: Addictive, Silly, Cartoony Arcade Game . . . 332

88 MacChess: You Versus Your iMac 335

89 Myth II: Soulblighter—Perhaps the
Best Mac Game Ever. 337

90 Pac the Man: It's PacMan for the Mac! 341

91 Slithereens 343

92 Tomb Raider II 346

MORE COOL STUFF **349**

93 Bartender's Friend: Drink Database with a Twist 350

94 Relax: Sit Back and Listen to the Birdies 352

95 Uli's Moose: The Stupidest Mac Trick of All Time
Is BACK! 353

96 UpdateAgent Online: Keep Your Mac OS Software
Up To Date 356

97 USB Overdrive: Use Any USB Device! 359

98 It's a Beep Sound Randomizer—YO! 361

Index *363*

Introduction

I love the iMac. Of course, it's a well-known fact that I just plain love Macs. But I really love the iMac. It's the first Mac in a long time that I've felt really good about recommending to the non-techie user—like my in-laws, my father, my brother Andy, and my cousin Nancy. All of them wanted a computer that was easy to set up, easy to use, and easy to connect to the Internet. All of them adore their iMacs. But they're always saying thing to me like, "But what else can I do with it?"

This book is the answer.

Why Me?

But before I get to talking about the book and why I think you'll enjoy reading it and using the software on the companion CD-ROM, let me tell you a bit about myself and what qualifies me as an expert on things Macintosh….

This is my 32nd computer book. Others I've written lately include, *Mac OS 9 For Dummies* for IDG Books, *Mac Answers: Certified Tech Support* for Osborne/McGraw Hill, and *Macworld Office 98 Bible* from IDG Books. My books have sold more than a million copies worldwide. Most of them have been exclusively about the Mac.

I am also the Mac columnist for the *Houston Chronicle* and the *Austin Amercian-Statesman* and write a weekly question and answer column for MacCentral (`http://www.maccentral.com`). In the past, I've been published in more than two dozen computer magazines.

If that's not enough, I've spoken at more than 200 seminars in the USA and abroad, presented keynote addresses in three countries, and produced a series of Macintosh training seminars in five cities. (I also won the Macworld Expo MacJeopardy World Championship three times before retiring my crown, undefeated.)

So that's my story and I'm sticking to it. I'm a Mac guy through and through. I would venture to say that I have forgotten more about Macs than most people know.

The point is, I know a lot about the Mac and this book is my way of sharing some of that knowledge with y'all.

How This Book Came to Be

As far as how this book came about, when the iMac came out, it got me to thinking, "I've got to write a book for iMac users." But then I got busy with another book project and forgot all about it. Before I knew it, there were ten books out for iMac users. They were all good books, too, but they were all the same book. It seemed that every iMac book I've seen is aimed at the same reader—the first-time Mac user!

Which made me wonder, "Why not a book for the iMac user who already knows how to use a Mac? For the iMac user who wants to explore what *else* their wonderful machine can do." Forget teaching them how to double-click; instead, teach them how to use AppleWorks better. Or how to make CDs run faster. Or the things you need to do to keep your iMac running strong and trouble-free.

This is that book.

From getting the most out of the bundled software you got with your iMac (or iBook—more on iBooks in a second…), to using the Web better and smarter, to running a home-based business, to talking to your iMac and having it talk back to you, I've tried to include something for everyone.

And I've collected nearly 70 of the best shareware, freeware, and commercial demo programs I know of, all of which I think you'll find useful, interesting, fun, or all three.

In a nutshell, if you know enough about your iMac or iBook to launch programs and use menus, you know enough to have a great time with this book.

NOTE By the way, the essays are not presented in any particular order; feel free to jump around the book reading the essays that interest you most.

About the iBook

In July 1999, this book was nearly complete. But then Steve Jobs introduced the iBook to the world at Macworld Expo in New York. He called it "iMac to go." And explained how it is really just a portable iMac.

Which got us (Sybex and me) to thinking. (I seem to do a lot of that, don't I?) The book was almost done. The software had all been selected. Was there any reason not to make this an "iMac and iBook" book instead of just an "iMac" book?

Well, there was just one—actual iBooks won't be available for about a month. So although I played with one for more than an hour at Macworld Expo, I don't have one here now.

Which means that I haven't actually tested any of the stuff in this book on an iBook. (Heck, I'm not even sure where the ports are on an iBook!) So I have to issue this proviso: I believe, with the iBook being so similar to the iMac, that everything in this book will work as shown on an iBook. But I can't promise anything as I don't actually have an iBook handy and probably won't until this book is on the shelves. So if you have an iBook and something doesn't work the way you think it should, please send me e-mail and let me know so I can correct it in future editions. My e-mail address is boblevitus@boblevitus.com.

NOTE Heck, feel free to send me e-mail even if it works perfectly. I'm always interested in hearing how you liked my work, and I'd love to know if you have suggestions for making future editions of this book better. Thanks!

Still, we didn't feel my lack of an actual iBook was a good enough reason to exclude iBook users from enjoying this tome. Which is why it's an "iMac and iBook" book now and not just an "iMac" book.

Conventions Used in This Book

This is the obligatory part where I tell you about the way things are presented in the book. For example:

When I want you to choose an item from a menu, I'll say:

Choose File ➤ New.

In plain English, that means, "Pull down the File menu and choose the item called New."

Keyboard shortcuts appear in parentheses after their menu item. Like this:

Help ➢ Quicken Help (Command+?).

In plain English, that means, "Pull down the Help menu and choose the item called Quicken Help or use the keyboard shortcut Command+?."

To use the keyboard shortcut, of course, hold down the appropriate modifier key (the Command key in the example above), then press the indicated key (the ? in the example above).

Step-by-step instructions appear in numbered lists. Like this:

1. Choose File ➢ New.

2. Click the Use Assistant or Stationery button.

3. Choose All Stationery from the pop-up Category menu.

4. Choose your template from the list, and click OK.

Follow instructions like these by completing each step in order.

When I want you to click a button on the screen, the button name will be capitalized. Like this:

Click Print Merge.

Notes from the author appear beside the banana icon. Like this:

NOTE This is an author note.

Finally, warnings about anything even remotely dangerous appear beside the banana peel icon. Like this:

WARNING This is a warning.

So there you have it—everything you need to know to use this book effectively and efficiently. What are you waiting for? Go ahead and turn the page!

Get the Most out of Stuff You Have

Part of the allure of the iMac and iBook is the tasty bundle of software that comes with each and every one of them. You all have AppleWorks. You all have Quicken. You all have AOL, Kai's Photo Soap, and Nanosaur. But are you using them to their fullest potential? Just because they're free doesn't mean they're not incredibly useful.

NOTE Actually, most of the original blue iMacs came with ClarisWorks rather than AppleWorks. But AppleWorks and ClarisWorks are just the same program with different names. I'm going to refer to it as AppleWorks from now on, 'cause that's its most current moniker.

So let's take a look at the stuff you have and see if we can make it more useful to you, or at least more fun.

Letterhead Just Like the Pros   Shows you how to create high-quality letterhead with AppleWorks and even includes a nifty template.

In Living Color(ing Book)   Contains instructions for using the included template and macro so that you can create literally thousands of cool coloring book pictures.

Certified Certificates   Shows you how to create a certificate of appreciation automatically, customized for one person or a thousand, with a handy mail merge template.

Instant Card   Is just what it sounds like—a cute, clever template for creating cards for any occasion almost instantly.

Quicken: It's Not Just for Checkbook Management Anymore   Gives tips and hints for keeping your house or small business in order and saving time and money, too!

AOL: It's Not As Bad As You Think   Shows you some cool stuff about America Online that you might not already know.

Nanosaur Play Action Guide   Shows you the ins and outs of the iMac and iBook's nifty bundled game plus how to cheat and win.

Sounds Good To Me: Recording Sound with Your iMac or iBook Shows you how to use your iMac or iBook to record your voice and other stuff.

Improve Scans and Digital Photos with Kai's Photo Soap SE Gives a quick glimpse at this fantastic tool for making scanned and digital photos look better.

1 Letterhead Just Like the Pros

I really like AppleWorks. It's a great program for most people, most of the time; it's fast, easy to use, and incredibly powerful. This part contains several AppleWorks essays, but this particular one is about creating letterhead that looks really professional.

NOTE I'd like to thank my friend Deb Shadovitz for creating most of the templates for this chapter.

Making Deb's Letterhead Template Your Own

Let's get started. Open the file entitled Deb's Letterhead Template (in the Templates folder on this book's companion CD-ROM) and follow along. Once you get the hang of it, you'll be able to create your own letterhead from scratch.

NOTE The official name for AppleWorks templates is *stationery*. But they'll always be templates to me. I use the two words interchangeably.

The letterhead you create using Deb's Letterhead Template prints your name and address on the first page, but not on subsequent pages. It also numbers your pages at the bottom of the page. If you have three pages, it will say page 1 of 3 or page 2 of 3. If your document grows or shrinks, this dynamic numbering will reflect the total page count.

Here's a quick lesson on customizing Deb's Letterhead Template:

1. Select the words "Type your name" at the top, then type your name.

2. Select the text in quotes and type the pertinent information for each text block.

3. Click each text block in the top header once to select it as an object, then choose a font for it.

4. Select the page number at the bottom of the page, and choose a font for it.

5. Resize each text block in the top header to allow your text to fit.

6. Add or delete the visible returns in the top section to size the length of the section to just fit your letterhead information.

7. Make sure you don't delete the section marker shown in Figure 1.1. This is what allows you to have subsequent pages that don't carry the name and address blocks.

FIGURE 1.1 Don't delete the section marker highlighted by the gray circle, or else the stuff in the top header will appear on every page instead of just the first one.

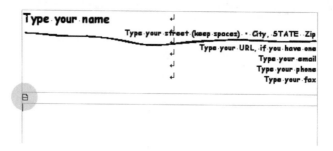

8. Choose File ➤ Save As, then click the Stationery button. Name your stationery, then click Save.

AppleWorks will automatically save the file in its AppleWorks Stationery folder. This is where you want it. Then, to use it in the future, follow these steps:

1. Choose File ➤ New.

2. Click the Use Assistant or Stationery button.

3. Choose All Stationery from the pop-up Category menu.

4. Choose your template from the list, and click OK.

NOTE There are a lot of templates in the list. You can find yours quickly by typing the first two or three letters of its name. The list will automatically jump to your template (or one near it). Open the AppleWorks Stationery folder, make an alias of this file, and put it either on your desktop or in your Apple menu. Then you can create new letterhead (by opening this alias) any time you like.

Other Stuff You Can Do to Your Letterhead Template

There's much more you can do before you declare your personalized letter-head template finished. For example, if you don't like Deb's squiggly line, don't forget that AppleWorks comes with a number of picture libraries. Choose File ➤ Library to choose a library, select a different image, then drag it onto your letterhead. This is your personal stationery—enjoy it! See Figure 1.2 for an example of what you can do with this template just by changing the picture and the font.

FIGURE 1.2 **This is my attempt at decent-looking letterhead.**

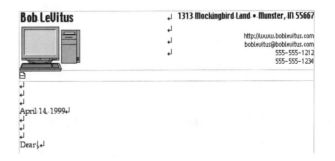

N O T E When you're looking at a library, choose By Object in the library windoid's View menu. This will let you see more than one library item at a time, which is handy for browsing.

If you prefer this design, it is also on the companion CD as Bob's Letterhead Template.

Change the Shape and Order of Things

Don't forget, you can, of course, change the shape and order of the information in the top header. Try moving everything to the right side or to the left side. Or, if you're really bold, try moving some of it to the bottom of the page!

Add a Live Date

You might want to add a live date, which automatically types the particular date on which you're working into new documents you create with this template. Here's how:

1. Make sure the cursor is in the body text area of the template, then press Return two or three times.

2. Choose Edit ➤ Insert Date.

3. Press Command+A to select all, then choose the font you want for the body of the letter (and the date).

4. Choose Edit ➤ Preferences, and then choose Text from the Topic menu.

5. Choose the date format you prefer.

6. Choose File ➤ Save As, then click the Stationery button. Name your stationery, then click Save.

The next time you use your template, the correct date will appear at the top of the body text area. (There is a live date in Bob's Letterhead Template; you can see it in Figure 1.2.)

Make It Merge with a Database Document

Did you ever want to send the same letter to a lot of different people, but personalize it so it said "Dear John" and "Dear Mary" instead of "Dear To Whom It May Concern?" AppleWorks makes this a piece of cake.

You can merge information from a database into this letterhead. The specifics are beyond the purview of this essay, but it's pretty easy.

NOTE If you're interested, open AppleWorks Help and search for Mail Merge. This tutorial offers good instructions for adding mail merge codes to this (or any) template. Also, take a look at the Certified Certificates essay later in this part and its associated templates for an example of what you can do with mail merge.

2 In Living Color(ing Book)

Here's another cool AppleWorks deal created by Deb. As you probably know, AppleWorks includes a library of thousands of graphics. Deb has created a template and macro that strips the colors out of them so you can colorize them yourself with crayons, markers, or whatever. You can also paint them in AppleWorks or import them into another painting program, such as KidPix, and colorize them there.

It's a nifty little hack, and if you have kids, it will provide them with hours and hours of fun. However, the template and macro also have a more serious use: You can use them to convert color clip art (you have a huge library of the stuff) to black and white line art for purposes other than coloring. For example, if you have a monochrome (black and white) printer, you might want to "decolorize" one of the pieces of clip art to use in your black and white letterhead.

How to Create a Coloring Book Page

Find the document entitled Deb's Coloring Book Template (in the Templates folder on your CD-ROM) and follow along.

1. Launch Deb's Coloring Book Template. A blank, untitled Drawing document will appear.

2. Choose File ➤ Library to open libraries that interest you.

NOTE   The libraries are where you'll find the clip art included with Apple-Works. There are more than two dozen separate libraries, offering many kinds of graphic images. If you've never explored them, take a look now—the collection contains many useful graphics. (And I don't just mean useful for making coloring book pages!)

3. Drag a picture (or more than one picture if you like) from the library onto the document.

4. Enlarge the picture(s) to approximately coloring book size.

5. Run the macro by choosing File ➤ Macros ➤ Play Macro. When the Play Macro dialog box appears, select the Make Coloring Book macro (it's probably already selected), and press Play, as shown in Figure 2.1

6. Save your document, then print it. Your decolorized picture will like the one in Figure 2.2.

FIGURE 2.1   Just click the Play button...

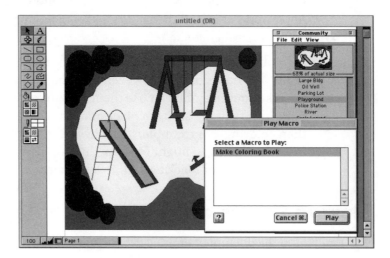

FIGURE 2.2   ...And just like that, the colored playground will become a coloring book page.

Coloring Your Pictures On-Screen with AppleWorks

As much fun as crayons, markers, and paints may be, there are times when painting with the computer is preferable. In times like that, follow these instructions:

1. Choose Edit ➤ Select All (Command+A).

2. Choose Edit ➤ Copy (Command+C).

3. Choose File ➤ New (Command+N), and create a new Painting document.

4. Choose Edit ➤ Paste (Command+V).

5. Use AppleWorks' paint bucket and brushes to colorize your picture to your heart's content.

NOTE   The reason you have to perform this procedure is that a Drawing document is different from a Painting document. So, you have to convert your Drawing document into a Painting document. Only then will you be able to use the paint bucket and brushes on it. AppleWorks Help has a lot more information on the differences between Drawing and Painting if you're interested.

Using Your AppleWorks Pictures in Kid Pix (or Another Program)

There may be times when you would prefer to work on an AppleWorks picture using a program other than AppleWorks. If that's the case, follow these instructions:

1. Choose File ➤ Save As.

2. Choose PICT from the pop-up Save As menu.

3. Save the document.

You will now be able to use your coloring book picture in KidPix and other paint programs.

3 Certified Certificates

I coach soccer and baseball, so I often have to come up with inexpensive morale boosters for my team. Nothing does the trick better (and cheaper) than a personalized certificate created in AppleWorks. I can knock out a dozen certificates in about 10 minutes, and, let me tell you, the kids love them. They put them on their bulletin boards and cherish them for years.

Even if you don't coach a sport or even play one, you'll be able to find a use for an award-type certificate whether it's for your Employee of the Month, Salesperson of the Year, or someone else who deserves to be recognized.

Making certificates relies upon AppleWorks' mail merge feature, and if you use the files I've provided (or even if you don't), it's a piece of cake.

How to Be a Certificate-Maker

Find the documents entitled Bob's Certificate Database and Bob's Certificate Template (in the Templates folder on your CD-ROM), and follow along.

1. Open Bob's Certificate Database and Bob's Certificate Template.

2. Choose Bob's Certificate Template from the Window menu to bring it to the front.

3. Choose File ➤ Save to name and save the file to your hard disk.

4. Modify the certificate's text to suit your needs. Surely, you can think of something more creative than "for outstanding performance." And don't forget to put your name or your company or team name where it says "Your Organization Name Here." Once you're satisfied with the certificate, save it again.

5. Choose Bob's Certificate Database from the Window menu to bring it to the front.

6. Choose File ➤ Save to name and save it to your hard disk.

7. Fill in the blanks (i.e., create a database record) for the first certificate recipient.

NOTE For the purposes of this demonstration, I used only the Name field. I added the other fields for your convenience, in case you want to use this database template for something other than certificates. The only field you need to complete for this exercise is the Name field. You can ignore all the other fields for the duration of this essay.

8. Choose Edit ➤ New Record, and create a database record for each certificate recipient. When you've added a record for every recipient, save it to your hard disk again.

9. Choose Bob's Certificate Template from the Window menu to bring it to the front. Now, you're ready to print.

10. Choose File ➤ Mail Merge. A mini-dialog box will appear. Select the Show Field Data checkbox if you want to see the name appear in the certificate, as shown in Figure 3.1 (otherwise, you'll see the merge field identifier, <<Name>>).

11. Click Print Merge. A standard Print dialog box will appear. Click Print.

That's it. Sit back and watch the personalized certificates pile up. You'll make someone (or a bunch of someones) very happy.

I've created a fairly generic certificate of appreciation and included it on the CD-ROM, but don't let your imagination stop there. You can use the same template to make a Most Valuable Player, a Salesperson of the Year, or a Good Sportsmanship award or just about any other type of award. And don't feel limited to my trophy artwork. AppleWorks has lots of appropriate art for certificates and awards in its libraries. (That's where I found the trophies.) Go wild!

FIGURE 3.1   The final step: Press Print Merge (then Print in the Print dialog box), and the certificates will pile up in your paper tray like magic.

hereby wishes to express
its sincere appreciation to

Bob "First name in the database" LeVitus

Other Stuff You Can Do with the Certificate Template

Most good stationery stores carry very cool specialty paper for printing awards and certificates. Most of these specialized paper sheets have a classy border and are printed on high-quality stock. They really look nice. I've bought some with a sports theme and others with a classy stock-certificate look to them. They're inexpensive and make your results much nicer.

You may have to adjust the margins of your certificate to get it to print properly on the special paper, moving everything closer to the center. If so, practice with plain paper, not the more expensive specialty paper. Then put your freshly printed copy and a piece of the stationery together and hold them up to a light. You will be able to tell if the printing is in the right place on the stationery. If not, adjust it in AppleWorks, print again on plain paper, and repeat the process. When you have it right, feed the expensive paper into your printer (make sure it's facing the right way, up or down, depending upon your printer) and choose Print Merge.

And hey, while you're at that stationery store, take a look at those official-looking foil stickers you can affix to your certificate to make it look even snazzier. Many stationery stores sell them.

Finally, don't forget that you can add other customized information to each certificate. For example, you could personalize each person's achievement by creating a field in the database entitled Achievement, then adding that field to the certificate template. So Charlie's certificate might say "Most Valuable Player," Jacob's will say "Fastest Runner," and Sam's will be for "Best Fielder." It won't take long to set up, and it makes handing out the certificates more fun if each one is different.

4 Instant Card

AppleWorks makes it easy and painless to create a card on demand for almost any occasion. Printed on an 8.5 × 11 piece of paper, then folded into quarters, the card really does look special, especially if you have a color printer.

Deb has developed a template for this type of card. It generates a birthday card as it's supplied, but by swapping art and text you can use the template for any type of card—birthday, wedding, anniversary, or whatever.

There's not much to it, so this essay will be short and sweet.

How to Make a Card

Find the folder entitled Deb's Birthday Card Template (in the Templates folder on your CD-ROM), and follow along.

1. Launch Deb's Birthday Card Template.
2. Edit the text and graphics any way you like.
3. Choose File ➤ Save if you want to save this card for reuse. Name and save the file.
4. Choose File ➤ Print.
5. Fold into quarters, following the light-gray lines.

NOTE Don't forget that the libraries contain lots and lots of art that you can use for a card. Specifically, look at the Events and Holidays and Awards libraries for ideas.

If You Have a Black and White Printer...

Let's face it, your cards won't look quite as nice. But there's no reason you can't still take part in the fun. Most of the pictures in the AppleWorks libraries print out quite nicely on monochrome printers. So, the first thing to do is create your card, then do a test print.

If the artwork is too big, small, dark, light, or whatever, you might want to run it through Deb's Coloring Book Template and decolorize it. I won't promise anything, but it will probably look better. To do so, follow these steps:

1. Open Deb's Coloring Book Template.

2. Drag or paste the art you want to decolorize onto an untitled document.

3. Make the art the size you want.

4. Run the macro by choosing File ➤ Macros ➤ Play Macro. When the Play Macro dialog box appears, select the Make Coloring Book macro (it's probably already selected), and press Play, as shown in Figure 4.1. If you're happy with the results...

FIGURE 4.1 Select the Make Coloring Book macro and press Play.

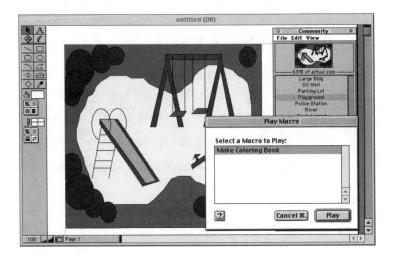

5. Choose Edit ➤ Select All (Command+A).

6. Choose Edit ➤ Copy (Command+C).

7. Open your card if it's not already open.

8. Choose Edit ➤ Paste (Command+V).

Resize and position the art, then try a test print. You may find you need to turn it upside-down or change its angle on the page. If so, choose Arrange ➤ Flip Vertically or Arrange ➤ Free Rotate. If something doesn't look right, go back to Deb's Coloring Book and try again, then copy and paste the art into the card again.

NOTE If you choose to use Deb's Coloring Book to decolorize your picture, consider coloring your card by hand with crayons, markers, or whatever after you print it in black and white.

I have a color printer and a black and white printer. I've created good-looking cards on both. All it takes is a little trial and error. And here's my last AppleWorks tip: Once you get a card "just so" and you're perfectly happy with the way it looks and prints, it's a good idea to save it for use in the future. You can change the name and message next time if you like, but the pictures, fonts, and other stuff can remain the same. It'll save you a bunch of time if you have saved a good birthday card for adults and another one for children. That way, you don't have to start modifying Deb's template from scratch every time.

5 Quicken: It's Not Just for Checkbook Management Anymore

Quicken 98, included with every iMac (but alas, not with the iBook), is an awesome program that can help you manage your checkbook. But it can also do much more. It can help you pay bills (my favorite feature) and do many other tasks to help you keep your finances (and, as you'll soon see, your household) organized. For example, you can use it to track investments, budget, pay bills electronically with no stamps or envelopes, and track your assets and debts to the penny. But did you know you can also use Quicken 98 to create an Emergency Records Organizer and a Household Inventory (an important item for insurance purposes)? Yes, Quicken 98 is a veritable cornucopia of handy tools for managing your money and your life.

Unlike the AppleWorks essays, this one contains no tutorials. I just don't have the space to tell you about all the cool features *and* show you how to use them. Fortunately, Quicken 98 is very easy to use and has extensive help and documentation available.

A Few Things You Should Know about before We Begin

First of all, since your copy of Quicken 98 didn't come with a printed user manual, all of your documentation is on the Quicken 98 CD. To use it, insert the Quicken 98 CD before launching the Quicken 98 program on your hard disk, then choose Help ➤ User's Manual. An Adobe Acrobat document containing the manual will appear on your screen.

In fact, Quicken 98's Help menu has a wealth of excellent help modules for learning to use the program. For example, choosing Help ➤ Quicken Basics lets you choose from eight well-produced QuickTime movies that show you how some of Quicken 98's features work.

NOTE Like the User's Manual, the QuickTime movies are on the Quicken 98 CD. So, the CD must be in your CD-ROM drive before you can use this feature.

If you choose Help ➤ Quicken Help (Command+?), you'll get a wonderful selection of interactive help tutorials, including dozens and dozens of How Do I entries that guide you through each process step-by-step.

If you choose Help ➤ Tips and Shortcuts, you can discover lots of ways to make it easier to use Quicken 98. A tip appears each time you launch Quicken 98, but if you want to see them all at once, this is the place to look.

Quicken 98 also offers balloon help. If you don't know what a button or feature does, try turning on the help balloons, then pointing at the particular button or feature you're wondering about. A balloon will pop up and tell you about it. This will often do the trick faster than the other Help modules.

Finally, if you choose Help ➤ About Help, you can even learn more about all of the different Help modules.

Getting Started

The first thing to do with Quicken 98 is create a data file. This is the document that contains all of the information you enter into Quicken 98.

NOTE You must back up this file regularly, or you risk losing vital financial data.

If you haven't already done so, create a new data file by choosing File ➤ New File. After you name and save the file, a dialog box will ask you if you'd like to watch a movie about accounts. I suggest you click the Play Now button and check it out.

NOTE Even if you're familiar with Quicken, I heartily recommend you watch the movie *Understanding Data Files* by choosing Help ➤ Quicken Basics, then clicking the Data Files button. An informative movie will begin playing almost immediately. In fact, you should probably watch all of the movies in the Quicken Basics Help module. They're a lot faster and easier than looking things up in the manual!

Once you've created a data file, a dialog box will appear asking you what kind of account you're creating—Bank, Cash, Credit Card, Asset, Liability, Portfolio, or Mutual Fund. Make that decision, name the account, and you're ready to rock and roll with Quicken 98.

Online Banking and Bill Paying

Of course, Quicken 98 can manage your checkbook automatically, help you reconcile your account, and print checks. You'd expect that much from a personal finance program, and Quicken 98 doesn't disappoint. But that's only the tip of the iceberg. If you have an Internet connection and bank at a cooperating bank, you can also use Quicken 98 to download up-to-date information about your transactions, automatically compare these transactions with those in your Quicken check register, and transfer money between accounts. Plus, you get my favorite feature of all: You can pay bills electronically without stamps, envelopes, or your printer.

NOTE   Note that there may be an additional charge for electronic bill-paying. In my case, the charges are roughly equal to what I'd spend on postage, so I have no qualms. But your bank could charge more. Or less. It is a good idea to ask your bank about their fees before you use this feature.

This is the killer feature, at least in my humble opinion. In the old days, I sat down with my checkbook, pen, and a pile of bills, envelopes, and stamps and did that bill-paying thing. It took the better part of an hour a week and gave me writer's cramp. Since I began using Quicken's online payments feature, the same number of bills takes less than 15 minutes and my hands don't ache. In a word, online payments are awesome.

To get started with online banking and payments, choose Online ➤ Getting Started with Online Banking. There you'll learn everything you need to know to get started, as well as which banks offer this service (many major ones do).

If your bank doesn't support online banking with Quicken 98, it might be a good time to shop for a new bank. Yes, this feature is that cool.

Create an Emergency Records Organizer

Quicken 98's Emergency Records Organizer helps you track all the essential information that may be important to your family in an emergency—such as emergency contact information, where important documents can be found, and information on property you own. Once you've completed the on-screen questionnaire, you can print the contents for a friend, relative, lawyer, or accountant.

To create your own Emergency Records Organizer document, click the Planning icon on the left side of the screen and then the Emergency icon at the top of the screen. The Emergency Records Organizer (ERO), a separate program, launches.

If you haven't used the ERO before, you'll start by creating a new file that you name and save to your hard disk.

NOTE You can password-protect this file to keep it from prying eyes if you so desire.

Once you've named and saved the file, a window will appear, as shown in Figure 5.1.

FIGURE 5.1   **The main Emergency Records Organizer window: Informational movies are in the middle, and questionnaire categories are listed on the right.**

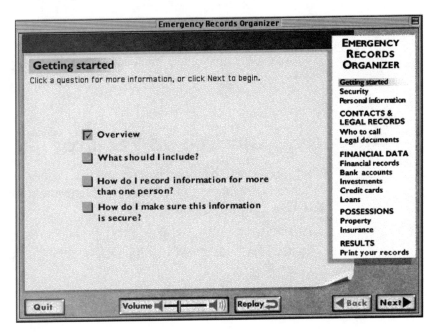

The first thing I would do is watch the informational movies by clicking the checkboxes in the middle of the screen—Overview, What Should I Include?, and so on.

Once you've done that, fill out your questionnaire by clicking the Emergency Records Organizer categories on the right—the list that begins with Getting Started, Security, etc. Each category should be self-explanatory; fill in the blanks and move on to the next category.

NOTE You don't have to do this all at once; you can quit in the middle and come back to it another time. Everything you've typed into the questionnaire will be saved automatically when you quit the program.

When you've filled out all the pages, click the Print Your Records button at the bottom to print a report (there are several to choose from). Now give it to a friend or relative (or lawyer or accountant) and forget about it for a while.

NOTE But don't forget about it for too long: You ought to update and reprint this document every so often. Things change. Someone may be depending on this document in an emergency, so keep it up to date.

Other Neat Quicken 98 Features

What you've seen so far barely scratches the surface of what Quicken can do for you to organize your finances and household. Other capabilities worth checking out include:

QuickEntry A little program that lets you enter a transaction without launching Quicken 98. Quite handy. It's in the Quicken folder if you care to use it.

Tax Deduction Finder A simple, easy-to-use questionnaire that helps you determine whether you overlooked any deductions you might claim. Very neat. Choose Activities ➤ Financial Fitness ➤ Tax Deduction Finder.

Free Credit Report You can get a free report on your credit rating just by being a Quicken user. Choose Activities ➤ Financial Fitness ➤ Free Credit Report.

Stock Portfolio Tracking The stocks in your portfolio can be updated with the latest prices by choosing Online ➤ Quicken Quotes.

NOTE Alas, this feature costs a dollar a minute, and since I get more or less the same information for free on my Excite home page, I don't use it.

Quicken Home Inventory Sure, you can just write down everything you own, but this little program makes it easier. Choose Activities ➤ Quicken Home Inventory.

Reporting If you have the numbers in your Quicken data file, choose Activities ➤ Reports and Graphs to sort, summarize, and otherwise massage them about a million different ways. Want to see visually what percent of your spending goes to credit card companies? No problem. Just create a graph comparing your expenses.

The Quicken Credit Card This is a Visa Gold card issued by Travelers Bank. You can review your account status online, download your transactions to your Quicken data file, and/or choose to participate in an optional TravelerMiles program. To apply, call Travelers Bank at 800-442-4939.

NOTE Last time I checked, the Quicken credit card had a higher interest rate than my other Visa card. I still use it but pay my balance in full every month to avoid paying the higher interest. It's a handy thing to have if you use Quicken, but caveat emptor (let the buyer beware).

6 AOL: It's Not As Bad as You Think

Let's get this straight right up front: I'm not a fan of America Online (AOL). Sure, they're the biggest ISP (Internet Service Provider) in the world, but I get better connections from my local ISP. Still, I recognize that for many people AOL is all the Internet/online access they need. So here is an essay describing some of the more interesting (and often hidden or buried) features.

NOTE Among the advantages of using a local ISP that I've discovered are features like no advertising, fewer busy signals, faster connections, and better tech support. But hey, like I said, AOL is easy and, for many people, the right choice for online and Internet access.

Taking Control of AOL

AOL offers a plethora of controls that manage what appears on your screen. Two cool examples are the controls that help you to manage the influx of those seemingly endless advertising pop-ups and the controls that AOL makes available to limit your kids' access to the Internet.

Since AOL can be annoying with its in-your-face advertising pop-ups, it's a good thing you can choose to turn them off if you so desire, which I do and you can too.

To turn off all pop-up ads and opt not to receive unsolicited e-mails from AOL or its affiliates, choose My AOL ➤ Marketing Preferences.

NOTE My AOL is a button and menu item at the top of the screen rather than a menu item in the menu bar, as shown in Figure 6.1. Click and hold the My AOL button to invoke the menu.

FIGURE 6.1 Use this menu item to turn off AOL's annoying pop-up ads and limit junk e-mail from AOL and its affiliates.

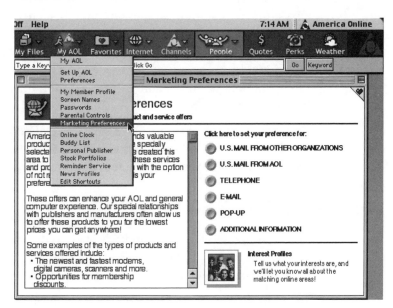

NOTE You must log on to AOL to set Marketing Preferences. Moreover, Marketing Preferences can only be set for one screen name at a time. So if you want to set Marketing Preferences for five screen names, you'll have to go through the process five times.

In Figure 6.1, notice that there are six buttons on the right side of the Marketing Preferences window. You'll have to set each of these preferences separately to stem the flow of junk.

In a different vein, if you have kids, you'll want to use Parental Controls, which can limit your kids' access to AOL. First create a screen name for each child for whom you want to set Parental Controls. Then, log on to AOL, and choose My AOL ➢ Parental Controls.

NOTE You have to log on to AOL using your Master Account, the first screen name you created, to set up Parental Controls.

There are several levels of restricted access. For example, Kids Only is the most restrictive and excludes access to all but the Kids Only channel. It also shuts off instant messages and member-created chat rooms and limits the use of e-mail to text only. Young Teen (ages 13–15) and Mature Teen (ages 16–17) provide more freedom while still restricting access to questionable areas and services. Once you've set up a control level for a screen name, use the Custom Controls option to adjust specific activities for each screen name.

If you have kids, this feature alone may make AOL your preferred ISP. It primarily enables you to leave your kids alone online and not worry (too much) about them stumbling across inappropriate material.

Finding What You Need

AOL is a huge service with hundreds of areas devoted to thousands of topics. It can be overwhelming, and the confusing click-heavy interface is no help. That's why the Find on AOL feature is so useful.

To use it, click the Find button on the Navigation bar, just below the Button bar at the top of the screen. Hold down the mouse button, and a menu will pop down, as shown in Figure 6.2.

FIGURE 6.2   The Find on AOL feature helps you to find topics of interest within the AOL service.

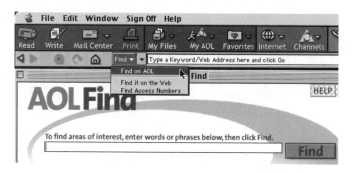

Choose Find on AOL, then type what you're looking for in the field next to the Find button.

NOTE Once you find an area you like, it's a good idea to create a shortcut (like a bookmark in an Internet browser) so you can get back to it easily. To do so, choose Window ➣ My Shortcuts ➣ Edit Shortcuts. Or, if you see a little heart in the upper-right corner, click it to add this area to your Favorites list.

If you can't find what you need on AOL, you might want to try finding it on the Web. To do that, click the Find button on the Navigation bar, just below the Button bar at the top of the screen, as shown in Figure 6.2. This time, hold down the mouse button and scroll down to Find It on the Web, then release the mouse button. AOL's built-in Web browser will launch, and a Search window will appear.

NOTE If the AOL search engine doesn't find what you're looking for, you might want to try a different one. My three favorite Internet search pages are: **HotBot** (www.hotbot.com), **Ask Jeeves** (www.ask.com), and **AltaVista** (www.altavista.com).

Finding Cool Mac Stuff on AOL

If you want to find the best information, discussions, shareware, fonts, clip art, games, and other tools and toys for your Mac, there are several areas on AOL you should explore.

The main one is the Mac OS Resource Center. To go to it, type **MacOS** in the Navigation Bar field over the message "Type a Keyword/Web Address here and click Go." Then click the Go button.

NOTE You might want to create a shortcut for this area, as it is the gateway to almost all Mac-related services on AOL.

From the MacOS Resource Center screen, you can access the Mac OS software libraries, the Mac OS message boards, and Apple's own area on AOL.

NOTE To get directly to the goodies—fonts, clip art, games, and other tools and toys—without visiting the Mac OS Resource Center, use the keywords **Download Software.**

The Mac OS message boards bear further discussion. These areas contain "bulletin boards" where Mac users can post questions and comments. They're easy to use and more useful than you might expect. Here are some suggestions on ways to use them:

◆ Browse through all of the categories, looking for topics that interest you.

◆ Post a message if you're looking for opinions on a piece of software or hardware that you're considering purchasing.

◆ Post a message asking for help with a bug or other problem that you're having.

◆ Search for messages regarding a bug or other problem you're having.

◆ Post a message asking for advice on any aspect concerning the use of your iMac or iBook.

NOTE One important thing to remember when you post a message is that you have to return later—in a day or two—to read the responses. So once you find a message board that you want to participate in, it's a good idea to click the little heart in the upper-right corner of its window and add it to your Favorites list.

Getting Help Using AOL

Even though AOL offers toll-free technical support by phone, it is known for making callers wait on hold for long periods of time. I've personally sat on hold for as long as an hour. And the last time I called, a recorded voice told me they were too busy to take my call and to call back later.

So you may prefer to get your help another way. Fortunately, there are several options.

If you can log on to AOL, type the keyword **Help** in the Navigation Bar field. There, you'll find several resources that may answer your question.

If you are unable to make a connection to AOL, try using the AOL Guide by choosing Help ➤ AOL Guide or using the keyboard shortcut Command+?. The AOL Guide has a lot of interactive guided help that may aid you in solving your problem. If that doesn't work, or you can't even launch AOL for whatever reason, you'll have to call them.

NOTE For the shortest waits, try calling early in the morning. The earlier, the better.

The toll-free number for Mac tech support is 888-265-8007. Other toll-free AOL phone numbers you may find handy include:

◆ 888-265-8004 for screen name and password help

◆ 888-265-8005 for help with AOL access phone numbers

◆ 888-265-8003 for help with billing

◆ 888-265-8008 to cancel your AOL service

7 Nanosaur Play Action Guide

Nanosaur is a 3-D action game that comes pre-installed on your iMac and iBook. It's a stunning demonstration of their built-in 3-D graphics capabilities and a lot of fun besides. For weeks after we got our iMac, my kids wouldn't play anything else. And even I have played it often enough to provide you with some tips for playing better and smarter.

The Premise and Basic Gameplay

In the far distant future, a species of dinosaurs known as Nanosaurs rule the earth. Your goal as a player is to travel back in time to retrieve the dinosaur eggs of five species before a giant asteroid wipes them out. You are equipped with a jetpack, a cannon, a GPS map locator, and a temporal compass for locating time portals. You have limited ammunition but can gather more as you explore the world of the Nanosaur. Your jetpack, for instance, can refuel from gas vents found near volcanoes and lava flows.

When you locate an egg, pick it up and deposit it in a time portal. The time portals will appear at regular intervals; your temporal compass will aim you toward the nearest one. Once you have transported all of the eggs to the future, your mission ends successfully.

Which Keys Do What?

To play the game well, you have to master the keyboard commands (the mouse is not used at all). They are as follows:

Arrow keys   Enable you to turn and move forward or backward.

< and >   Enable you to spin the camera around.

1 and 2   Make the camera zoom in and out, respectively.

Command   Enables you to jump (or double-jump if you tap the Command key quickly twice).

Shift   Makes your next weapon available to you.

Option   Allows you to pick up and throw an item.

A and Z   Increase and decrease your jetpack thrust, respectively.

Control+M   Toggles the music on and off.

Control+B   Toggles the ambient sound on and off.

+ and –   Raise and lower the volume, respectively.

ESC   Pauses the game.

TAB   Changes the camera mode to normal or head-cam.

G   Toggles the GPS map.

Command+Q   Enables you to quit the application at any time.

The first thing to do is launch the program, start a game, and practice with these keys until they become second nature to you. Without doing this, you will never make any progress. (But hey, practicing is lots of fun....)

Playing Hints

The most important hint I can give you is that you have to move quickly. This is a timed game, and if you don't complete your mission before time runs out, the game ends—even if you're doing great. So, move fast.

Here are a few more tips:

◆ Learn to jump and double jump (using the Command key). You'll die a thousand horrible deaths otherwise.

◆ Learn to use all the weapons at your disposal. Some weapons kill certain dinosaurs better than others.

◆ Keep an eye on your map so you don't waste effort exploring terrain more than once.

NOTE If you'd like a fuller explanation of the game, there's a complete walkthrough of the game's six levels at www.octec.org.au/ajtrade/nano.html.

Cheats

Some people hate cheating and think it ruins the game; others love the built-in cheats you can use to make things easier. If you're in the former category, stop reading now. If you're in the latter category, here are a few cheat codes I discovered on the Pangea Software (makers of Nanosaur) Web page at www.pangeasoft.net/.

While playing the game, hold down the F12 key and then press:

◆ F1 to restore your health

◆ F2 to get all weapons

◆ F3 to get your shield

◆ F4 to win the game

◆ F5 to get more fuel

NOTE If these cheats don't work on your copy of Nanosaur, you may need to download a newer version. They worked with version 1.0.8 (on my newer tangerine iMac) but not with version 1.0.5 (on my original first-generation iMac). To see which version of Nanosaur you have, click the Nanosaur Application icon, then choose File ➤ Get Info (or press Command+I). If you don't have version 1.0.8 or later, you can download the latest version, for free, from www.pangeasoft.net/.

There is one other cheat that I know of: If you jump on one of the Pteranodons and fly really high, so high that you can't see the ground, you'll get 100% health, all weapons, 999 items, a full jetpack, and a shield.

NOTE Use your jetpack to return to the ground level; avoid landing in lava.

8 Sounds Good to Me: Recording Sound with Your iMac or iBook

Did you know that your iMac has a built-in microphone and that you can record your voice or songs from music CDs? Or that you can connect an inexpensive microphone to your iBook's USB port and do the same? Well, that's what this essay is all about.

We'll look at how to record your own sounds with the built-in mic on iMacs or external mic on iBooks, as well as how to record sounds from other sources, such as your CD-ROM drive. I'll also show you how to create your own "beep" or alert sounds.

Where Is That Darn Microphone Anyway?

If you look at your iMac, you'll see a little slit right above the monitor, in the very center. That's where your built-in microphone lives. When you record sound, it's best to place your sound source—your lips or whatever—no more than 12-24 inches directly in front of the mic, rather than way above or below it.

NOTE If you have an iBook, you'll need to use an external microphone connected via your USB port. The iMic universal audio adapter from Griffin Technology is a USB device that allows the connection of virtually any microphone or sound input device to the iBook. Find out more at www.griffintechnology.com/.

Recording Your First Sound

Recording a sound with your iMac or iBook is simple. In fact, the program you're going to use for recording is so simple it's called SimpleSound. But before we get to SimpleSound, there's one thing you need to do or this little experiment won't work properly.

First, open the Monitors and Sound control panel, click the Sound button at the top of the window, and choose Built-in Mic from the Sound Monitoring Source pop-up menu.

NOTE If you have an iBook with an external microphone, choose External Mic instead of Built-in Mic.

Now, close the Monitors and Sound control panel, and you're almost ready to record.

Next, open the SimpleSound application (it should be in your Apple menu, unless you've moved it). To record a sound using the built-in microphone, just follow these easy steps:

1. Choose File ➢ New.

2. Choose a quality level from the Sound menu.

NOTE CD quality is the best, and phone quality is the worst. The other two choices—music quality and speech quality—are in-between. The higher the quality you choose, the more space your recorded sound will consume on your hard disk. So, experiment with the various quality choices, and use the lowest one that gives you the results you find acceptable.

3. Click the Record button.

4. Make your sound or sounds.

5. Click the Stop button.

6. Choose File ➤ Save to save your sound to your hard disk.

Now that you have a sound, you might want to hear it. To do so, open the sound file (double-click it if it's not already open), and choose Sound ➤ Play.

To record a sound from your iMac or iBook's built-in CD-ROM drive (using a music CD, not a CD-ROM, of course), open the Monitors and Sound control panel, click the Sound button at the top of the window, and choose CD from the Sound Monitoring Source pop-up menu. Now, close the Monitors and Sound control panel, and you'll be (almost) ready to record from your music CD.

Before you start recording, there's one last thing you have to do. Open the AppleCD Audio Player program (it should be in the Apple menu), locate the exact portion of the CD you want to record, then click the Pause button. Once your CD is queued up, open SimpleSound (but don't close AppleCD Audio Player). Now, with SimpleSound as the active application, follow these steps:

1. Choose File ➤ New.

2. Choose a quality level from the Sound menu.

NOTE Remember what I said earlier about quality. Since this is a recording from a CD, choosing CD quality will provide the best results but will also create the largest files. Experiment.

3. Choose AppleCD Audio Player from the Application menu in the upper-right corner of the screen.

4. Click the Play button.

5. Choose SimpleSound from the Application menu in the upper-right corner of the screen.

6. Click Record.

NOTE The recording will start immediately, so you might want to "rewind" the CD to a few seconds before where you want to begin recording and then click Play (in AppleCD Audio Player). This way, you'll be able to time your click of the Record button (in SimpleSound), so the recording begins precisely where you want it to.

7. When you're finished recording, click Stop.

8. Choose File ➢ Save to save your sound to your hard disk.

Making Your Own "Beep" Sounds

You may be sick of the built-in alert ("beep") sounds your iMac or iBook offers. If so, it's easy to create your own. Just launch SimpleSound (if it's not already running), then follow along with the steps below:

1. Choose Sound ➢ Alert Sounds.

2. Choose a quality level from the Sound menu.

3. Click the Add button in the Alert Sounds window.

4. Click Record.

5. Make your sound or sounds.

6. Click the Save button.

7. Name your sound.

8. Click OK to save this recording automatically as an alert sound.

If you want to hear your new alert sound, double-click it in the Alert Sounds window. If you hate it, click it once in the Alert Sounds window, then click Remove.

Finally, to use your new sound as your alert sound, open the Monitors and Sound control panel, click the Alerts button at the top, then choose your new sound from the Alert Sound list by clicking it once. Your sound will play immediately and become your active alert sound. It remains active until you click a different alert sound.

9 Improve Scans and Digital Photos with Kai's Photo Soap SE

There is a reason this is the last essay in the chapter. That reason is that it may not be of any use to you. Unless you have a scanner or digital camera or routinely edit scanned images or digital photos, you won't get much use out of Kai's Photo Soap SE. Even worse, it doesn't come with the iBook, so if you're an iBook owner you're doubly out of luck.

What is Kai's Photo Soap SE ("Soap" for short)? It's a very cool program that can repair, enhance, mend, and otherwise improved scanned images and digital photos. With Soap you can repair red-eye, erase cracks and creases from old pictures, improve color and contrast, and much more. You can also add borders, backgrounds, and text to your pictures if you so desire. All things considered, if you work with photos on your iMac, you're gonna love this program.

Unlike the other programs in this chapter, Soap does not come pre-installed on your iMac. Instead, you received a CD called Kai's Photo Soap SE. If you want to check out the program, insert that CD, open the English folder, and install Soap on your hard disk.

Getting Started with Soap

Once you have it installed, launch Soap. Surprise! It's not your father's Mac interface. Kai Krause, the brilliant and talented Photoshop guru and imaginative interface designer, created Soap. As you can tell from Figure 9.1, he's not exactly a fan of the traditional Mac interface.

FIGURE 9.1   The In Room interface. Think different indeed!

The first thing you'll notice is that there are no ordinary menus in Soap. So, probably the first thing you'll need to know is how to quit, as you won't find a Quit command in the non-existent File menu. That's easy. When you're ready to leave Soap, just press Command+Q, then click the Checkmark button or press Enter or Return.

Learning Soap

Soap was designed using a "room" metaphor; each room is dedicated to a specific task. There are seven actual rooms—In, Prep, Tone, Color, Detail, Finish, and Out Rooms, plus the Map Room, which is more like a hallway that provides access to the other seven rooms. It's probably best, at least until you get to know the program better, to follow the order above (it's the same order as that in the Map Room), moving from one room to the next in the order prescribed. Once you're familiar with Soap, you don't have to use every room, nor do you have to use them in a particular order; you can skip from room to room instantly via the Map Room.

There are three ways to become familiar with Soap. The first is to just dive right in and click stuff. This is fun, but probably not that efficient. The second is to read the Adobe Acrobat version of the manual, which you'll find on the Soap CD in the English folder. This is probably the most effective but will take the longest. A good compromise is to spend some time looking at Soap's built-in Help, shown in Figure 9.2, then dive right in and start clicking stuff.

To access the Help system, click the Help button in any room or click the word MetaTools in the upper-right corner.

FIGURE 9.2   **The fast way to learn Soap—use the Help system!**

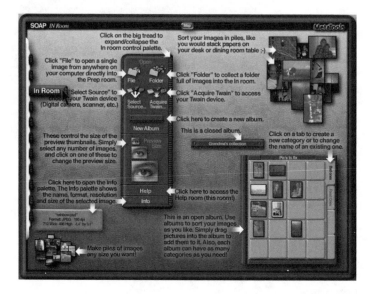

To get help for a particular room (or help with tools), move your cursor (the arrow) near the side of the window. A tab for each room pops up when your cursor is over it. The tab for the In Room is shown in Figure 9.2.

NOTE   The bottom tab is the Exit tab; you must exit Help before you can continue using (or quit) Soap.

Once you've absorbed this stuff, open one of the sample pictures and go to town.

How to Do a Few Cool Things...

The Detail Room is where much of the magic of Soap occurs. So, we'll focus on it.

NOTE Does your picture have blemishes, folds, wrinkles, dust spots, creases, or other imperfections? If so, visit the Detail Room and try the Heal tool and/or the Clone tool. While you're in the Detail Room, you might also want to use the Smooth tool to soften skin texture and eliminate distracting detail or the Sharpen tool to bring out details in images that are soft or fuzzy. Be careful not to overdo it with the Sharpen tool; a little sharpening goes a long way.

NOTE If your subject has red eye, use the Red Eye tool to remove or at least reduce it. The Red Eye tool has tinting options for brown, blue, and hazel eyes, a neat touch.

When you're happy with the quality of your image, move to the Finish Room where you can add a background, apply edge effects, and add objects such as calendars, cartoons, frames, or text.

Finally, when everything is just so, move to the Out Room and save your image.

There's a lot more to the program than I have space for here, but I hope you've gotten a feel for what it can do. It's a very cool program, but it requires an investment of some time to master. If you work with scans or photos, I think you'll find it's well worth it.

Your iMac or iBook and the Web

The *i* in *iMac* or *iBook* allegedly stands for *Internet*. Every iMac or iBook is Internet ready, so this chapter should appeal to you. Whether you are a surfer or a Webmaster, this chapter is full of tips and hints for getting more out of the Internet with your iMac or iBook.

Your Dream Start Page   Is a tutorial showing how to tailor the default iMac or iBook home page on Excite to better suit your needs.

Seeing the Sites   Offers a wealth of wonderful Web sites for keeping up with all things Macintosh and with the capabilities of your iMac or iBook.

Buy It on the Net   Shows you how to shop for iMac or iBook hardware and software (and more) without leaving the comfort of your home.

Getting the Most out of Sherlock   Shows you how to maximize the new Find File's functionality and use it to search the Internet.

Safety First on the Internet: Using the EdView Internet Safety Kit Shows you how to protect your family (more or less) from smut on the Web.

Home Sweet Web Page with Adobe PageMill   Is a quick look at the Web page builder included with "fruit-flavored" iMacs.

Publish or Perish on the Web   Talks about using your iMac or iBook as a Web server or using an ISP (Internet Service Provider) to serve up your Web pages. It also covers the advantages and disadvantages of each technique.

Fixing Pix for E-mail   Shows you how to prepare pictures so that you can send them by e-mail to Mac or PC users.

So log onto the Internet and get ready to rumble!

10 Your Dream Start Page

The first time you launch a browser—Netscape Communicator or Microsoft Internet Explorer—on your iMac or iBook, you will automatically be taken to a sign-up page for Excite's My Excite Start Page service, which is part of the iMac or iBook package. It's a great jumping off point for your Web-surfing adventures as it comes right out of the box; but as you'll discover in the coming pages, you can customize almost every aspect of it to suit your tastes and needs. If you haven't already done so, sign up for this service now and get ready to make this start page your own.

NOTE If you've changed the start page in your browser preferences (you don't see an Excite page when you launch your browser), you can surf to `http://apple.excite.com/?cobrand=apple` and follow along. If you like what you've done, be sure to bookmark the page or use your browser's preferences to choose it as your new start page.

Personalize Your Page

To get started, click the Personalize Your Page link. If you've not already done so, you'll be asked to register and choose a password. After you've done this, a page will appear that describes all the wonderful services you're now entitled to as an iMac or iBook user. Let's begin with My Excite Start Page, the prototype for your personalized start page.

Click the My Excite Start Page link. Notice the start page features: My News, My Stocks, My Weather, My Sports, and so on. You can customize each of these to suit your personal tastes.

Now that you've looked at the start page, scroll to the bottom where all the customization options appear. You will see a box called Personalization Manager, as shown in Figure 10.1.

FIGURE 10.1 Excite's Personalization Manager lets you personalize your start page in many ways.

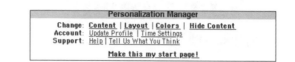

Content Is King

To personalize the content—the items that your start page will show—click the Content link in the Personalization Manager. The Personalize My Content page will open.

In the first section of this page, you can choose the name your start page will use to address you. I changed mine from "Welcome, Bob" to "Hey Good Lookin'," but that's not required. If you do not customize this option, the start page will call you by your first name, as you entered it during registration.

The second section is where the action is. You'll see a plethora of checkboxes representing all the different items you can choose to appear on your start page—news, business, sports, weather, entertainment, and more. Select the checkboxes that appeal to you.

In the third section, you can choose password protection if you want to password-protect your start page so that nobody else can modify it.

If there's anything you'd like to change, or an item you'd like to get rid of, go back to the Personalization Manager, click the Content link, and make any necessary changes. When you're finished, click the Submit button at the bottom of the page.

NOTE If you see a dialog box that says something about insecure information, ignore it and click OK.

Make a Layout You'll Love

Next, we'll customize the layout of the items on your page. Click the Layout link in the Personalization Manager and you'll see the Personalize My Layout page. This is where you arrange the order in which the items you chose in the previous section will appear on your start page.

For each item you selected in the previous section, you'll see a box denoting its order on the page. Item 1 appears at the top; the highest numbered (I have 11) item appears at the bottom. There's even a preview layout that you can use to see how the start page is going to look before you submit it. Enter a number for each item on your start page and click the Redraw button to preview it. When everything on your start page is in the order you prefer, click the Submit button.

NOTE Your stock portfolio will always appear at the top of the page if it includes seven or more columns, and the TV listings will always appear at the bottom of the page due to their size.

Colorize Your World (or at Least Your Start Page)

You can even specify the colors for your start page by clicking the Colors link in the Personalization Manager. On the Personalize My Colors page, you can choose your background, header, text, link, and other colors. Click the Redraw button to preview your handiwork. Click the Submit button when you have it just the way you like it.

Making the News Your Own

Now that you've tuned up both the look and the content of your start page, you can choose the kind of news that will appear on it. There are two different adjustments you can make: You can decide exactly what types of news will appear on your start page, and you can set up a customized clipping service that will search the Internet for stories that match your criteria. This is one of my favorite features and I'm sure it'll become one of yours, as well.

Tuning Up My News

Find the My News section on your start page and click the Change link, as shown in Figure 10.2.

The Personalize My News Categories page will open, and you'll see a massive list of topics that you can choose from. Select topics that appeal to you

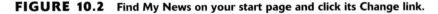

FIGURE 10.2 Find My News on your start page and click its Change link.

by holding down the Command key and clicking them. Once all the topics you desire are selected, click the Add button to add them to your start page. Click the Submit button to view your changes.

If you're feeling adventurous, go back to the Personalize My News Categories page and click the Advanced Personalization button. This lets you choose how many of each topic's headlines will appear on your start page. It also lets you choose how old the oldest headline should be. When the news topics and number of headlines you see for each topic are just the way you like them, click the Submit button.

Your Own Clipping Service, Too

Now you can create a clipping service that searches the Internet for stories about topics that you specify. To set it up, find the news section called News-Tracker Clipping Service and click the Create Your Own Personalized News Topics link. (If you've created a topic before, it won't say that. Instead, click the NewsTracker Clipping Service link, then click the New Topic link on the next page you see.)

For each NewsTracker topic you create, you can choose keywords. For each keyword, you can decide whether it's a "must have," a "good to have," or a "must not have."

Being an egomaniac, I have one NewsTracker topic set up that must contain *Bob* and *LeVitus*. And since I'm an avid Apple watcher, I have another search topic that must have *Apple Computer, Inc.* I have also created a search for news items containing the words *Steve Jobs*.

There are many uses for this feature. If you follow a stock, set up a topic for the company. If you are only interested in news about a company's stock (and not the company itself), include the word *stock* as a "must have." If you want all the news on your favorite singer or movie star, set up a topic just for that. It's fun, it's easy, and it's incredibly useful. (In other words, it rocks!)

Once you've set up a topic and filled in all its keywords, click the Create My Topic button. You'll see another page filled with suggestions that may be of use. Check any that apply (or none if you like) and click the Make Changes button. For instance, one of the words suggested for my Apple topic was *iMac*. I thought that was a good suggestion, so I accepted it. Now my News-Tracker Apple topic clips stories with iMac in them, too.

After you've created your topic or topics, you can view a summary of articles that match your criteria by clicking the topic's name in the News-Tracker Clipping Service section of your start page.

Taking Stock of Your Portfolio

I love the fact that my start page can keep track of my stock portfolio and tell me at a glance how every stock I own is doing as of 15 minutes ago. (Stock quotes are delayed 15 minutes.) And unlike Quicken, this tracking is free.

To set up your own portfolio, find the My Stocks section on your start page and click the Change button next to it, as shown in Figure 10.3.

FIGURE 10.3   **Find My Stocks on your start page and click its Change link.**

The Personalize My Stock Portfolio page appears. Choose which indices (Dow Jones, NASDAQ, etc.) you want to track in the first section. In the second section, enter the ticker symbol, shares owned, and price paid for each stock you want to track. In the third section, customize your portfolio layout and choose which columns will appear in your full portfolio view. When you're satisfied with your entries, click the Submit button to save your changes.

From now on, the My Stocks section will show all the stocks in your portfolio, their current price, and their price change (plus or minus) since the market opened that morning.

NOTE   For more detail, click the Full Portfolio link. You'll see a large grid that shows items such as current price, the day's change in dollars and percent, share volume, number of shares owned, current value, gain/loss, and links to charts and stories about each stock. This is also where you can view the total value of your holdings.

Your total holdings—the only number that really matters at the end of the day—will appear at the bottom of the Current Value column. If you don't *have* a Current Value column, go back to the Personalize My Stock Portfolio page and choose Value from one of the pop-up menus in the last (Customize Your Portfolio Layout) section.

You can also choose to view additional data about stocks in your portfolio by choosing one of the following views at the bottom of the My Stocks section: Holdings, Fundamentals, Price Performance, or Day Trader. Each view uses different columns to show your portfolio.

NOTE   Don't forget, once you've customized your start page to your liking, you can set it to be the first thing that your browser brings up when you start it. To do so, use your browser's Preferences dialog box, Internet Config, or the Mac OS 8.5 Internet control panel—whichever appears on your particular iMac or iBook. Browser preferences can be found in the Edit menu of both browsers on all types of iMacs and iBooks. If you have an original Bondi Blue iMac, you can use the included Internet Config application. If you have one of the newer "fruit-flavored" iMacs or an iBook, use the Internet control panel. All three methods will achieve the same effect—making this the first page your browser displays when you launch it.

11   Seeing the Sites

The World Wide Web is full of wonderful sites with a wealth of useful information about Macs in general and iMacs or iBooks in particular. In this essay, I'll try to provide you with a list of the best and brightest, along with brief descriptions of what you will find at each site.

There are a couple of things I need to mention before we begin. The first is that sometimes Web sites move and leave no forwarding address. I checked every link in this book before it went to press, and every single one worked at that time. But that doesn't mean that they'll still work by the time you get this book home to read it. I hope they will; but as you know, stuff happens. Bottom line: If you encounter a dead or broken link, I apologize; but don't blame me. I did all I could.

Second, you'll find a pair of files on the CD-ROM that came with this book, entitled Bookmarks (Explorer) and Bookmarks (Navigator).

NOTE These files are both the same; the only difference is in which browser will launch.

These files contain links for every URL (Web address) in the book, grouped by chapter. Rather than tediously typing in URLs, select the appropriate bookmark file from the CD-ROM and click it. Don't forget that you can use your browser's Find command (Command+F) to find a particular bookmark in this file.

NOTE It's also a good idea to use your browser's bookmark feature to save sites you like and wish to return to in the future.

Great iMac-Specific Web Sites

The iMac has spawned hundreds of Web sites dedicated to every aspect of using our favorite computer. Here are a few of my favorites.

Ric Ford's iMacInTouch pages are great. 'Nuff said. This is one of the few iMac sites I visit every single day. You'll find it at http://www.macintouch .com/imac.html.

The iMac Channel, which the *San Diego Union-Tribune* referred to as "the most comprehensive set of [iMac] links and news," can be found at `http://lowendmac.com/imac/index.shtml`. If all you care about is the list of iMac Web site links, you'll find it at `http://lowendmac.com/imac/links .shtml`. This is another site worth visiting regularly.

Two more excellent places for news and iMac-related links are the iMac2day site at `http://www.imac2day.com/` and the iMac.com site at `http://www.theimac.com/`. Both are updated frequently and filled with interesting information and late-breaking news about iMacs or iBooks.

There's also *Macworld* magazine's iMacworld site at `http://www .imacworld.com/`.

Finally, if you just can't get enough iMac Web sites, visit the iMac WebRing home page at `http://www.webring.org/cgi-bin/webring?ring=1imac3;list`. A WebRing is like a club for Web pages. This page is a list of more than 45 interesting sites that are members of the iMac WebRing.

N O T E   My favorite feature of WebRings is the Visit a Random Site link or button that you'll find on every member's pages. Click it and you'll be transported to a member site at random, which is kind of neat. Random ring surfing can be both fun and informative; so if you've never visited a WebRing, be sure to give it a try.

More Great Web Sites

Every morning after I read the morning local newspaper and the *Wall Street Journal*, I spend a few minutes surfing the Mac-related Web sites and seeing what's new in the Mac world. After all, iMacs and iBooks are also Macs. This section consists of six sites that cover the entire spectrum of things Macintosh (these are six great Mac sites that I read every day), followed by four other sites that are incredibly useful when you need them.

My Morning Reading (Web Sites I Visit Daily)

Just as iMacInTouch is a great resource for iMac owners, Ric's MacInTouch site is a great resource for all Mac users. A compelling blend of news, opinion, discussion, special reports, and product reviews, MacInTouch is a site I look forward to reading every single day. It's at `http://www.macintouch.com/`.

Conflict of interest alert: I write a column every Saturday for *MacCentral* and I'm about to recommend them as another site I visit daily. But I was a fan of *MacCentral* before I was a columnist there; and I still believe it's one of the best, with a great staff of writers, including yours truly. You'll find MacCentral Online at `http://www.maccentral.com/`.

Another great site for news and views is the Macintosh News Network at `http://www.macnn.com/`. This is primarily news about Apple and vendors of hardware and software for Macs; but it's updated twice a day or more and is often one of the first places I see a story.

There's nothing nutritious about MacOS Rumors. It's the *National Enquirer* of Mac Web sites, and I read it religiously the same way I read the *Enquirer* whenever I'm stuck in a grocery store line. You'll find it at `http://www.macosrumors.com/`.

Ted Landau, the proprietor of the MacFixIt Web site at `http://www.macfixit.com/`, is an old friend of mine. His book *Sad Macs, Bombs, and Other Disasters* is the classic Mac troubleshooting guide. His Web site continues the tradition with complete coverage of numerous ongoing issues about Macs , iMacs, and iBooks. It's published Monday, Wednesday, and Friday of every week, except during Macworld Expo.

The last place I stop for my daily fix of Mac news and information is MacSurfer's Headline News page at `http://www.macsurfer.com/`. This is a links page. It scans the Internet for stories about Apple and Macintoshes and offers you the headlines and links to select if you care to read more. It's updated several times a day, so it's a good place to find up-to-date information on a breaking story or issue.

Four More Great Mac Sites

The more pieces of software you use, the more useful you'll find MacUpdate and VersionTracker Online. Both sites offer up-to-date news on the latest versions of almost every Mac application, Control Panel, or extension. They also offer links to download any updates that you might need. They're at `http://www.macupdate.com/` and `http://www.versiontracker.com/`, respectively.

Apple's Technical Information Library (TIL) is another great site to remember. It's Apple's keyword-searchable knowledge base of product information, technical specifications, and troubleshooting information. It's updated daily and contains more than 14,000 articles. You will find the

TIL at `http://til.info.apple.com/`. If something is wrong with your iMac, this is a great place to begin your search for a solution.

NOTE   If you find yourself needing the TIL, you might want to jump ahead to Chapter 7, which is packed with troubleshooting tips and hints.

The last site I want to tell you about is Apple's Macintosh Products Guide Web site, another searchable database with listings and descriptions of more than 14,000 Mac products.

NOTE   14,000 articles in the TIL. 14,000 products in the Macintosh Products Guide. Coincidence? You be the judge.

You'll find the Macintosh Products Guide at `http://guide.apple.com/`. It's a great place to find more information about software or hardware items for your iMac.

12   Buy It on the Net

Basically, you have two ways to buy software and hardware for your iMac. You can get in your car, drive to the local CompUSA, park the car, go into the store, and find that they either don't carry what you're looking for or that they're out of stock on your desired item. Or, you can fire up your Web browser, find the best price on the item, order it with a few clicks of the mouse, and wait for it to be delivered to your door (which is often the next day).

As an iMac user, you've no doubt noticed that most of the computing world uses another operating system—Windows—and that the selection of Mac hardware and software in many local stores is downright meager. (But, to paraphrase my friend Peter Lewis of the *New York Times*, "Cockroaches also outnumber humans. That doesn't make them better.")

I rarely get in my car anymore for computer stuff because it's faster, easier, and usually cheaper to order it online. I know that I'll get exactly what I want at the best price and that it will be delivered to my door promptly.

> **NOTE** There are a handful of great Mac retail stores scattered around the world. The ComputerWare chain in Northern California is one. There are others in many cities. If you're fortunate enough to have a retailer who specializes in the Mac, give them whatever business you can. Unfortunately, no such thing exists in my neck of the woods.

Shopping on the Net is easy, it's safe, and it's fun. So let's go shopping!

Shopping on the Web

Being able to compare prices is probably the best thing about shopping on the Internet. When I want or need something for one of my Macs, I visit several online stores and see what they have to offer and how much they charge. Or I use a ShopBot, one of the comparison-shopping Web sites. After I've done my homework, I order from the vendor offering the best price or the most timely delivery, whichever is more important to me at that moment.

Good Mac Stores Online

If you want the most detailed information on a new Mac, visit The Apple Store (`http://store.apple.com/`). You can order a Mac from this site if you like, but the big four vendors listed next often have better prices.

If you want detailed information on third-party hardware and software for the Mac, visit the Macintosh Products Guide (`http://guide.apple.com/`). But when it comes time to buy, the MPG doesn't offer online shopping. Fortunately, there are at least four major online vendors with huge selections of both Apple hardware and third-party hardware and software.

The big four are Cyberian Outpost (`http://www.outpost.com/`), Mac-Warehouse (`http://www.warehouse.com/macwarehouse/`), MacConnection (`http://www.macconnection.com/`), and MacZone (`http://www.maczone.com/`). Each is an authorized Apple reseller, so you can buy a new or refurbished Mac. Also, they all offer literally thousands of third-party Mac hardware and software products, accessories, and supplies.

It's easy to compare prices; just visit all four sites and use their search feature to find the item you're looking for. All four indicate whether a product is in stock, which is important if you need the item quickly. Finally, each vendor has a different policy and price for standard and overnight shipping, so don't forget to take those charges into account.

That's it. You have all the information you need. Choose a vendor, order your item, and wait for it to be delivered to your door. Each vendor's checkout procedure is a bit different, but all are easy to use.

NOTE Having been totally fair so far, I want to say that I usually don't bother with any of the above. I generally just buy whatever I need from Cyberian Outpost. They usually have the lowest price; they offer free overnight delivery in the U.S. and a 30-day money-back guarantee on most items; and they have a great order-tracking system. Over the course of dozens of transactions, they've always been a pleasure to deal with; so I am a loyal Cyberian Outpost customer.

Shopping for Non-Computer Stuff

There are so many great places to buy things online, it's hard to know where to start. For books, look at the big three: Amazon.com (`http://www.amazon.com/`), Barnes & Noble (`http://www.barnesandnoble.com/`), and Borders (`http://www.borders.com/`). For technical and computer books, try FatBrain.Com (`http://www.fatbrain.com`), formerly known as Computer Literacy and home of one of the largest selections of computer book titles.

If music is your bag, all three big bookstores also sell music CDs. Or you can visit a site that specializes in music, such as CDNow (`http://www.cdnow.com/`), CD Universe (`http://www.cduniverse.com`), or Tower Records (`http://www.towerrecords.com/`).

NOTE If you can't find the music CD you're looking for at one of those six sites, I suspect it's going to be very hard to find that CD anywhere on earth.

Truth is, you can buy almost anything online these days. Why, just last week, I ordered some shorts and swimsuits from Lands' End (`http://www.landsend.com/`) and sent a gift from Sharper Image (`http://www.sharperimage.com/`). The bottom line is that if you have a favorite printed catalog or store, chances are that they also have a Web site with online shopping.

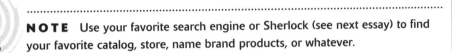

NOTE Use your favorite search engine or Sherlock (see next essay) to find your favorite catalog, store, name brand products, or whatever.

Online Auctions

Another great way to shop on the Internet is by frequenting online auctions. My family and I are big fans of eBay (`http://www.ebay.com`), which offers literally millions of items on the world's largest online auction Web site. There are hundreds of auctions for Mac hardware, peripherals, and software—almost all used—going on at any given time. If it's collectable—beanie babies, coins, art, baseball cards, or whatever—you'll find auctions galore on eBay.

An all-Mac auction started up recently at `http://www.auctionmac.com/`. I haven't used it, but it looks promising. I plan to check this site every so often.

Buying and selling at online auctions is easy and fun. You might even get something at a bargain-basement price. I say online auctions are well worth checking out.

Online Shopping Tips

You may have reservations about shopping online. Perhaps you've heard that it's not safe to use your credit card on the Internet or that sometimes you get—and get charged for—things that you didn't order. Don't worry. Shopping on the Net is as safe as shopping at a mall, as long as you use good sense. Here are some tips.

Security and Safety Issues

You may have heard that your credit card number or other personal information can be stolen if you send it over the Internet. In some cases, this is true; but it's not the threat that it's made out to be. Most reputable Web sites that offer online shopping offer a secure connection between your browser and the vendor. Your personal information, including your credit card number, is encoded and encrypted before it's sent over the Internet. It cannot be deciphered by anyone but the vendor at the other end of the secure connection.

NOTE   I believe all of the sites mentioned in this chapter offer secure connections. Sites that are secure usually display this information prominently. Still, before you submit credit card information over the Internet, it's a good idea to check that the connection is a secure one. Look for a link called Security, or About Our Secure Server (or something like that) on the vendor's pages. Both browsers that come with your iMac—Netscape Navigator and Microsoft Internet Explorer—support secure connections.

Your credit card is safer on a secure Internet connection than with a waitperson or salesperson who takes your card who-knows-where and does who-knows-what with it for five minutes, while it is completely out of your sight. So, if that's what has held you back from shopping on the Net, you have nothing to fear.

One other thing: Always use a credit card on the Internet. Never use your debit card or a check or money order. Why? Because using a credit card almost always provides you with rights if the product isn't up to snuff or if a dispute arises between you and the vendor.

If you use a credit card for a purchase and then have a dispute with a vendor, your credit card company may very well do battle for you. Write them a letter explaining the circumstances and request that the charge be disputed. They will try to work things out with the vendor for you. Having a 900-pound gorilla fight your battle for you usually gives you a better chance of having the situation resolved to your liking. If you use cash, check, or debit card, you don't get the benefits of the 900-pound primate.

Comparison Shopping Services

One last thing that bears discussion is the comparison shopping services (ShopBots), such as BottomDollar (`http://www.bottomdollar.com/`), Excite

Search (http://www.jango.com/), Yahoo! Shopping (http://shopping
.yahoo.com/), and PricePulse (http://www.pricepulse.com/). These Web
sites purport to "search the Internet and find you the lowest prices." For the
most part, they work.

There are some things to consider when you use a ShopBot. The first is that
some vendors seem to be arbitrarily excluded from some ShopBots' searches.
Don't think your ShopBot search is a sure thing; there still may be a lower price
out there on the Net. The answer is to surf to your favorite sites after using a
ShopBot and see if it really did find you the lowest price, because sometimes
they don't.

The second thing is related to the first: The ShopBots often find a low price
from a vendor I've never heard of and have never done business with. What
they don't tell me is that my favorite online vendor offers the same item for
a few cents more. And for a few cents (or even a few bucks), I'll order from
Cyberian Outpost even if the ShopBot doesn't check their prices for me.

Finally, don't forget to check shipping prices and whether the product is in
stock or back-ordered. Most ShopBots don't take these things into account,
so check them out for yourself before you order.

The bottom line is that if you're the kind of person who likes to know you
paid the absolute lowest price for something, the ShopBots are worth a try,
as long as you remember that they're far from flawless.

13 Getting the Most out of Sherlock

If you have Mac OS 8.5 or higher, you have Sherlock, Apple's remarkable
new search application.

N O T E If you aren't sure which version of Mac OS you have, choose About
This Computer from the Finder's Apple menu.

Like earlier versions of Find File, it can search your hard disk for files by name or attributes, such as creation date, size, and kind. But unlike earlier Find File incarnations, Sherlock has two hot new features:

◆ Sherlock can search for words within document files on your hard disk.

◆ Sherlock can search for words on selected Internet Web sites.

Since this is the Internet chapter, we're going to focus on that aspect of Sherlock for now.

NOTE Suffice it to say that if the ability to search for words in documents on your hard disk appeals to you, click the question mark (?) in Sherlock to learn more about searching by content. Then click the Find by Content tab in Sherlock and index your hard disk. That's pretty much all there is to it.

If you don't have OS 8.5 (many early iMacs didn't come with it), consider upgrading your iMac to the latest version of Mac OS. You'll get Sherlock, plus much more. You can find information about operating system upgrades for your iMac at http://www.apple.com/macos/.

Search the Net with Sherlock

As far as I'm concerned, Sherlock's coolest ability is that it can search multiple Web sites simultaneously (and very quickly) and rank the results according to their relevancy. The relevancy ranking is occasionally quirky, but you'll probably find it helpful more often than not.

There is only one requirement before you can use Sherlock's Internet search: You must have an active Internet connection established. If you're not connected to the Internet, log on via AOL or your ISP. Once you're connected, launch Sherlock by doing one of the following:

◆ Choose Apple menu ➤ Sherlock.

◆ Choose File ➤ Find.

◆ Use the keyboard shortcut Command+F (for Find).

Searching the Internet for the First Time

Once Sherlock is running, click the Search Internet tab and you'll see a window like the one in Figure 13.1.

FIGURE 13.1   Sherlock, ready to search the Internet

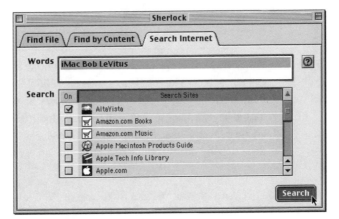

Type a word or phrase into the box at the top (where it says "iMac Bob LeVitus" in Figure 13.1) and click the Search button. Sherlock combs the Internet and returns its findings, as shown in Figure 13.2.

FIGURE 13.2   The results of my search, ranked by relevance

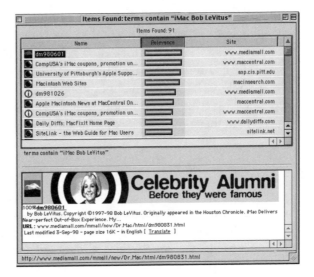

The Items Found window, shown in Figure 13.2, has two panes. The top pane shows the results of the search ranked by relevance. If you select an item in the top pane (dm980601), the bottom pane displays a synopsis, the item's URL, and an advertisement. To view an item, double-click it in the top pane. Your browser will launch automatically if it's not open already, and the item will be displayed.

NOTE Let's see how the relevance ranking worked for my search. The most relevant link, according to Sherlock, was dm980601. This document is a review of the iMac article I wrote for the *Houston Chronicle*. So this is a very relevant document for the keywords *iMac, Bob,* and *LeVitus.* Unfortunately, the next three items in the list are not relevant at all. The fifth item is relevant. The sixth through tenth aren't. So don't depend heavily on the relevance ranking. It misses as often as it hits.

To sort your search results by name or Web site in the Items Found window (instead of by relevance), click the Name or Site column header.

Choosing Sites to Search

What you've seen so far is just the tip of the iceberg. Sherlock can search not only the entire Internet but also only the Web sites you want it to search; and you can choose from literally hundreds of different sites. (I'll show you how in a minute.)

Open Sherlock and click the Search Internet tab. It should look like Figure 13.1. Notice the list in the lower portion of the window, which is a list of search sites Sherlock knows about. Your iMac comes pre-loaded with 16 sites: AltaVista, Amazon Books, Amazon Music, Apple, AppleTIL, Barnes & Noble, CNN, DirectHit, Encyclopedia, Excite, GoTo, Infoseek, LookSmart, Lycos, MacGuide, and Yahoo. You can choose to have Sherlock search any or all of these sites by clicking the On checkbox beside the site's name.

NOTE Sherlock knows which sites it can search by using plug-ins. A folder called Internet Search Sites in your System folder contains 16 plug-ins, one for each of the aforementioned sites. To have Sherlock search a site, download a plug-in for that site (see next section) and put it in this folder.

You can download hundreds of additional plug-ins for Sherlock. The official Apple Sherlock Plug-In Directory is at http://www.apple.com/sherlock/plugins.html. But it has only a handful of them. To get the good stuff, hit the Sherlock Internet Search Archives, the other official Apple Sherlock plug-in page, at http://www.apple-donuts.com/sherlocksearch/index.html. This site has several hundred plug-ins for your downloading delight and has links to Sherlock add-ons and news, too. Finally, if you are a fan of Sherlock, check out the Sherlock Resource Site at http://www.macineurope.com/sherlocksite/. It is a great unofficial site with lots of interesting information about Sherlock and its add-ons and plug-ins.

NOTE If you get the plug-in bug like me (I have more than one hundred of them so far), a program like Baker Street Assistant can help you manage things by letting you enable and disable plug-ins in sets. You can download a copy of Baker Street Assistant from http://www.casadyg.com/.

If Sherlock Crashes or Freezes

If you add a lot of plug-ins, Sherlock may crash or freeze when you launch it. This is simply Sherlock's way of telling you it needs more memory. To give it what it needs, follow these steps:

1. Click the Sherlock icon to select it. It's in the Apple Menu Items folder inside your System folder.

2. Choose File ➢ Get Info or use the keyboard shortcut Command+I.

3. Choose Memory from the Get Info window's pop-up menu and increase the Minimum Size to 2,000K and the Preferred Size to 3,500K.

4. Close the Get Info window.

If Sherlock still crashes, repeat these steps, but this time increase the Minimum Size to 3,000K and the Preferred Size to 6,000K.

14 Safety First on the Internet: Using the EdView Internet Safety Kit

EdView Internet Safety Kit (EISK) blocks your browser from visiting any Web site that hasn't been authorized. Once it's installed and activated, you can only access pages that you have authorized yourself or that are in the EdView Smart Zone.

The Smart Zone contains a database of thousands of sites categorized by both subject and grade level that have been verified by a team of educators as being safe and having educational value. It works with most Internet connections, including ISPs and America Online. This is a heavy-handed approach; but it does block most, if not all, inappropriate content. When you request a site that is not authorized, you'll see the message shown in Figure 14.1.

FIGURE 14.1 **This is what you'll see if you try to access a site outside the Smart Zone.**

The EdView Internet Safety Kit is bundled with all "flavored" iMacs and all iBooks, but you may not have even noticed that you have it. If your iMac came with it, you'll find its installer on the iMac or iBook Install CD-ROM in the Internet folder.

If you didn't get a copy with your iMac, you can download a 30-day demo from EdView at `http://www.edview.com/download/fastdownload.asp`. It'll cost you $40 if you decide to keep it after the 30 days expire.

NOTE If you didn't get a copy of the EdView Internet Safety Kit with your iMac and you don't want to buy one, you may still use EdView's Smart Search for Kids search engine at `http://school.edview.com/search/`. It blocks out most age-inappropriate material, and it's free. However, it doesn't prevent kids from finding inappropriate sites on their own once they leave this site. That's what the Internet Safety Kit does.

Getting Started with EdView Internet Safety Kit

Once installed, EISK limits your browser to Web sites in the Smart Zone. You can also add pages manually. To get EISK up and running, follow these steps:

1. Insert your iMac Install CD-ROM.

2. Open the Internet folder or open the EdView Internet Safety Kit folder.

3. Double-click the Install EdView Family icon.

4. During the installation process, you'll be asked to enter a password. Do this and try not to forget the password.

5. Click the Set button and wait a few seconds. Another dialog box appears.

6. Click the Restart button.

When your iMac reboots, you'll notice a new item—the EV (EdView) menu on the right side of your menu bar. This tells you that your iMac is now protected. Notice how the *V* is red. If you use the menu to turn off protection, the *V* changes to gray. A red *V* means that the protection is on, and a gray *V* means that it's off.

Now let's see if it works. Make sure the EV is red, then connect to the Internet and launch your browser. Now type in any URL that should be blocked. Try your favorite search engine, for example, or try www.garbage.com. You should see a message telling you that this site is outside of the EdView Smart Zone.

NOTE   There are thousands of sites that are in the Smart Zone. So some innocuous sites—like Dell and Apple—come up properly, while others—like Gateway and Outpost—don't. Also notice that sites that you may not mind your kids visiting, such as Disney.com or Nationalgeographic.com, may be blocked by default.

Fortunately, there are two ways to view sites outside the Smart Zone.

Viewing Sites outside the Smart Zone

The easy way to view sites that aren't a part of the Smart Zone is to turn off EISK by choosing Disable Channel Lock from the EV menu. As long as you know the password, disabling EISK takes only a second and allows you to access anything on the Internet.

When you turn EISK back on (choose Enable Channel Lock from the EV menu), you'll see a dialog box that recommends that you clear your browser's cache immediately. If you've visited any sites you wouldn't want the kids to see, be sure to do that. The cache is in your browser's Preferences dialog box.

But this doesn't answer the bigger question: How do I allow my kids to see a site that isn't included in the Smart Zone without disabling EISK? Fortunately, this is easy, too; though not quite as easy as shutting the thing off completely.

To add a site, choose Edit Preferences from the EV menu. In the Preferences dialog box, click the Sites tab. Now comes the hard part: This dialog box doesn't want to know the name of the site you want to enable; instead, it wants the site's IP address. No problem! Assuming you're already connected to the Internet, just click the little Go To NSLookUp link in the dialog box, as shown in Figure 14.2.

FIGURE 14.2 **Clicking the Go To NSLookUp link in the EdView Channel Lock Preferences dialog box lets you look up any site's IP address.**

EdView™ Channel Lock Preferences

General | Services | **Sites** | Servers

IP Addresses where all services are allowed

☑ 17.254.3.196 – livepage.apple.com
☑ 198.3.98.160 – my.excite.com
☑ 208.218.3.18 – Disney.com

[Add] [Remove] Go To NSLookUp

[Cancel] [OK]

Your browser will launch and you can type in the name of any site you want the IP address for. Type in a keyword, such as **Disney** or **National Geographic**, and press Return. The IP address will appear. Write it down. Now click the Add button in the EdView Channel Lock Preferences dialog box and type the IP address and domain name for this site. Click OK. That's it. The site is now enabled and EISK will no longer block it. In Figure 14.2 you can see that I've added Disney.com as an approved site.

NOTE Quite frankly, although this program worked fine in my limited testing, I feel more comfortable being nearby when my kids, ages 6 and 10, surf the Internet. On the other hand, this site is better than nothing, and the price (free if you have one of the later-model, "flavored" iMacs or an iBook) can't be beat. However, I ultimately found it a hassle and uninstalled it, but that doesn't mean it's not worth a try.

15 Home Sweet Web Page with Adobe PageMill

This essay will briefly show you how to create a Web page. Read the next essay for a discussion of how to actually get pages you create onto the Web.

NOTE   PageMill is included with all "flavored" iMacs. If you don't have an Adobe PageMill CD-ROM (or you are an iBook user) and you still want to join in the fun and create a Web page for yourself, you can download a 30-day examination copy from Adobe's Web site at `http://www.adobe.com/prodindex/pagemill/demodnld.html#mac`.

To understand what PageMill is and what it does, you have to understand a little about how Web pages work. All Web pages are constructed using HTML (HyperText Markup Language). HTML looks like English, but it's a pain in the keister for mere mortals to program. Since a picture is worth a thousand words, here's a quick demonstration. Figure 15.1 shows a simple Web page viewed with the Netscape browser.

Figure 15.2 shows the HTML code for the simple Web page shown in Figure 15.1.

It's ugly, isn't it? Suffice it to say that creating Web pages by typing out HTML code isn't fun or easy. That's what Adobe PageMill is all about. It lets you create Web pages, or even entire Web sites, without having to type one line of HTML code. You don't really even need to know anything about HTML code (though you may want to if you're serious about creating Web pages).

Adobe PageMill is a visual Web page and Web site builder. It's a rich, complex program that lets you construct individual Web pages, as well as manage entire Web sites. Alas, I don't have the space to show you very much about PageMill. What I hope to do in our brief time is show you how easy it can be to construct a simple Web page using PageMill.

FIGURE 15.1 A simple Web page viewed with a browser

FIGURE 15.2 The HTML code for the Hello World page

```
<HTML>
<HEAD>
  <META NAME="GENERATOR" CONTENT="Adobe Pagemill 3.0 Mac">
  <TITLE>myhome</TITLE>
</HEAD>
<BODY BGCOLOR="#009999">

<P><CENTER> </CENTER></P>

<P><CENTER><FONT SIZE="+4"></FONT> </CENTER></P>

<P><CENTER><FONT SIZE="+4"></FONT> </CENTER></P>

<P><CENTER><FONT COLOR="#ff0000" SIZE="+4">Hello World!</FONT></CENTER></P>

</BODY>
</HTML>
```

The Five-Minute Web Page

First, install PageMill if you haven't already done so. Now launch it. An untitled document will appear on your screen. This will become your Web page. Next, save the Web page. If I haven't mentioned it before, it's always a good idea to save important documents often. To save the page, follow these steps:

1. Choose File ➢ Save Page As.

2. Use the New Folder button to create a new folder for your Web site.

3. Name the folder **Website**.

4. Name the file **homepage**.

5. Save it inside the Website folder.

> **NOTE** Although we're only going to create a single page in this exercise, it's a good idea to dedicate a separate folder to each Web site you create. Most Web sites consist of numerous text and graphic files. It is a good habit to have one folder for all the text and graphics files that belong to a site. That way, as your site grows, it'll be much easier to keep track of its content if it's all saved in a single folder.

Now we're ready to create the five-minute Web page.

1. Near the top of the page, you'll find the Title field. Double-click the words *untitled document* and replace them with the words **My Home Page**.

2. Click in the gray area below the Title field. This is where you design your page. Press the Return key 3 or 4 times to move the cursor down toward the middle of the page. Type **Welcome to my home page** or something equally creative.

3. Choose Edit ➤ Select All or use the keyboard shortcut Command+A.

4. Click the Center Align Text button (Figure 15.3).

FIGURE 15.3 **PageMill's Center Align Text button**

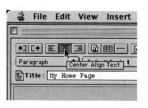

5. Choose Largest Heading from the pop-up Style menu (Figure 15.4).

6. Choose Site ➤ Show Settings. In the Site Settings dialog box, click the Add button.

7. Type **My Home Page** for the Site Name.

FIGURE 15.4 PageMill's pop-up Style menu

8. In the upper section of the dialog box (Local Site Location), click the folder icon next to Local Site Location. Find your Website folder in the dialog box and click the Choose button.

9. In the lower section of the dialog box (Site Destination), click the Local Folder radio button at the bottom, click the icon of a folder next to it, and find your Website folder in the dialog box. Create a new folder and name it **Webstuff**. (You can't use your Website folder for this step; it requires a unique and separate folder.) Click the Choose button. The dialog box should look like Figure 15.5.

FIGURE 15.5 Your Site Settings dialog box should look like this.

10. Click the Close button to dismiss the Site Settings dialog box. Choose File ➤ Upload ➤ Page. You'll see a brief flash as the file is created on your hard disk.

You have created a Web page and uploaded it to your hard disk! To check your handiwork, use your browser to open the homepage file inside the Webstuff folder.

NOTE If you want to see the HTML code for this page, choose View ➤ Page Source (in Netscape Navigator) or View ➤ Source (in Microsoft Internet Explorer).

This page is not yet live on the Internet. You'll have to read the next essay to find out how to do that. But before we get to that, here is a quick look at some other stuff you can do to your Web page with PageMill.

Other Stuff You Can Do with PageMill

PageMill lets you do more than just put a few words on a Web page. For example, you can easily add a picture to spice up your page. Or, you can add a link to another Web page or another site.

Adding a Picture

You need a .gif or .jpg (GIF or JPEG) graphics file for this. If you don't have one of your own, there are some in the Tour folder in the PageMill folder on your hard disk. You'll find additional graphics files on the PageMill CD-ROM in the Web Pages and Content folder.

NOTE AppleWorks and GraphicConverter can open many kinds of picture files and can save the picture as either a GIF or JPEG file. There's more about GIF and JPEG and what it all means in the last essay in this chapter, which covers how to prepare pictures to send by e-mail.

To add a picture to your home page, follow these steps:

1. Open your homepage file in PageMill if it's not already open.

2. Click just above the text you typed earlier.

3. Choose Insert ➢ Object ➢ Image.

4. Choose your graphics (JPEG or GIF) file from the dialog box and click Insert.

The picture will appear in your page, as shown in Figure 15.6.

FIGURE 15.6   Just like that, I added a picture to my home page.

Of course, there is much more that you can do with your picture now—resize it, reposition it, make it a link, and other stuff. But this is supposed to be a tantalizing look at creating your own Web pages. After I show you how to create a link, you're on your own.

Making a Link

Now you have a page with words and a picture. But how do you create a link to another page, which is the cornerstone of modern Web page design and implementation? To link to another Web page, follow these steps:

1. Type the words you want to make into your link anywhere on the page.

2. Select the words you want to make into your link.

3. Choose Edit ➢ Make Link or use the keyboard shortcut Command+M.

4. Type the URL of the page you want to link to in the Make WWW Link field.

5. Click the Make WWW Link button.

That's it, you've got a link, as shown in Figure 15.7.

FIGURE 15.7 And just like that, a link is born.

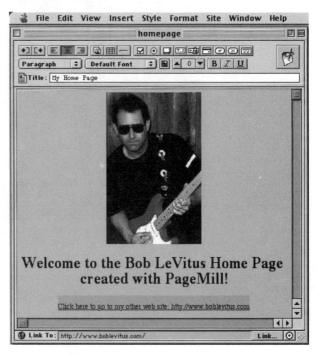

There is much more that PageMill can do, but that's all we have space for. I hope I've, at the very least, shown you how very easy it can be to create a Web page from scratch.

NOTE PageMill is a very capable and feature-rich program. If you are serious about building a Web page, be sure to read the *Getting Started* and *User Guide* .pdf files on the CD-ROM and check out the extensive PageMill help system.

16 Publish or Perish on the Web

Unlike most of the essays in this book, this one isn't a hands-on tutorial. The subject matter—hosting a Web site or page—is just too broad. Instead, this essay will discuss the pros and cons of hosting a Web page or site locally on your iMac or iBook using Personal Web Sharing versus having an ISP or America Online host your page or site for you. Each approach has its advantages and disadvantages; we'll look at both approaches.

Using Your iMac or iBook As a Web Server

Mac OS 8.1 and above include the Web sharing control panel, which can turn your iMac or iBook into a personal Web server with just a few clicks. It's not designed to host a big, complex Web site; but it can host a simple home page. Moreover, Personal Web Sharing makes it extremely easy to share files with any Internet user.

The Advantages of Using Your iMac or iBook As a Web Server

Probably the biggest advantage of using your iMac or iBook as a Web server is that it's free (assuming you have an Internet connection already). Another plus is that it's very easy to set up a page that allows you to share files with others on the Internet, complete with password protection if you so desire. Finally, you can use your Mac to share files this way without having to create a Web page at all. Your Mac will automatically create a page listing files you have made available for others to download.

NOTE If you want to try Personal Web Sharing yourself, open Mac OS Help and search for Web Sharing. There you'll find a bevy of articles and interactive guided tutorials that will have you up and running in minutes. Good luck.

The Disadvantages of Using Your iMac or iBook As a Web Server

First and foremost, your iMac or iBook Web server is available only when you are connected to the Internet. So, if you have a dial-up connection (you use a modem and not ISDN, cable modem, or DSL), you have to be connected for your page to appear on the Web. If you want a full-time site, you'll have to remain connected to the Internet 24 hours a day. A related drawback is that if you are connected by modem, your Web server will be fairly slow for users. Finally, Personal Web Sharing can handle only a single page or a list of files or both. But it can't handle a huge multi-page Web site, nor can it handle more advanced Web site features, such as guest-logging, e-commerce, and searching within your site.

NOTE I could not get Personal Web Sharing to work using AOL as my Internet connection. I'm told that it can be done, but I couldn't make it work for me. (However, it worked fine when I used a local ISP to connect to the Internet.) If you use AOL for your Internet connection, you may not be able to use Personal Web Sharing.

Using an ISP or AOL to Host Your Web Site

If you want a full-time Web site or if your needs are greater than the single-page Personal Web Sharing offers, your best bet is to let someone else host your site. That way it will be faster; it will be available 24 hours a day, whether or not your iMac or iBook is turned on; and you'll have professional assistance if you need it.

The Advantages of Using an ISP or AOL to Host Your Web Site

First and foremost, an ISP or AOL host's connection to the Internet is guaranteed to be faster than yours; so your pages will be served up faster and can be seen by more users simultaneously. Another advantage is that your site will be available 24 hours a day. You can also add services like e-commerce, streaming audio or video, or secure transactions if you like (with an ISP but not with AOL). Finally, most ISPs (but not AOL) offer great technical support for your site.

The Disadvantages of Using an ISP or AOL to Host Your Web Site

The biggest disadvantage is that it's going to cost you something. If you use AOL and your needs are modest, you get 2 megabytes of space for a Web page included with your monthly fee. But if your site exceeds 2 megs, you'll have to find another host. AOL doesn't have an option for bigger sites. ISPs charge anywhere from $15 a month to hundreds of dollars a month, depending upon what services you require and the size of your site.

The only other disadvantage I can think of is that hosting a site remotely is somewhat more complicated than turning on Personal Web Sharing. Be prepared to invest substantial time if you want to set up and run a Web server hosted remotely.

The Bottom Line

If your needs are few and all you want is a simple home page or the ability to allow people to download files from your Mac via the Internet, Personal Web Sharing is for you. Don't forget that your iMac or iBook has to be connected to the Internet for your page to be available to others.

If you want a feature-rich, multi-page Web site that's fast, available 24 hours a day, and can include advanced features, your best bet is to find a good ISP and have them host it.

17 Fixing Pix for E-mail

This is a quick tutorial about how to prepare pictures—optimizing both the file size and quality—and send them via e-mail to Mac or PC users. If you don't work with pictures or don't e-mail pictures to others, you'll find this essay totally irrelevant. Otherwise, read on.

The basic premise is that pictures sent via e-mail should almost always be converted to the JPEG file format before sending.

NOTE JPEG is the Joint Photographic Experts Group file format. It creates smaller files than almost any other file format and preserves the integrity of your photos better than other compressed file formats, such as GIF.

There are two ways that you can accomplish this: the quick-and-dirty method using AppleWorks and the slightly more complicated (but more controllable) method using GraphicConverter, which you'll find on the CD-ROM that came with this book. Let's take a look.

Quick-and-Dirty Picture Fixing with AppleWorks

First, let's try the easy way to get your picture saved in the JPEG format:

1. Launch AppleWorks.

2. Open the picture file.

NOTE This is the part that may throw you: AppleWorks cannot open all pictures. For example, if your picture is saved in the TIFF format, AppleWorks may or may not be able to open it. If you can't open your picture using AppleWorks, skip to the next section now.

3. Edit, resize, and otherwise manipulate the picture until you're satisfied.

4. Choose File ➤ Save As.

5. Choose JPEG from the pop-up Save As menu.

6. Name your file and click Save.

You're now ready to e-mail that file (see the final section of this essay). Using this technique, I slimmed a 636K PICT file into a 40K JPEG file with almost no loss of quality.

While this method is easy and creates a JPEG file, which is what you want, you have no control over the quality or size of the JPEG file. This may well be all you want or need. But if you would like some additional control over the quality of your picture, you'll want to use GraphicConverter instead of AppleWorks.

Picture Fixing with GraphicConverter

GraphicConverter is a great shareware program that can open almost every graphics file format ever invented and can save your file using almost any graphics file format ever invented. There are two reasons you might prefer GraphicConverter over AppleWorks. First, Graphic-Converter can open many types of graphics files that AppleWorks can't open. Second, GraphicConverter lets you adjust the image quality of your picture, allowing you to tweak both the quality of your picture and the size of the resulting file.

NOTE GraphicConverter is shareware. If you use it more than a few times, you are honor-bound to send its author, Thorsten Lemke, $35. Don't be a creep—if you use it, please pay for it.

Here's how to make a better JPEG file:

1. Install *GraphicConverter* from this book's companion CD-ROM if you haven't already done so.

2. Launch GraphicConverter.

3. Open the picture file.

4. Edit, resize, and otherwise manipulate the picture until you're satisfied.

5. Choose File ➢ Save As.

6. Choose JPEG/JFIF from the pop-up Format menu.

7. Click the Options button. This brings up the Options dialog box, where the real fun happens.

8. Click both the Preview and Calculate File Size check boxes. These two items make the Options dialog box much more useful.

NOTE If you want to see a different part of your picture in the preview, click directly on the preview picture and drag. That will allow you to move it around.

9. Slide the Quality slider left or right. When you do so, keep an eye on the Preview so you can see how the quality setting affects the way your picture looks. While you're playing with the slider, keep your other eye on the file-size information so you know how big your file will be at this quality setting. See Figure 17.1 for an example. Ignore the Library section of this dialog box for now. Leave it set to JPEG 6.0 with the Progressive option unchecked.

FIGURE 17.1 Compare the quality and file size at the lowest setting (left) and highest setting (right).

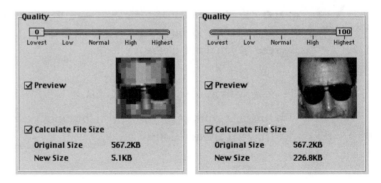

NOTE You'll achieve the best balance of file size and quality near the middle of the scale, where it says "Normal."

10. Once you're happy with the quality and size, click OK.

11. Name your file and click Save.

That's it. You're ready to e-mail that file (see the final section).

Sending Your Picture via E-mail

The hard part is over. Now just launch your e-mail program, prepare a message to your recipient, then add the JPEG picture as an enclosure. Now send the message. Your recipient will receive the JPEG file; and, assuming they have a program that can open a JPEG file (which almost every computer user—Mac and PC—does), they'll be able to download and view your picture.

NOTE If your e-mail program offers the option of compressing the file before sending, don't bother. When you saved the file in the JPEG format, you compressed it. Using your e-mail's compression won't make the file (much) smaller and may complicate things for the recipient.

SOHO: The Small Office/Home Office iMac or iBook

The iMac or iBook is a near-perfect computer for the small business or home office. I've worked out of my home using my Macs for 12 years and I've picked up a tip or two along the way. In this chapter, we'll look at ways of using an iMac or iBook to run your business, as well as ways of using your iMac or iBook to become more efficient and effective at what you do.

Here's what we'll cover:

Just the Fax, Ma'am   Shows how to install and get the most out of FAXstf, which is included with all iMacs and iBooks.

Quicken Can Manage Your Business (Maybe)   Contains tips and hints for using Quicken to handle finances for your small businesses.

Getting Along with the Aliens   Contains tips and hints for working with our less-fortunate brethren (and sister-en), Windows users.

Organize This   Introduces you to the powerful personal organizer, Consultant (demo version on CD), and shows how it helps you manage contacts, appointments, reminders, alarms, and more.

Windows on Your iMac or iBook   Talks about emulation software— SoftWindows and Virtual PC—programs that let you run Windows software on your iMac or iBook.

18   Just the Fax, Ma'am

Did you know you have a complete fax machine living inside your iMac or iBook? All you need to use it is a phone line, an internal modem, and the included FAXstf software.

Is FAXstf Right for Me?

Is FAXstf the right choice for your small business or home office? That depends. Let's look at the pros and cons of having your iMac or iBook double as your fax machine.

Pros:

◆ It's free.

◆ You don't have to print documents before sending them.

◆ It's easy.

◆ You can file away incoming faxes on your hard disk.

◆ You can read incoming faxes onscreen and never print them if you don't want to.

◆ It doesn't require additional desk space.

◆ QuickNote (FAXstf's instant fax feature) is handy and fast.

◆ It's free. (I know I listed it twice, but it's an important consideration for many!)

Cons:

◆ You have to leave your iMac or iBook on all the time.

◆ You can only fax documents created by applications on your iMac or iBook. (In other words, you can't fax hard copy—magazine pages, handwritten documents, etc.—unless you have a scanner. Even if you have a scanner, the results of this approach are usually worse than those you'd get from a stand-alone fax machine.)

◆ You may notice a slowdown of other operations on your iMac or iBook while it's sending or receiving a fax.

◆ If you want a printed copy, you must print the fax after it's received (an additional step).

It's a toss-up. If you do little faxing and have no need to fax hard copy, or if you're on a tight budget, FAXstf is just the ticket. On the other hand, if you have heavy fax needs or often fax articles or other hard copy, you'll be happier with a stand-alone fax machine.

So, if you think FAXstf might work for you, read on….

Getting It On…

Before we begin, make sure FAXstf is both installed and enabled on your iMac or iBook. To do this, open the Extensions Manager control panel and click on the Package column heading, then scroll down the list so you can see all four FAXstf items. Make sure all four are checked, as shown in Figure 18.1.

> **NOTE** On both of my iMacs, FAXstf was installed but not enabled. On a third iMac, it wasn't installed. Go figure. I have no idea if it's installed on an iBook, having not yet received mine.

FIGURE 18.1 If all four FAXstf items are turned on in Extensions Manager, you're ready to begin sending or receiving faxes (you may need to restart your Mac first).

On/Off	Name	Size	Version	Package
☒	Speech Manager	32K	1.5.3	English Text-To-Speech 1...
☒	FAXstf PPC Shared Library	308K	5.0.5	FAXstf from STF Technologi...
☒	STF Toolbox	96K	5.0.5	FAXstf from STF Technologi...
☒	FaxMonitor	20K	5.0.5	FAXstf™ • FaxMonitor
☒	STFInit	40K	5.0.5	FAXstf™ • STFInit
☒	AppleScript	996K	1.3.4	iMac 1.5

If you don't see all four items, you'll need to reinstall (or install) FAXstf. You'll find an installer in the FAXstf folder, in the Applications folder on the Install Software CD-ROM that came with your iMac or iBook.

After you've enabled all four items (or installed FAXstf from the CD), you'll need to restart your iMac or iBook.

That's it! Your iMac or iBook (assuming it's plugged into a phone line) is now a full-blown fax machine!

Getting Ready

Before you can send or receive your first fax, you need to set FAXstf's settings. Here's how:

Launch the Fax Browser application and choose Edit ➤ Settings. Configure the settings by clicking the icons on the left and completing the information on the right for each icon (Cover Page, Dialing, Fax Browser, etc.)

NOTE You'll find complete instructions for choosing your settings in the FAXstf User Manual, which is in the FAXstf folder on your hard disk. I'm afraid that if you are going to use FAXstf, you'll have to read the manual. It's full of important information that I don't have room for in this essay, such as which settings you should use in the Settings dialog box.

When you've selected all your settings, click Done.

OK, you're ready to fax.

Sending a Fax

This is so easy you're going to laugh. Open AppleWorks (or any application that has a Print command). Create a document that you want to fax to someone. Save it (just in case something happens during the creation and sending of your fax). When it's ready to fax, try this experiment:

Pull down the File menu. You see a Print command, but no Fax command, right? Now press the Command and Option keys and pull down the File menu. You should now see a Fax command instead of the Print command. Choose it.

NOTE This assumes you didn't change your activation keys in the Fax Menu section of the Settings dialog box. If you changed the activation keys to something other than Command and Option, press those keys instead.

That's the magic of FAXstf. In whatever application you are using, holding down Command and Option changes the Print command into the Fax command in the File menu. Neat, huh?

OK, just one more thing to do before you can send your fax. Choose Temporary Address from the pop-up menu (it should say Fax Numbers before you pop it up) or use the keyboard shortcut Command+N. Fill in the blank fields for Company, Fax Number, First and Last Name, etc., then click OK.

N O T E Actually, the only field that's required is the fax number field; the others are optional but it's considered good form to fill them in anyway.

That's it. Click Send and your fax will wing its way to wherever.

Sending a QuickNote

Every so often you may find you need to dash off a quick fax to someone. That's what FAXstf's QuickNote feature is all about. It's easy and fast and doesn't require you to create your document in another program. To send a QuickNote, follow these steps:

1. Launch Fax Browser.

2. Choose File ➤ Send a QuickNote, or use the keyboard shortcut Command+K.

3. Fill in the Company, Fax Number, Title, and both Name fields, as shown in Figure 18.2.

N O T E Again, the only field that's required is the Fax Number field; the others are optional but it's considered good form to fill them in anyway.

4. Type your brief note in the Cover Page Note field.

5. Click Send Fax.

And that's all. Just like that, a half-page fax will be sent to the recipient.

Receiving a Fax

Again, this is such a no-brainer, you're going to laugh. Launch Fax Browser and choose Edit ➤ Settings again. Click the Fax Modem icon on the left, then make a choice from the Answer On pop-up menu. This tells your modem how many rings to wait before answering and receiving a fax. After you've selected the number of rings, click Done. Presto! It's done. Your iMac or iBook will now answer the phone after the number of rings you selected and receive your fax automatically.

FIGURE 18.2 My QuickNote is ready to send.

Untitled QuickNote

Company	Bungie Software
Fax Number	312-555-1212
Title	Myth II Rocks
First Name	Doug
Last Name	Zartman

FAXstf™

Cover Page QuickNote

Cover Page Note

Doug,

Just wanted to tell you that Myth II is the best multi-player game I've ever tried. I just love it. Keep up the good work.

Regards -- Bob LeVitus

Clear   Send Fax

19 Quicken Can Manage Your Business (Maybe)

If you use your iMac or iBook to run a small business or sole proprietorship, chances are you can use Quicken (which came free with your iMac or iBook) to track your business's income and expenses. And while it's not a full-blown business accounting software package, it may well have all the capabilities you need. So the next section is dedicated to helping you figure out whether you can use Quicken instead of a more expensive and complicated accounting package. The section after that shows you some of the tips I've discovered in the years I've used Quicken to manage my business's finances.

NOTE My accountant tells me that using Quicken over the course of the year saves me time and money at tax time. It reduces the fees I would otherwise have to pay him for organizing my finances for filing and saves me hours that I would otherwise have to spend putting my financial information together.

NOTE In a related note, Quicken has built-in links to MacInTax (another Intuit program you can buy each spring). If you generally fill out your own tax return, using Quicken during the year may save you even more time come April 15.

How to Decide If Quicken Will Work for You

Let's start with an easy situation: If you have employees and are responsible for payroll taxes, Quicken is probably not right for you. While you can jury-rig it to handle FICA and SSA and the like, it's not really designed to handle payroll. If you want to handle your own finances, you'll probably need a more capable accounting program such as MYOB Accounting Plus 8.0 from BestWare or QuickBooks from Intuit (Quicken's big brother).

NOTE I have never used either program (I use Quicken!) so I can't recommend one or the other.

On the other hand, if you have only one or two employees, you may be able to get away with using Quicken anyway. My best advice if that describes your situation is to talk to your accountant or bookkeeper and explain what you're trying to do. A financial professional is best equipped to tell you whether Quicken's capabilities are sufficient for your needs.

Here's another easy one: If your business has product inventory and/or transacts multiple sales every day, Quicken may not be powerful enough for your needs.

So who is a prospect for using Quicken to run their business? If you are a one-person shop and provide a service (as opposed to physical goods and inventory), Quicken is nearly perfect. If you're a consultant, freelance writer, or almost any type of freelancer, it could be just the ticket. Or, if you sell physical goods but have few sales to record each day, it may work for you.

If you fall into one of those categories, here's what you can do with Quicken: You can track your income and expenses to the penny, record every check you write, and view or print detailed reports about your finances. Not bad for a program you got free with your iMac, eh? Alas, this is one time you iBook users lose out: Apple made the decision not to include Quicken in your software bundle. Still, you might want to read the chapter to see what Quicken can do for you, then perhaps (gasp) buy a copy.

Tips for Using Quicken to Manage Your Business Finances

First, create a separate Quicken file for your business transactions. When you create it, you'll want to select Business categories, as shown in Figure 19.1.

FIGURE 19.1 When you create your Quicken file for business, be sure to check the Business categories checkbox.

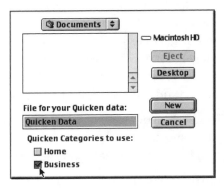

Doing so will start your file with a selection of appropriate categories. You'll probably want to add categories as you go along, but you'll start off with most of the important ones you're likely to need.

The type of account you want to create for your main business file is almost always Bank, but some of Quicken's other account types—Cash, Asset, Credit Card, Liability, Portfolio, etc.—may also be helpful, depending upon the kind of business you run.

NOTE I use only a Bank account, but your needs may be different.

Using Categories

The heart of making Quicken work for your small business is its categories. If you use Quicken categories for every transaction you enter, you'll be able to create meaningful reports that track just about anything you need to know about your financial situation.

NOTE Quicken's reports are very flexible, so you don't really have to create categories to generate meaningful reports. Still, it makes things a lot easier in the long run. Trust me, I've been doing this for years…. If you create useful categories up front, creating meaningful reports down the road will be easier.

Although Quicken created several dozen income and expense categories when you created your file initially, it's generally helpful to add categories of your own. For example, since my work is project based, I create a separate category for each project's income and expenses. That way, I can quickly create a report that shows how I'm doing on each project—or generate an income and expense report that shows how all my projects are doing at once.

To add categories, choose Lists ➤ Categories and Transfers or use the keyboard shortcut Command+L. Then click the New button near the bottom of the window to create your new category.

You don't have to create them all at once or create them at the beginning of the year. When you add a new vendor, for example, or a new revenue source, it's perfectly acceptable to add a new category at that time.

Finally, categories can have sub-categories. So, for example, I have a category called Royalties, with sub-categories for each book I've written. While I don't expect this exact model to work for you, you should plan ahead as you create your categories; sub-categories may make things even easier for you.

To use your categories, be sure to assign a category to every transaction you enter into your register. Quicken makes it easy. Merely type the first letter or two of your category into the Category field of the register and Quicken will fill in the name for you. Or click the black triangle next to the Category field in the register and choose your category from the pop-up list.

Using Reports

Quicken has two types of reports that help you understand your financial situation at any moment. If you've created meaningful categories and assigned them religiously to each transaction, you'll be able to find out just what's going on with either a QuickReport or regular report, in seconds.

QuickReports are fast and easy to set up but relatively inflexible. Quicken's regular reports are more comprehensive and configurable, but take more time to set up.

To create a QuickReport, choose Activities ➢ QuickReport. Choose the subject of your report—Category, Payee, Description, etc.—from the pop-up menu, type a keyword into the Contains field, then choose a time period, as shown in Figure 19.2.

FIGURE 19.2 This QuickReport will tell me in an instant how much money I've spent on hardware this year.

```
┌─────────────────────────────────────────────────┐
│ ▢            Create QuickReport             ▤    │
│ ┌─────────────────────────────────────────────┐ │
│  Show transactions in all accounts where         │
│                                                   │
│   Category ▼    contains      Hardware           │
│                                                   │
│  Date : Year-to-date ▼                           │
│                                                   │
│            ┌────────┐   ┌──────────┐             │
│            │ Cancel │   │    OK    │             │
│            └────────┘   └──────────┘             │
└─────────────────────────────────────────────────┘
```

That's it. Click OK and your report will be generated in an instant.

NOTE If you choose a category in the Categories and Transfers window before you choose QuickReport from the Activities menu, that category will automatically be typed into the Contains field.

To print your QuickReport, choose File ➢ Print Report.

To create a regular report, choose Activities ➢ Reports and Graphs ➢ Reports. This brings up the Reports window, as shown in Figure 19.3.

The Standard and Business tabs are probably the most useful, so examine the reports they offer. Once you've decided which report you want, click the Customize button to tailor it precisely to your needs.

FIGURE 19.3 The Reports window lets you tailor a report to your specific needs.

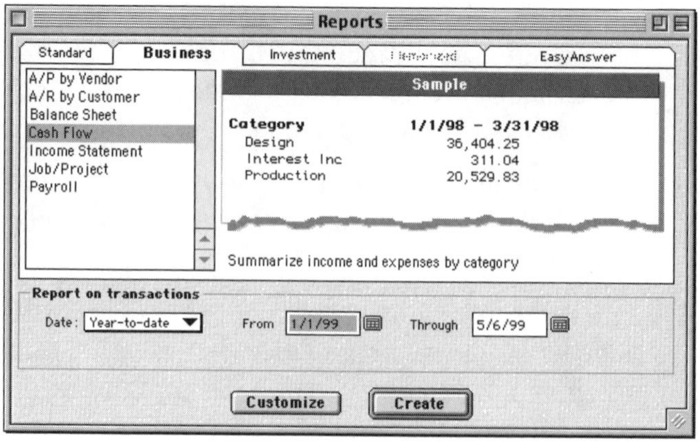

The Customize window offers three tabs: Layout, Content, and Organization. Be sure to visit all three to ensure your report contains what you want and looks the way you like it to.

Once everything appears just as you like it in the Customize window, click OK. Quicken will generate your report instantly.

To print your report, choose File ➢ Print Report.

20 Getting Along with the Aliens

Not everyone is as smart as we are. Not everyone uses a Mac (or an iMac or iBook). In fact, most people use another type of computer, commonly known as a PC. PCs don't use the same operating system as Macs. They use an inferior one from Microsoft, called Windows. (I have seen Windows and trust me, it's no Macintosh!) Alas, Windows and Macintosh are only marginally compatible. So this chapter will show you how to exchange files and messages with your less-fortunate brethren (and sister-en), Windows users, without breaking a sweat.

There are two ways you might want to exchange files or messages with PC users—electronically (via e-mail) or by disk. Let's look at both.

Sharing with PC Users via the Internet

Sharing files and messages with PC users via the Internet is a piece of cake. But before we get into the specifics, I need to define two things—e-mail *messages* and e-mail *attachments*.

An e-mail message is all text. You type the message, fill in the recipient's e-mail address, then click Send. The PC user receives the text of your message. It really is that easy. I'll show you how in a moment.

An e-mail attachment is a file from your hard disk (usually) that is attached to your e-mail message. In this case, you need to make sure the file you attach is in a form that a PC user can read. Attaching a file is also relatively easy if you know what you're doing. I'll show you how to do this, too, in a moment.

Sending E-mail Messages to PC Users

An e-mail message is, by its nature, all text. So, since PCs understand text as well as Macs, you don't have to do anything special to send an e-mail message to a PC user.

As long as you have an e-mail account and a connection to the Internet, all you need to do to send e-mail to a PC user is create it, then send it. Here's how:

Open your preferred e-mail program (usually AOL or Outlook Express). Now create a new e-mail message (Mail Center ➢ Write Mail for AOL, File ➢ New ➢ Mail Message for Outlook Express). When the form appears, fill in the recipient's e-mail address and a subject, then type your message in the body of the form. Finally, when everything looks right, click Send Now. That's it. Your message will arrive in the PC user's mailbox shortly.

Sending Files (Enclosures or Attachments) to PC Users

This takes a bit more forethought. That's because PCs can't read every kind of file on your Mac hard disk. You have to make sure the file you enclose (sometimes called attach) is a type of file the PC will be able to decipher. For example, you can't send a Mac program, control panel, extension, or other Mac OS file to a PC user.

NOTE Actually, you can send it and they can receive it, but their PC won't know what to do with it and it'll appear on their end as junk.

But documents created by Mac applications are another story. As long as you save them in a format the PC can understand, your recipient will be able to use them. So before you enclose a document to send to a PC user, the first thing you need to do is make sure to save that document in a file format a PC can understand.

Among the file formats that work pretty much flawlessly across platforms are…

For graphics files:

◆ TIFF

◆ JPG (sometimes called JPEG)

◆ GIF

For text files:

◆ Text (sometimes called ASCII)

◆ RTF (Rich Text Format, which will work if they have a current version of Microsoft Office on their PC)

Other file formats PCs can read:

◆ Microsoft Office 98 files created by PowerPoint, Excel, or Word (assuming they have a recent version of Office on their PC)

NOTE This list is by no means exhaustive. It's just a few file formats I know for sure will work on either platform. If you use some other program that is available for both Macs and PCs—Photoshop, CorelDraw, WordPerfect, etc.—their native file format may very well work too. The bottom line is that the above-mentioned formats will work for sure; you'll have to experiment to see if other formats work also.

In other words, use the Save As command in whatever program you're using, then choose one of formats listed above from the list of available file formats in the Save As dialog box.

Once you've saved the file in a compatible format, follow the instructions in the previous section for creating an e-mail message, but don't perform the final step (clicking Send Now) yet.

Before you send the message, you have to add the enclosure. If you're using America Online, click the Attach Files button and find the file (or files) you want to attach.

NOTE Be sure you do not enable the Compress Attachments checkbox in the Attach Files dialog box. Files you send to Windows users should never be compressed.

If you're using Outlook Express, click Add Attachments and find the file (or files) you want to attach. You needn't do anything special to make sure the file is not compressed before sending.

NOTE If you use Outlook Express, you may have to tinker with the settings in the Preference dialog box's Message Composition section. The portions you're interested in are the Attachment encoding pop-up menu and the Compress Attachments checkbox. Make sure that AppleDouble or Base64 is selected from the former and that the latter is unchecked. These settings should allow you to send attachments to PC users without any problems.

Sharing Data with PC Users on Disk

Macs are great. They can create disks (floppy, Zip, Jaz, SuperDisk, etc.) that PCs can read. Better still, a Mac can read a floppy disk, Zip, Jaz, or Super-Disk disk created on a PC.

A PC, on the other hand, can't read or write Mac disks.

So, to share files with a PC user, you have to do two things:

1. Format the disk so their PC can read it.

2. Make sure the files you want to deliver on the disk are saved in a format a PC can understand.

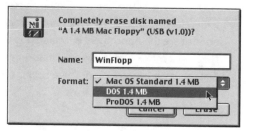

N O T E Read the previous section about file formats a PC can understand when you send files as enclosures with e-mail. The same rules apply to files you deliver to PC users on disk—they must be saved in a format a PC can understand.

If you have a floppy disk drive, you can create a disk that your PC-using friends can use with Windows. Just follow these steps:

1. Insert a floppy disk.

2. Click on it once to select it.

3. Choose Special ≻ Erase Disk.

4. Name the disk. (Note that it can only have 11 characters in its name—8 characters with a 3-character extension—like this: WINSLAME.DOC. That's because Windows is lame.)

5. Choose DOS 1.4MB from the pop-up menu, as shown in Figure 20.1.

FIGURE 20.1 It's a cinch to create a floppy disk a PC can read.

6. Click Erase.

Your iMac or iBook will whir and click as it formats the disk so a PC can read it. Now just copy your files to that disk and give it to the PC user. It's a piece of cake.

N O T E You can also format Zip, Jaz, SuperDisk, and other removable media devices so the disks will be readable by a PC. See your owner's manual for instructions for your specific device.

That's all there is to it. In summary, you need to do just two things to share your files and disks with a PC user:

1. Save your files in a format a PC can understand.

2. Format your disks so a PC can read them.

Do these two things and you'll hardly notice you're dealing with a Windows machine and not a Mac.

21 Organize This

This essay introduces you to the powerful personal organizer, Consultant (there's a demo version on the companion CD that comes with this book), and shows how it helps you manage contacts, appointments, reminders, alarms, and more.

N O T E Although I describe most of the software on the CD in Chapters 8–14, and describe Consultant in Chapter 12, Consultant is so useful for a small or home office worker that I made an exception and gave it its own essay in this chapter.

Consultant is awesome. Chronos, the makers of Consultant, call it the "intelligent way to organize your life." I concur. When I reviewed it in the *Houston Chronicle*, I said, "Consultant is the best personal organizer I've ever used. Period."

And here's the best part: You can try it free for 30 days with the demo version supplied on your CD. If at the end of that time you wish to continue using it—and I'm sure you will—you merely use the included order form and pay as little as $40. Chronos will send you an authorization number and your demo copy will become a real, registered copy you can continue to use in perpetuity.

NOTE Consultant will cost you $39.95 without Palm synchronization, $49.95 with Palm synchronization, and $59.95 + $5 shipping and handling (inside the USA) for a boxed copy with a CD and printed user manual.

Alas, all I can do here is give you a tantalizing taste of what Consultant can do by showing you a few cool tricks. Fortunately, Consultant includes excellent online help (Choose Help ➢ Consultant Help) and a system called RealHelp that explains each feature when you move your cursor over it, as shown in Figure 21.1.

FIGURE 21.1 I'm pointing to the Translate button near the top of the screen; the RealHelp explanation appears at the bottom of the screen.

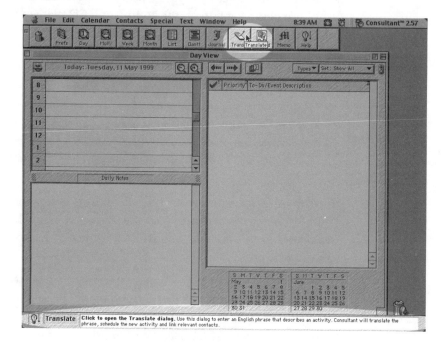

To find out what almost any feature of Consultant does, merely point to it with RealHelp turned on.

NOTE For RealHelp to work, it must be turned on in the Help menu. If the item in the Help menu says "Disable RealHelp," then it's turned on. If it reads "Enable Real Help," then it's turned off. Select RealHelp to turn it on.

Installing Consultant

Like most Mac software, Consultant is easy to install. Just follow along:

1. Locate the file called `Consultant Installer` on your CD and launch it.
2. Click Continue at the first (splash) screen.
3. Read the license agreement, then click Accept to accept it.
4. Read the installation instructions (or you'll be sorry), then click Continue.
5. The main installer window will appear. Click Install.
6. Click Fresh Install to install a full working copy of Consultant on your hard disk, and wait a few moments.
7. Click Restart to restart your iMac or iBook and enable the extensions that come with Consultant (more about them in a moment).

That's it. Consultant and its two extensions (Consultant Contacts and Consultant Activities) are installed.

Getting Started with Consultant

Open the Consultant folder on your hard disk and double-click the Consultant 2.5.7 application to launch it. Then follow these steps:

1. Click Not Yet. A standard Open File dialog box will appear.
2. Click New.
3. Name your file, then click New.
4. A dialog box will ask if you want to make this your primary file. You do.
5. A dialog box will ask you if you want to password-protect your Consultant data file. If you do, click Add Password and follow the directions. If you don't, click No Password.

The next thing you'll see is a QuickTip window, with tips regarding Consultant's features. Read its contents (the first one is about Consultant's myriad Help features), then click OK. If you want to read more QuickTips at this time, click Next Tip instead of OK. When you've finished reading QuickTips, click OK to continue.

NOTE A new QuickTip will appear every time you launch Consultant unless you uncheck the "Show at Startup" checkbox in the QuickTip window or turn QuickTips off in the Preferences dialog box. It's a good idea to leave them enabled until you get the hang of using Consultant. They're interesting and often useful.

Consultant opens and displays the Day View for today. One of Consultant's most powerful features is its ability to let you to look at your data (contacts, appointments, to-do items, etc.) in a variety of views. Look in the Calendar menu and choose MultiDay, Week, Month, Year, etc., to check out what other views look like.

NOTE Since you haven't entered any data yet, there's nothing to see in any of the views. We're going to fix that in a moment.

Adding Data to Consultant

Now let's see what Consultant can really do. We'll enter a contact, create an appointment, link the contact to the appointment, and create a to-do item.

NOTE If you use another personal organizer (and want to try using Consultant), you can export your data from that program's file and import it into Consultant. Look in Consultant's Help system for details (they're in the section called Import/Export).

Creating a New Contact Record

Let's add a person to your contacts list. It'll only take a moment, as you'll see:

1. Choose Contacts ➤ New Contact (or use the keyboard shortcut, Command+5). A blank contact form will appear.

2. Fill in the fields (First, Last, Title, Company, etc.).

NOTE You can press the Tab key to move from field to field if you like, or just click in a field and start typing. Pressing Shift+Tab moves your cursor backward from field to field. Try it, you'll like it.

3. Close the contact form window.

NOTE You don't have to fill out every field on the form, only the ones you want or need. Also, you don't have to type the hyphens in phone numbers—Consultant is smart and can do that for you. Try typing a phone number with no blanks or hyphens, then press the Tab key. See!

It's that simple. You have created a contact. Once you have created a contact or contacts, you can do many things with it, including linking it to a to-do item or appointment, using it to dial your phone (assuming it's hooked up to the modem port on your iMac or iBook), or adding notes to it. Let's look at how to do all three.

Creating Events Using the Translate Feature

Now let me show you one of Consultant's neatest features: the unique way that Consultant can translate a typed sentence into an appointment linked to a contact.

Here's how it works:

1. Choose Calendar ➤ Translate.

NOTE Or, use the keyboard shortcut Command+T, or click the Translate button in the button bar at the top of your screen. Any of these three methods will work.

2. Type **lunch with (name of contact you entered in previous section; in my case it was Bob LeVitus) at noon on Saturday.**

3. Click Translate.

An Activity window will appear with your appointment typed in. It will be set up for the next Saturday on the calendar, at noon, as shown in Figure 21.2.

FIGURE 21.2 I typed "lunch with Bob LeVitus at noon on Saturday" in the Translate window, clicked Translate, and Consultant created this activity automatically!

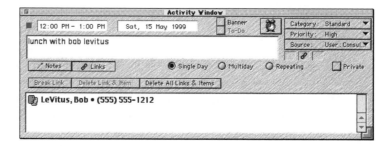

Now click the Links button at the bottom of the window, and you will see that the appointment has been linked automatically to the proper contact.

Double-click the name of your contact at the bottom of the window (it appears only after you click the Links button). The Contact window for that person will open. You can now type other information in the Notes field if you like.

Isn't that slick!

You can use the Translate feature to create a to-do item just as easily:

1. Choose Calendar ➤ Translate.

NOTE Or, use the keyboard shortcut Command+T, or click the Translate button in the button bar at the top of your screen. Any of these three methods will work.

2. Type **Call (name of contact you entered in previous section; in my case it was Bob LeVitus)**.

3. Click Translate.

An Activity window will appear with your to-do item typed in. It will be set up for today since you didn't specify a date. Again, if you click the Links button, you'll see that Consultant automatically linked this to-do item to the proper contact.

Creating Events Manually

You don't have to use the Translate feature to create an appointment or to-do item. You can also create them from scratch just as easily.

Here's one way to do that:

1. Choose Calendar ➢ New Appointment or use the keyboard shortcut Command+1.

NOTE You can also choose Calendar ➢ New To-Do, Calendar ➢ New Event, or Calendar ➢ New Banner, or use the keyboard shortcuts Command+2, Command+3, or Command+4, to create these types of events instead of an appointment.

2. An Activity window will appear. Type the name of the activity.

3. Click the start or end time to change them if you like.

4. Click the date, month, or year to change them if you like.

NOTE After you click, you can type new start or end times or use the little up and down arrows that appear.

5. Click the Notes button at the bottom of the Activity window if you want to add additional information.

6. Click the Links button if you want to link this appointment to a contact.

7. Close the Activity window. The event now appears on your calendar at the proper time and on the proper date.

Here's another way to create an appointment (or to-do item, event, or banner):

1. Choose one of the calendar views from the Calendar menu.

2. Click the calendar at the appropriate time (day or multiday views) or date (week or month views).

3. An Activity window will appear. Type the name of the activity.

4. Click the start or end time to change them if you like.

5. Click the date, month, or year to change them if you like.

NOTE After you click, you can type new start or end times or use the little up and down arrows that appear.

6. Click the Notes button at the bottom of the Activity window if you want to add additional information.

7. Click the Links button if you want to link this appointment to a contact.

8. Close the Activity window. The event now appears on your calendar at the proper time and on the proper date.

And that's all there is to creating an event—an appointment, to-do item, event, or banner—on your calendar.

NOTE It doesn't matter which view you choose. Once you create it, the event appears on the proper day and at the proper time in all of Consultant's views.

Six More Cool Things You Can Do with Consultant

I could write a book about all the neat things you can do with Consultant—and someday I might. But for now, here are six more cool things you can do with Consultant:

1. You can have Consultant read you your daily schedule. Choose Special ➢ Speak Today's Schedule (or use the keyboard shortcut Command+/). You can also have Consultant speak the current time and date by choosing Special ➢ Speak Time (or use the keyboard shortcut Command+,).

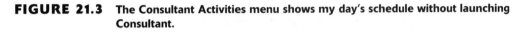

NOTE The Speech control panel and Speech Manager extension must be installed and enabled on your iMac or iBook or these features won't work. Unless you turned them off or de-installed them, they should be operative.

2. You can type a memo using Consultant's built-in word processor. Choose Text ➤ Memo View to try it.

3. You can see today's events and to-do items by pulling down the Consultant Activities menu, as shown in Figure 21.3.

FIGURE 21.3 The Consultant Activities menu shows my day's schedule without launching Consultant.

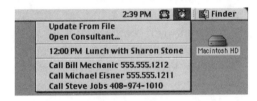

4. You can see the phone number of any contact you've marked as a favorite by pulling down the Consultant Contacts menu, as shown in Figure 21.4.

FIGURE 21.4 The Consultant Contacts menu shows my favorite contacts without launching Consultant.

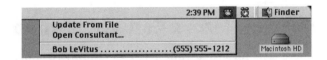

5. You can have Consultant dial a contact's phone number with your iMac or iBook's built-in modem (see "Dialing" in Consultant Help for details).

6. You can transfer (and synchronize) your Consultant data with a Palm Connected Organizer, a tiny, portable electronic device (prices start around $200). That way, you can have all your appointments and contacts at your fingertips even when you're away from your iMac or iBook.

Sigh! There's so much more, but I'm afraid I've run out of space. I hope this quick glimpse has convinced you that Consultant can help organize your life. I know it's helped me organize mine; maybe that's why I use it every single day.

22 Windows on Your iMac or iBook

A few pages ago, in the Getting Along with the Aliens essay, you learned how easy it is to share files and disks with those less fortunate than us, users of PCs running Windows. But did you know that your iMac or iBook can actually run programs designed for the Windows operating system? Well it can, but it's going to cost you around $175. All you need is a copy of one of the PC emulation programs—SoftWindows or Virtual PC—running on your iMac or iBook. These programs turn your iMac or iBook into a "virtual" PC. When one of them is running, you see Windows running on your iMac or iBook screen, as shown in Figure 22.1. What a hoot!

For more information on SoftWindows, visit `http://www.insignia.com/4.0/products/pc_comp.htm`. For more information on Virtual PC, visit `http://www.connectix.com/html/connectix_virtualpc.html`.

But do these emulators work? And if they do, do they work well? The answer to both questions is: Pretty much. Read on to learn more.

What Emulators Can and Cannot Do

The biggest advantage of emulation, of course, is that you can run programs created for Windows on your Mac.

NOTE If, on the other hand, if you're scratching your head and thinking, "why on earth would I ever want to do that," you can safely skip this essay.

FIGURE 22.1 Here you see Virtual PC running ClarisWorks 5.0 for Windows on my iMac.

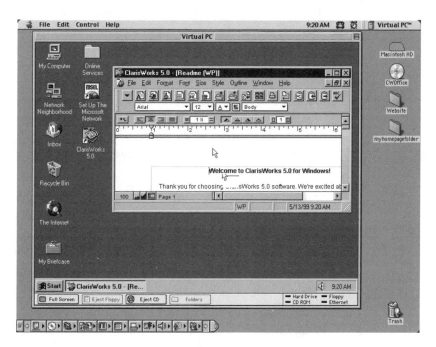

If you occasionally need to run a Windows program on your iMac or iBook, an emulator may be just the ticket. Both SoftWindows and Virtual PC work quite well on an iMac or iBook and can run most Windows programs at quite acceptable speeds.

Notice that I said "most." That's because one thing both emulators do poorly is run most popular Windows *games* at a usable speed.

NOTE The makers of both SoftWindows and Virtual PC will argue this point. They'll tell you that their product can run many games well. Don't believe it. I've tried and tried and have become totally frustrated. The fact is that neither emulator is fast enough, even on my fastest iMac (running at 333MHz), for most popular Windows games. So if your reason for wanting an emulator is to run Windows games, give it up. Unfortunately, the only way I know of to play Windows games at acceptable speeds is to buy a WinTel box, a computer that runs the Windows operating system.

What they can do, and do quite well, is run Windows programs not available on the Mac—such as ACT, Microsoft Access, or other Windows productivity applications—at reasonable and usable speeds.

NOTE I wrote *ClarisWorks 5 for Dummies* not too long ago. It is a cross-platform book, covering both the Mac and Windows versions of AppleWorks. I was able use the Windows version with Virtual PC (instead of buying a PC), which saved me a ton of both time and money. It worked flawlessly the entire time.

Another thing both programs can do is use your Mac modem (or cable modem, or ISDN, or whatever) to access the Internet for browsing, e-mail, or downloading files. Again, while performance is not what I'd call "zippy," it is perfectly acceptable and usable if, for some reason, you must use a Windows program to access the Internet. (See the next section for the differences between SoftWindows and Virtual PC, when used to access the Internet.)

Finally, both programs can, for the most part, use Mac peripherals such as printers, Palm organizers, CD-ROM drives, and the like. (See the next section for the differences between SoftWindows and Virtual PC, when used to access iMac or iBook peripherals.)

Differences between SoftWindows and VirtualPC

In the big scheme of things, both programs do what they promise—run Windows programs on your iMac or iBook. And both programs do it relatively well. But there are some differences.

First, SoftWindows makes it easier to use your iMac or iBook's Internet connection. The big advantage is that you don't have to configure Windows for Internet access to make it work. If your Mac has an Internet connection, SoftWindows uses it automatically, with no configuration hassles on the Windows side of things. And you don't have to log your iMac or iBook off the Internet to make a connection using SoftWindows.

Virtual PC requires you configure Windows for TCP/IP, which can be a daunting task. It also requires you to quit your iMac or iBook Internet connection before connecting with Windows (something you don't have to do with SoftWindows).

I have to say, while it sounds like SoftWindows is much better in this regard, I've configured Virtual PC to work with the Internet on two computers, and while it's somewhat of a hassle, once you've done it you never have to do it again. Still, SoftWindows is easier.

The second major difference is in the way the programs handle peripherals. I've heard from several users who were unable to get peripheral devices such as a GPS locator to work with SoftWindows. Virtual PC did work with such devices. So, if you're going to connect an external device to your iMac or iBook and use it with one of the emulators, Virtual PC may have an advantage.

Either way, for most people most of the time, both Virtual PC and Soft-Windows are fine choices for running Windows on your iMac or iBook.

You Can Do It, but It'll Cost You

This chapter is more conceptual than most of the others. It has no tutorials and it doesn't cover software on the CD-ROM or even software that came with your iMac or iBook. What it does cover are add-on technologies, hardware devices you can buy to make your iMac or iBook more useful. I hope that these are things you didn't know you could do.

We'll begin by looking at the different ports on your iMac or iBook and what you might use them for. Then we'll move on to discussions of specific devices that can make using your iMac or iBook better and easier.

Ports in a Storm   Discusses all the ports (holes you plug stuff into) on your iMac or iBook and talks about what each one can be used for.

Getting Your Stuff from an Old Mac to an iMac or iBook   Shows you how to move your files quickly and easily from an old Mac to an iMac or iBook.

Making Memories with Your iMac or iBook   Talks about using digital cameras and scanners to get pictures into your iMac or iBook.

Backup/Storage Solutions for Your iMac or iBook   Discusses external storage and who needs what and why.

Cable Modems, ISDN, ADSL: Fast Alternatives to Your Built-in Modem   Talks about faster Internet access technologies available for the iMac or iBook.

Memory Is Made of This   Explains iMac and iBook memory and why you might want more than you already have.

What to Do About Your Legacy Hardware...   Talks about how to use your old Mac or its peripherals with your iMac or iBook.

23   Ports in a Storm

Your iMac or iBook has a bunch of *ports*, a fancy name for the holes in your computer that you plug stuff into. If you open the little door on the right of your iMac, you will see, from left to right:

◆ The Sound Input (microphone) port

◆ The Sound Output (speaker) port

- A pair of USB ports, one atop the other
- The Ethernet port
- The Internal Modem (telephone line) port

On the front of your iMac, you'll see another pair of ports with a little icon next to them that looks like a pair of headphones. These, of course, are the Headphone ports.

N O T E Since I don't have an iBook yet, I can't tell you where exactly these ports are on an iBook. I trust you'll find them.

The differences between iMac and iBook ports are few; the iBook doesn't have a sound input port and only has one USB port. Otherwise, the two machines are the same, port-wise.

N O T E You can find additional information about these ports in Mac OS Help. Open Mac OS Help, click the About Your iMac or About Your iBook topic, then click Connecting Equipment.

You use these ports to connect external devices to your iMac or iBook. Let's take a look at each of them and see what they do:

Audio Ports

Your iMac or iBook can record and play back sounds. And while your iMac has a built-in microphone and built-in speakers (the iBook has built-in speakers but no microphone), neither is exactly the finest money can buy, which is why you may want to connect a higher-quality device for recording or listening to audio. Luckily, your iMac or iBook has ports that make this easy.

External microphones and speakers connect via the Sound Input and Sound Output ports, which you'll find inside the door on the right side of your iMac. They have illustrative icons, as shown in Figure 23.1.

FIGURE 23.1 The Sound In (microphone) port (left) and Sound Out (speaker) port (right) look like this.

Both ports accept the 3.5mm miniplug connectors found on many audio components. There are two kinds of 3.5mm miniplug connectors, stereo and extended, as shown in Figure 23.2.

FIGURE 23.2 Your iMac or iBook can use either type of 3.5mm miniplug—stereo (left) or extended (right).

Stereo miniplug   Extended miniplug

If you have an iMac, you can connect a stereo plug to either the Sound In or Sound Out port. An extended plug, on the other hand, will work properly only in the Sound In port. If you have an iBook, you'll need to connect your microphone via the USB port.

To connect a microphone or external speakers to your iMac, simply plug them into the appropriate port.

NOTE All modern Macs require a special type of microphone called a Plain-Talk microphone. This type of mic is available wherever fine Mac hardware is sold. Make sure yours is the proper type, or it won't work. All PlainTalk microphones come with an extended plug.

If you plug external speakers into the Sound Out port, you needn't do anything further. Your iMac will automatically mute the built-in speakers and use the external ones.

If you want to use an external microphone, on the other hand, you must tell your iMac or iBook that you want to do so. Here's how:

1. Open the Monitors and Sound control panel.

2. Click the Sound button at the top of the window.

3. Choose Sound In from the pop-up Sound Monitoring Source menu.

N O T E To use the built-in microphone, choose Microphone instead of Sound In from the Sound Monitoring Source menu.

The main reason you'd want to plug in a new microphone or speakers is that the ones built into your iBook (speaker) or iMac (speakers and microphone) aren't particularly good ones. So, if you're not happy with the way your iMac or iBook sounds, or the way it listens, these ports let you hook up higher-quality microphones and speakers quickly and easily.

You'll find a selection of speakers and microphones at a variety of prices at any of the online Mac vendors mentioned in Chapter 2 or at any store that stocks Mac hardware and software. Any speakers with a 3.5mm connector will work, but you'll get the best results from powered or amplified speakers. (Un-powered or un-amplified speakers won't be very loud if they work at all.) If you want deep, rich bass (low-frequency) sound, look for a speaker system that includes a sub-woofer.

One last note about speakers: You can, in a pinch, connect your iMac or iBook to a home or bookshelf stereo system or a boom box, as long as you have the proper plug.

N O T E If you have a pair of speakers (or stereo system or boom box) that doesn't have a 3.5mm connector, try Radio Shack or other electronics stores. They often have converters that can turn another type of plug into a 3.5mm plug.

USB Ports

The Universal Serial Bus (USB) is the iMac or iBook's main port for connecting peripherals such as mice, keyboards, printers, scanners, and removable-media drives such as floppy drives, SuperDisk drives, Zip drives, CD recorders, etc. The iMac was the first Mac to use the USB.

The USB ports on an iMac appear one on top of the other, as shown in Figure 23.3.

FIGURE 23.3   Your USB ports look like this.

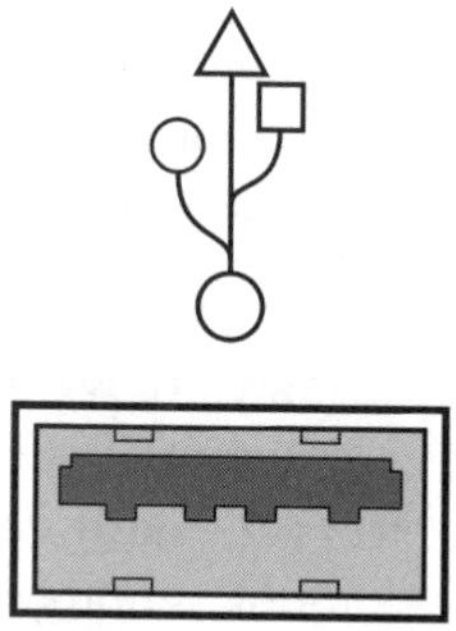

With all previous Mac models, peripheral devices such as those listed above connected to the Apple Desktop Bus (ADB) port, the SCSI port, the Printer port, or the Modem port. Your iMac or iBook has none of these ports; a pair of USB ports replaced all four.

USB has some distinct advantages over these other ports. First, USB can support up to 127 devices. The four older ports could support only a handful of devices each.

NOTE   If you run out of USB ports, you can buy an inexpensive device called a USB hub that adds additional USB ports to your iMac or iBook.

Second, USB devices can be hot-swapped. That means you can disconnect or connect a USB device without turning off your iMac or iBook. None of the four older ports supported hot-swapping.

NOTE That doesn't mean it's safe to disconnect a disk drive while your iMac or iBook is running. If you do, you run the risk of corrupting data or damaging the media (disk or cartridge).

I strongly recommend that you turn off your iMac or iBook before you connect or disconnect any device that reads or writes data. Apple warns, "Do not plug or unplug USB devices while you are using a device." On the other hand, it is usually OK to hot-swap non-recording devices such as keyboards, mice, modems, printers, and scanners.

So what does all this USB stuff mean to you? First and foremost, it means that older Mac peripherals won't connect to your iMac or iBook without a converter. There's an entire essay later in this chapter about connecting legacy devices, so we'll skip that subject for now.

Another important point is that not all USB devices are compatible with the Macintosh. Some work only with Windows. Since most hardware devices require certain software be installed on your iMac or iBook (usually called *drivers*), you have to look for devices that say they are "Mac compatible" or "work with iMac."

The bottom line is that if you want to connect a mouse, keyboard, printer, scanner, external hard disk, or removable-media drives such as floppy drives, SuperDisk drives, Zip drives, and CD recorders, you need to buy ones that connect via the USB port. We'll talk more about USB devices in upcoming essays in this chapter, so let's move on.

NOTE I hate the iMac mouse and keyboard. I am planning to replace them with a third-party USB keyboard and trackball (instead of a mouse).

Ethernet Port

The Ethernet port, shown in Figure 23.4, is a high-speed port that is generally used for one of two things—connecting your iMac or iBook to other computers via an Ethernet network or connecting a high-speed Internet access device such as a cable modem, ISDN modem, or ADSL modem to your iMac or iBook. We'll be discussing both uses in upcoming essays in this chapter, so let's move on.

FIGURE 23.4 Your Ethernet port looks like this.

Internal Modem (Telephone Line) Port

The last port inside the little door on the right side of your iMac is the Internal Modem port. This is where you plug in a telephone line to be used with your internal modem or for faxing using FAXstf (see chapter 3).

FIGURE 23.5 Your Internal Modem port looks like this.

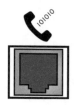

There's not much to say about this one; I include it only for completeness. If you're going to use your internal modem for Internet connections or faxing, you need to plug a phone line into this port.

NOTE Radio Shack and other electronics stores sell telephone jack splitters, which let you plug two phone cables into a single wall jack. This may be handy if you have a telephone handset you want to connect to the same phone line as your modem.

The Headphone Ports

On the front of your iMac you'll see a pair of ports with a little headphone icon next to them, as shown in Figure 23.6. The Headphone ports, like the Audio In and Audio Out ports, accept 3.5mm stereo plugs. When one or both Headphone ports are in use, the iMac's internal speakers are muted.

NOTE The iBook doesn't have headphone ports. But, you can easily connect headphones to its Audio Out port.

FIGURE 23.6 The headphone jacks on the front of your iMac or iBook look like this.

NOTE If you have a pair of headphones that doesn't have a 3.5mm connector, try Radio Shack or other electronics stores. They often have converters that can turn another type of plug into a 3.5mm plug.

To control the volume of headphones, use the volume control in the Monitors and Sound control panel or on the Control Strip.

24 Getting Your Stuff from an Old Mac to an iMac or iBook

This essay shows you how to move your files quickly and easily from your old Mac to an iMac or iBook. Of course, if your iMac or iBook is your first Mac and/or you don't own another Mac, you should probably skip ahead to the next essay. If, on the other hand, you have other Macs or upgraded to an iMac or iBook from an older Mac, you may be interested in reading about several ways to move files from any Mac to your iMac or iBook painlessly.

If Your Other Mac Has Ethernet

If your other Mac has Ethernet, you have your work cut out for you, but all you need is an inexpensive Ethernet crossover cable. Almost any computer store, even one that doesn't carry Macs, should be able to supply you with this cable for around $10 or less. Or, you could order one online at almost any computer store on the Web.

To transfer files from one Mac to the other:

1. Connect the two Macs using your Ethernet crossover cable.

2. On both computers, open the AppleTalk control panel and choose Ethernet Built-in from the pop-up menu. Close the AppleTalk control panel. (If you're asked to save your changes, click Save.)

NOTE On some Macs (i.e., non-iMacs or iBooks), you may see "Ethernet," or "Ethernet Slot #X" instead of "Ethernet Built-in." Choose it.

3. On both computers, open the File Sharing control panel and enable File Sharing if it's not already turned on. Close the File Sharing control panel.

4. On the iMac or iBook, open the Users & Groups control panel and create an account and password for yourself.

5. On the other computer, open the Chooser and click the AppleShare icon on the left. Select your iMac or iBook's hard disk from the list of file servers on the right. Click OK.

6. Type in your user name and password, then click Connect.

The iMac or iBook's hard disk should magically appear on the other Mac's desktop. Just copy your files from the old Mac to the iMac or iBook and you're good to go.

NOTE You may not have noticed, but you just set up a small AppleShare network that allows you to share files between two Ethernet-equipped Macs. If you have more than two Ethernet-equipped Macs and want to have them *all* be able to share files, or if you want to include an Ethernet printer or cable/ISDN/DSL modem in your mini-network, you need an inexpensive Ethernet hub. You'll find hubs almost anywhere computers are sold for around $50 or less for a five-port model that will support up to five computers/devices. You also need enough standard (not crossover) Ethernet cables to connect each device to the hub.

If Your Other Mac Doesn't Have Ethernet

If your other Mac doesn't have Ethernet (or even if it does), you have several choices.

E-mail the Files to Yourself

One of the easiest (and least expensive) ways to move files from another Mac to your iMac or iBook is to e-mail them to yourself. The other Mac, of course, must have a modem, and you must have e-mail.

To use this method, start out on the non-iMac, prepare an e-mail message, enclose the files you want to move to the iMac or iBook, then send the e-mail to yourself.

Now switch to the iMac or iBook and retrieve your e-mail.

Alas, this solution is useful only if you don't have a lot of files to move. If you have many, many megabytes of stuff you want to move to the iMac or iBook, one of the other solutions may be more useful and expedient to you.

Buy an Ethernet Card for the Other Mac

If your other Mac doesn't have Ethernet, but does have NuBus (very old Macs), PCI (most new Macs), or PC Card (most PowerBooks), you can buy an Ethernet card for them. Prices vary but start at under $50. Install the card, then follow the instructions in the previous section.

Buy a SuperDisk Drive for Your iMac or iBook

Assuming your other Mac has a floppy disk drive, another option would be a SuperDisk drive for your iMac or iBook. A SuperDisk drive is a nifty little device that can read your run-of-the-mill standard 1.4MB floppy disk, and it can also read special 120MB SuperDisks. It's becoming more common now that it's available for both iMacs and G3s. The drive itself will cost you about $150. While1.4MB floppy disks run about 50¢ each; 120MB Super-Disks go for around $10.

You'll also be able to use this device to back up important files on your iMac or iBook, so it could be a good investment even after you use it to move files from an old Mac to the iMac or iBook.

Buy or Borrow a Pair of Zip, Jaz, Orb, or Other Removable-Media Drives

This could be expensive, too, but if you often need to share files and can't, for whatever reason, hook up an Ethernet network, a pair of removable-media devices may work for you.

NOTE   Notice that I said "a pair," not "a." That's because unless your other Mac has a USB port (only very recent "blue G3" models, other iMacs, iBooks, and late-model PowerBooks do), you'll need a device that connects via the USB port for your iMac and a device that connects via the SCSI port for the other Mac.

Buy or Borrow a CD-Recorder for Your Older Computer

Granted, this could prove to be an expensive solution, but you *could* buy (or better still, borrow for a day) a CD-Recorder for the other Mac. Use it to burn a CD with your files on it that your iMac or iBook can read.

NOTE CD-Recorders can usually create two types of disk: single-session and multi-session. Your iMac or iBook's CD-ROM drive should be able to read single-session disks but may or may not be able to read multi-session disks. Read the CD-Recorder's documentation carefully to learn how to create single- and multi-session disks.

25 Making Memories with Your iMac or iBook

Your iMac or iBook can easily manipulate and edit graphic images and photographs. In fact, Chapter 1 contains an essay about how to fix and improve photographs with the copy of Kai's Photo Soap that came with your iMac or iBook. But how do you get pictures into your iMac or iBook?

Never fear. That's what this essay is all about. It talks about the two peripheral devices you might use to import pictures—digital cameras and scanners—and the pros and cons of each.

Digital Cameras 101

A digital camera is a special type of camera that stores images as digital files instead of recording them on film. You take pictures as you would with a film camera, but the images are saved on the camera's internal storage system. Later you can download these digital files to your iMac or iBook and manipulate them with a graphics program and/or print them on a color printer.

Most digital cameras include a built-in LCD screen that lets you review your pictures immediately.

The big advantage of digital cameras is that making photos is both inexpensive and fast because there is no film processing.

You'll find digital cameras from Kodak, Canon, Epson, Minolta, Olympus, Sony, and other manufacturers. Prices range from under $200 for low-end discontinued models to $1,000 or more for a state-of-the-art camera. With digital cameras you get what you pay for. The less-expensive models generally take poorer quality photos and have fewer features. More-expensive ones take better pictures and have additional features such as a built-in flash, zoom lens, removable lenses, and expandable storage capacity.

Alas, even the best digital camera connected to the best printer cannot produce film-quality photos. On the other hand, a high-end digital camera and one of the new Epson or Hewlett-Packard photo-quality printers can come pretty darn close.

One last thing: You want a camera that connects to your iMac or iBook via the USB port. Or, if you choose a camera that uses the serial port found on earlier Mac models, you'll need a serial-to-USB adapter.

NOTE A serial-to-USB adapter may or may not work depending upon the camera and the serial-to-USB device you choose.

The essay, "What to Do about Your Legacy Hardware," later in this chapter, has more information on such devices.

Scanners 101

A scanner is an electronic device that can take any image—a photograph, a magazine or book page, a crayon drawing, etc.—and digitize it into an electronic file you can manipulate with your iMac or iBook.

The big advantage of using a scanner to get images into your iMac or iBook is that you can scan almost anything, including hand-drawn pictures and book or magazine pages. You'd have a hard time using a digital camera to do that. Another advantage is that a decent scanner can create higher-resolution (read: higher quality) images than any digital camera. Finally, many scanners include optical character recognition (OCR) software, which lets you scan a page of text and turn it into a word processing file you can edit.

Scanners fall into two major categories: sheet fed and flatbed. Sheet fed scanners can only scan a single page—you feed a page into the scanner's slot and it's scanned and saved on your hard disk. Most sheet fed scanners are inexpensive and have limited feature sets. Flatbed scanners allow you to scan thicker items such as magazines, books, or even 3D objects. They are similar to photocopy machines with a large glass surface where you place the item you want to scan. A flatbed scanner will require significantly more desk space than a sheet fed scanner.

You'll find sheet fed and flatbed scanners from Hewlett-Packard, Canon, Umax, Microtek, Agfa, and other manufacturers. Prices range from under $100 to well over $1,000. The more expensive the scanner, the better the quality of your scanned images.

One last thing: You want a scanner that connects to your iMac or iBook via the USB port. Since older scanners generally used the Mac SCSI port, they are of no use to iMac and iBook owners (there are SCSI-to-USB adapters that have been announced, but none have shipped as of this writing).

Which Is Better: Scanner or Digital Camera?

You know the expression: "Good, cheap, or fast—pick two?" It certainly applies to the scanner-versus-digital camera issue.

A digital camera can be cheap and fast (remember, no film to develop), but even the most expensive models don't provide digital images as good as a film camera and a decent scanner. So, if superb image quality is important to you, you'll be better served by a film camera and scanner.

A scanner can be both good and cheap, but since you'll have to have your film developed before you scan your photos, it's never going to be particularly fast. So if speed is important to you, a digital camera will be a better choice than a scanner.

Another thing to consider is whether you will ever need to scan magazine or book pages, or other flat or 3D objects. If so, you need a flatbed scanner, not a digital camera.

Finally, would optical character recognition be helpful to you? Do you ever need to turn a printed page into a word processing document? If so, you want a scanner.

Other Options

If you don't like the digital camera or scanner route for whatever reason, there are still a couple of ways to get photos onto your hard disk. One is the QuickCam cameras by Logitech (http://www.logitech.com/us/cameras/). These devices connect to your iMac or iBook and use software to capture images directly to your hard disk. They can't be detached from the computer and the picture quality is not nearly as good as with a digital camera or scanner, but they are relatively inexpensive and can also be used for video conferencing between two computers.

Another option is to take your film to a Kodak processing location and request that it be delivered to you on a PhotoCD. For around $15 to $20 a roll, you'll receive your photos on a CD-ROM that your iMac or iBook can read. You can find out more about PhotoCD at http://www.kodak.com/global/en/professional/support/PCDWeb/welcome.shtml.

Software You Might Want or Need

Once you get the images from the camera or scanner onto your iMac or iBook hard disk, you'll probably want to edit them—crop, resize, fix colors, etc. So you'll probably need an image-editing software program.

On the other hand, your iMac or iBook came with some software you might find useful. AppleWorks can open, crop, add text, and save digital images, but not much more. Kai's Photo Soap can manipulate and improve digital images but can't paint or otherwise edit your graphics. Finally, Graphic-Converter, which you'll find on the companion CD-ROM, can do some of these things as well.

But if you want to really manipulate your images—add text with varying degrees of transparency, seamlessly combine two pictures into one, and so on—you'll need an image-editing program such as Adobe Photoshop, Adobe PhotoDeluxe, or Corel Draw. A discussion of these programs is beyond the scope of this book, but if you're serious about modifying your digital pictures, you'll probably want one of these programs.

Many scanners and some digital cameras include image-editing software in the purchase price. If you plan to modify or edit your pictures extensively, this feature may be something to consider.

26 Backup/Storage Solutions for Your iMac or iBook

Why back up your files? Because you must. If you care a tiny bit about your Quicken data, the novel you're working on, your lesson plan, or whatever it is on your hard disk that means anything to you, you need to know that unless these files are backed up—somehow—you run the very real risk of losing them forever.

Since the iMac and iBook don't come with a floppy disk drive, you're just going to have to bite the bullet and buy a storage device (or use an Internet backup service; more on this in a moment). Your storage options as I write this are a SuperDisk or Zip drive, or a recordable/rewritable CD-ROM device. You'll also want some backup software that automates the backup process for you.

Hardware Solutions

The three most popular storage devices for iMacs are SuperDisk, Zip, and CD-Recordable drives. All three connect to the USB port on your iMac. The first two are less expensive initially than a CD-R drive but will cost you more for media (disks) in the long run. Which you choose depends almost entirely upon how many files you have to back up. The more you have, the more attractive you'll find CD-R. Another consideration is what your friends and co-workers have. If they have floppy disks, a SuperDisk drive may appeal to you. If they have Zip drives, that may appeal to you. And since almost everyone has a CD-ROM drive, a CD-R drive is universally appealing.

Let's take a quick look at each:

SuperDisk Drive

The Imation SuperDisk drive is a device that can read old-fashioned 1.4MB floppy disks as well as new 120MB SuperDisk disks. I have one and it works great.

The drive costs around $150, and each 120MB SuperDisk will run you around $10. That means it'll cost you about 8.3¢ per megabyte of storage, not including the cost of the drive itself.

Zip Drive

The Iomega Zip drive comes in two flavors, 100MB and 250MB, but only the 100MB version is available for USB connections as of this writing. I've had several Zip cartridges die on me, and reports of Zip failure are fairly widespread. So I'm not comfortable recommending them. Still, if you're interested, here are the specifics.

The drive costs around $130, and each 100MB Zip disk will run you around $10. That means it'll cost you about 10¢ per megabyte of storage, not including the cost of the drive itself.

CD-Recordable and CD-Rewritable

CD-R and CD-RW drives are available from several vendors. CD-R drives can "burn" (copy your files to) a 640MB CD-ROM that can be used in your iMac or iBook CD-ROM drive. But each disk can only be used until it's full, then it's "frozen."

CD-RW drives do the same thing, but they can also use a special re-recordable disk that you can use over and over again.

CD-R drives cost around $300, and blank CDs will run you around $1.25. This means it'll cost you about 2¢ per megabyte of storage, excluding the cost of the drive itself.

CD-RW drives cost around $400. They can use blank CDs that cost around $1.25 or re-recordable disks that cost around $10.

Software Solutions

This is an easy one: There's only one software solution I recommend for iMac or iBook backup—Retrospect Express from Dantz Development.

Here's what I said in my review for the *Houston Chronicle* last year:

"Retrospect Express does everything you'd want your backup software to do—full backups, incremental backups, real archiving, filtering, scripting, unattended execution and much more…. It's easy to use, yet powerful enough to let you create a backup strategy that fits your needs and budget."

You need it. It'll run you less than $50 and is worth every penny.

And no, I am not being paid by Dantz. I'm just a satisfied customer who has depended upon Dantz backup software for almost 10 years. In all that time I've never found a reason not to use Retrospect. And so I give it my highest recommendation.

You can learn more about Retrospect Express at `http://www.dantz.com/dantz_products/express.html`.

Internet Backup

While I recommend buying an external storage device and backing up your valuable data to disks or CDs, if you're unable to do so for whatever reason, you may want to consider backing up your most valuable files to an Internet backup storage facility.

I know of four:

- ◆ iMacBackup/Committed to Memory:

    `http://www.macbackup.com/`

- ◆ RecoverIt:

    `http://www.forest.net/backup/recover-it.html`

- ◆ BackJack:

    `http://www.backjack.com/`

- ◆ iMac Floppy:

    `http://imacfloppy.com/`

Each offers a free trial so you can see if this scheme will work for you. If you have a lot of files to back up, it probably won't. But if you have only a few files you care deeply about, it may be the most cost-effective solution.

27 ISDN, ADSL, and Cable Modems: Fast Alternatives to Your Built-in Modem

Your iMac or iBook's built-in modem runs at 56kbps, or 56,000 bits per second.

NOTE Actually, due to the way phone lines work, a 56K modem's maximum is closer to 53,000bps. But hey, what are a few thousand bits per second between friends?

While this is a decent speed for connecting to the Internet, and should be sufficient for many of you, others will crave faster Internet access. With faster Internet access, Web pages will load in your browser faster, files will download faster, e-mail will be retrieved faster, and streaming media—audio and video you receive over the Internet—will work better.

Luckily, as an iMac or iBook owner, you have a myriad of options—IDSN, ADSL, and cable modems—available for faster Internet access. All you need is a cooperative telephone or cable company and some cash.

ISDN

Your local telephone company provides ISDN (Integrated Services Digital Network). ISDN runs at up to 128kbps (128,000 bits per second), or more than twice as fast as your iMac or iBook's internal modem. It requires an ISP (Internet Service Provider) that supports ISDN connections.

NOTE Your phone company may provide this service, but you don't have to buy it from them. Check with some local ISPs in your area to compare prices and services offered.

You'll need an ISDN modem (sometimes called an ISDN router or ISDN adapter; it is often supplied by the phone company) and a special phone line.

This same phone line can also be used for voice or fax at the same time you're using it to access the Internet. So you may be able to do without your regular phone line if you install ISDN.

Installation charges of up to several hundred dollars may apply. And the service itself will run you somewhere between $50 and $125 a month, depending on your provider's pricing and competition in your area.

NOTE In locations where all three services—ISDN, cable modem, and ADSL—are available, prices are generally lower than in areas where only one or two of the three are available. Ain't competition grand?

ADSL/DSL

ADSL (Asymmetric Digital Subscriber Line, sometimes referred to as just DSL) also comes from your local phone company. It's a new technology that transforms ordinary phone lines into high-speed digital lines for ultra-fast Internet access (384kbps to 1,500kbps). ADSL is often more expensive than ISDN and is only available in limited areas; only a few ISPs and phone companies offer it so far.

NOTE Your phone company may provide ISP service, but you don't have to buy it from them. Check with some local ISPs in your area to compare prices and services offered. ADSL availability is expected to grow rapidly in the next year or two. So, if it's not available in your area, ask when it will be.

You'll need an ADSL modem (sometimes called an ADSL router or adapter; it is often supplied by the phone company) and a dedicated phone line.

NOTE This same phone line can also be used for voice or fax at the same time you're using it to access the Internet. So you may be able to do without your regular phone line if you install ADSL.

Installation charges of up to several hundred dollars may apply. And the service itself will run you somewhere between $50 and $150 a month, depending on your provider's pricing and competition in your area.

The bottom line is that ADSL is fast, reasonably priced Internet access. While cable modems are faster and cheaper, they may not be available in your area.

Cable Modems

Cable modems, provided by your cable TV operator, are faster (downloading up to 10,000kbps and uploading up to 768kbps) and cheaper than either phone-based technology (ISDN or ADSL). Unlike ISDN and ADSL, you won't need a separate phone line and you don't pay a separate ISP fee. The two most popular services, TCI's @Home (http://www.tci.net/) and Time Warner's RoadRunner (http://www.rr.com/), are currently available in more than 50 markets and are expected to become available in hundreds more in 1999.

You'll need a cable modem (supplied by the cable company) but not an additional phone line. The cable operator will act as your ISP. Installation charges of up to several hundred dollars may apply.

NOTE Cable operators, hoping to get you to commit to this technology, often discount or waive installation charges if you purchase a one-year or longer contract.

Cable modem service will run you around $35 to $60 a month.

Cable is what I have now. I used to have ISDN, but when cable became available in my area, I was among the first to switch. Cable is faster and much less expensive. Mine costs $44 a month and is worth every penny.

The Bottom Line

If you're unhappy with the speed at which you access the Internet, you can use any of three solutions we've shown you. Watch for aggressive pricing and introductory offers as the three technologies compete for your Internet connection dollars.

Unfortunately, not all services are available in all households. ISDN is probably the most widespread, available now in most parts of the United States and the rest of the world. Alas, ISDN is the weakest choice—it's usually more expensive and not nearly as fast as cable modem or ADSL.

Cable operators (cable modems) and local phone companies (ADSL) are scrambling to make these services more widely available. But for now, only about ten percent of households can get one or the other.

NOTE To find out which service, if any, is available in your neighborhood, call your local phone company, a local ISP (Internet Service Provider), and/or your cable television operator and ask.

One last thing: It's possible to network several computers to use a single high-speed connection using an inexpensive hub. If you have more than one Mac that you want to have high-speed Internet access, ask your ISP or cable operator for details.

28 Memory Is Made of This

This essay will discuss your iMac or iBook's Random Access Memory (RAM), how to get the most out of what you have, and why you might want more.

What Is RAM Anyway?

Think of your hard disk as long-term memory and RAM as short-term memory. Everything you use on your iMac or iBook—the operating system, many control panels and extensions, applications, games, etc.—has to be copied from the hard disk into RAM when it is in use.

Your iMac or iBook came with 32 megabytes of RAM unless you have had extra memory installed. This is enough to run the Mac operating system and one or two programs under ordinary circumstances.

To find out how much RAM your iMac or iBook's operating system uses, choose Apple menu ➢ About This Computer. The About This Computer window will open, as shown in Figure 28.1.

FIGURE 28.1   **This iMac's operating system uses 16.7 megabytes of RAM.**

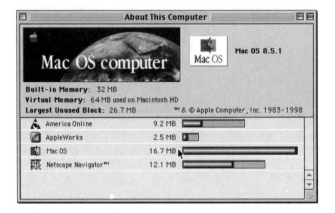

NOTE If your iMac or iBook's operating system uses more RAM than this, it's probably because you have more extensions and control panels enabled than I did when I created Figure 28.1. Another reason your iMac or iBook might use more RAM is that you have Virtual Memory disabled in the memory control panel. On the other hand, if your iMac or iBook uses less RAM than mine, you probably don't have some of the extensions and control panels—most of which use RAM—that I have enabled.

Virtual Memory

Virtual Memory (VM) is a scheme by which your Mac uses hard disk space in place of RAM. It can allow you to run programs you wouldn't ordinarily have enough RAM to run, or open more programs at once than would fit in your 32 megabytes of RAM. One of the best things about VM is that system software and applications require significantly less real memory (installed RAM) when it is turned on.

VM is turned on by default on your iMac or iBook. That's because Mac OS 8 and above run more efficiently with Virtual Memory turned on. Unless you have a good reason—like a program that is incompatible with VM or more than 128MB of real RAM—you should keep Virtual Memory turned on.

The advantages of VM are:

1. The iMac and iBook OS uses less RAM when VM is turned on.

2. Applications require less RAM when VM is turned on.

3. You can run more programs simultaneously with VM turned on.

4. Most applications launch somewhat faster with VM turned on.

So I recommend you keep Virtual Memory turned on in the Memory control panel, and set it to double your installed RAM. If you have 32MB, set it to 64MB. If you have 64MB, set it to 128MB. And so on.

The big disadvantage of Virtual Memory is that it creates a large invisible file on your hard disk. The VM partition (the invisible file) can be no smaller than the amount of RAM installed in your Mac. If you have 64MB of RAM and turn Virtual Memory on, you'll lose no less than 64MB of disk space. Of course, increasing your Virtual Memory to 128MB would eat up at least 128MB of hard disk space. And so on.

Another downside is that VM is slower than RAM. So if you have a program that requires more RAM than you have available without VM, it'll run slower with VM than with real RAM. But at least it will run.

N O T E Connectix RAM Doubler is a Virtual Memory replacement that works quite well and doesn't use any space on your hard drive. It also works with some games that won't run if Virtual Memory is turned on and may be somewhat faster than VM. It's what I use; you might want to try it.

Finally, many programs, including lots of games, slow down or refuse to run completely if Virtual Memory is enabled.

In these cases, you may be able to turn off Virtual Memory in the Memory control panel, restart your iMac or iBook, and try the program again. If you have enough RAM installed, they will work (or work better) now. But don't forget to turn Virtual Memory back on and restart your iMac or iBook again when you've finished.

Why You Might Want More RAM Than You Have

The bottom line is that your iMac or iBook will run slower when you use more RAM than you have installed. In other words, if you have 32MB of RAM and you do what I'm doing in Figure 28.1—running more than 32MB of programs ($9.2 + 2.5 + 16.7 + 12.1 = 40.5$MB)—your iMac or iBook will run slower than it would if you had 40.5MB (or more) of RAM.

Alas, RAM comes only in 32 megabyte increments. So you can buy:

- ◆ a 32MB upgrade (bringing your total RAM to 64MB)
- ◆ a 64MB upgrade (bringing your total RAM to 96MB)
- ◆ a 128MB upgrade (bringing your total RAM to 160MB)

You can buy up to a maximum of 256MB of RAM, which is the most an iMac or iBook can hold. Prices as I write this are roughly $50 per 32MB of RAM, but RAM prices fluctuate even more than gasoline prices, so you may pay significantly more or less.

The main reason you might want more RAM is so that you can open more programs and have them run noticeably faster.

The other reason you might want more RAM is if you use a RAM-hungry program such as Adobe Photoshop or Apple Final Cut Pro. Both work best if they have at least 50MB or more of real (not Virtual Memory) RAM available to them.

29 What to Do about Your Legacy Hardware...

If you owned another Mac before your iMac or iBook, chances are you have one or more peripherals you used with your old Mac—printers, modems, scanners, etc.—that don't have the right connector to use with your iMac or iBook. Can they be salvaged? Should you try?

That's what this essay is about.

Printers

If you have an older printer, you have a good chance of being able to buy a serial-to-USB adapter that will let it work with your iMac or iBook. Several vendors make them. Or, your printer's manufacturer may sell (or recommend) a serial-to-USB adapter for use with your printer.

Check with your printer manufacturer and see what they have to say.

I've never used one of these devices, so I'll point you to some resources on the Web:

iMacInTouch report on iMac devices
http://www.macintouch.com/imacusb.html#serial

The iMac.Com product guide
http://www.TheiMac.com/imacproducts.shtml

iMac2Day's USB adapter page
http://www.imac2day.com/peripherals/USBadapters.shtml

Peripherals.net device guide
http://www.peripherals.net/

NOTE Not every adapter works with every printer. Get a confirmation from either the adapter-maker or printer-maker that a particular adapter will work with your printer.

Another thought is that you can get a brand new USB printer for as little as $200 these days. Maybe it's time for a new printer anyway.

Other Devices

Some devices—modems, some scanners, Palm devices, Newtons, etc.—hook up to your old Mac through the Printer or Modem port. Other devices—external hard drives, CD-ROM recorders, tape drives, Zip or Jaz drives, etc.—hook up to your old Mac through the SCSI port. Keyboards and mice hook up to your old Mac through the ADB (Apple Desktop Bus) port. An iMac or iBook doesn't have a SCSI, Printer, Modem, or ADB port, so you will need an adapter to use these devices.

NOTE Adapters are funny. They work with some things and not others. It's important to determine that your device and your adapter support each other.

If you have a device that used your old Mac's Printer or Modem port, there are adapters available now that may let you connect the device to your iMac or iBook. Some devices—modems and MIDI (Musical Instrument Digital Interface) devices in particular—may not be adaptable. Again, it's important that you make sure the adapter will support your device. Not every adapter will.

If you want to use an old ADB keyboard or mouse, at least one manufacturer—Griffin Technology—has an ADB-to-USB adapter (more info at: http://www.griffintechnology.com/imac/imate.html). But it's $50, so you might just be better off buying a new keyboard or mouse.

If you have a SCSI device—hard drive, Jaz, SyQuest, Zip, or whatever—several vendors have announced SCSI-to-USB adapters. But none have shipped as I write this. And even when they do ship, a SCSI-to-USB connection will be much slower than a SCSI-to-SCSI connection.

NOTE Don't forget: If you have data on an external SCSI device on your old Mac, you don't have to connect it to your iMac or iBook to copy files from it. You may be able to transfer its files to your iMac or iBook via Ethernet. For details, see the essay "Getting Your Stuff from an Old Mac to an iMac or iBook," earlier in this chapter.

Again, since I've not used any of these devices personally, I'd advise you to find out more at one of these Web sites:

iMacInTouch report on iMac devices
http://www.macintouch.com/imacusb.html#serial

The iMac.Com product guide
http://www.TheiMac.com/imacproducts.shtml

iMac2Day's USB adapter page
http://www.imac2day.com/peripherals/USBadapters.shtml

Peripherals.net device guide
http://www.peripherals.net/

More Cool Stuff
You Can Do with
an iMac or iBook

We're just getting warmed up now. There's so much more you can do with your iMac or iBook. In fact, here are a few more things you may want to consider:

How to Talk to Your iMac or iBook   Shows you how to make your iMac or iBook respond to your voice.

How to Get Your iMac or iBook to Talk to You   Shows you how to have your iMac or iBook speak to you and even read documents.

Turn Your iMac or iBook into a Virtual Sony PlayStation   Shows how to run Sony PlayStation games and many other types of software written for other hardware devices such as Apple II, Atari, and Sega.

How to Make Most CD-ROMs Run Significantly Faster   Does just that—by showing you a secret trick that will speed up most CD-ROMs.

Tune Up Your Monitor   Shows you how to change the way things look on your screen, perhaps for the better....

30 How to Talk to Your iMac or iBook

You can talk to your iMac or iBook. Well, of course you can, but did you know that your iMac or iBook is capable of listening and responding intelligently? Well it is. All you need is Apple's Speech Recognition software, which they, nicely enough, will let you download for free from `http://asu .info.apple.com/swupdates.nsf/artnum/n11400`.

NOTE Since the iBook doesn't include a microphone, you will need to connect one via the USB port.

Download it now; I'll wait.

NOTE If you don't download and install this software, you can't talk to your iMac or iBook. (Or at least you can't have it understand you.)

When the download is finished, you should have a file called `English Speech Rec 1.5.4.smi` on your hard disk. This is a self-mounting image file. When you double-click it, it will mount a virtual disk on your desktop. The installer is on the virtual disk.

NOTE If the file you downloaded has the suffix `.bin` or `.hqx`, your browser did not decode it properly. Drag the `.bin` or `.hqx` file onto StuffIt Expander to decode it.

Use the Installer to perform an Easy Install, then restart your iMac or iBook.

Your First Time

I know you're eager to try this "talking to your Mac" thing, so we'll dive right in.

The first thing you must do is make sure your iMac's sound input is set to the built-in microphone (for iBooks, set it to External Microphone). So open the Monitors & Sound control panel, click the Sound button, and make sure your Sound Monitoring Source is set to Built-in Mic for iMacs and External Mic for iBooks.

Now open the Speech control panel and choose Speakable Items from the pop-up menu. Click the radio button to turn Speakable Items on. The Speech Recognition window should appear somewhere on your screen.

There are other configurations for Speech Recognition—and we'll talk about them all in the next section—but for now, close the Speech control panel and get ready to talk to your iMac or iBook.

Now—and this is very important—face it with your lips about six inches away from the top of the monitor (iMac) or external microphone (iBook). If you're an iMac user, look for the little hole right in the middle of the plastic above the monitor? That's the microphone. Speak directly into it.

Press the Escape key on your keyboard and keep it depressed while you say, "Tell me a joke," loudly and clearly and directly into the microphone.

If all has gone properly, your iMac or iBook should respond with a knock-knock joke, as shown in Figure 30.1. Press and hold the Escape key and say, "Who's there?" and "_____ who?" at the appropriate times.

FIGURE 30.1   Say "Tell me a joke," and your iMac or iBook will!

OK, so that was a silly demonstration. But Apple Speech Recognition can be useful. Let's take a look at how it works, then at some useful things you can do with it.

The Speech Control Panel

Let's look at the options available in the Speech control panel. Open it and choose Voice from the pop-up Options menu.

The Voice pane is where you choose the voice that responds to you. Listen to them all by choosing a name from the pop-up menu, then clicking the speaker icon.

Now choose Listening from the pop-up Options menu. The Listening pane is where you set the key you use for listening. Escape is a good one, though. So leave it alone unless you have a good reason to change it.

There are two options in the Listening pane for *when* you want your iMac or iBook to listen. If you choose Listen only while key(s) are pressed, your iMac or iBook will listen for your voice only when you press *and hold down* the Escape key (or other key(s) if you've changed that in the previous step). But if you choose Keys Toggle Listening On and Off, the key will act as a toggle for listening. Press it once and listening is on. Press it again and listening is off.

If you choose this option, you need to give the computer a name, then use that name to let your computer know you're talking to it. The default name is "computer." So you would press the Escape key once, then say, "Computer, tell me a joke." There's also a pop-up menu that lets you choose whether the computer name is optional.

I think you'll get better results using the Listen Only While Key(s) Are Pressed option, but feel free to try it the other way if you like.

Now choose Feedback from the Options pop-up menu. This is where you select the character that appears in the Speech Recognition window. I'm partial to Phil, with the goofy eyebrows. But that's probably just me. You can also choose a sound to alert you when your words are recognized.

Choose Speakable Items from the Options pop-up menu. You've already turned Speakable Items on, but there's one other item here you might enjoy: a checkbox that lets you say "OK" or "cancel" to respond to dialog boxes by voice. Check it if that capability interests you.

That's it. You now know all there is to know about Speech Recognition. Now let's look at some uses for it....

Using Speech Recognition

Speech recognition can be a useful tool. Not only can your Mac tell you jokes, it can tell you what time it is (Ask: "What time is it?"), what the date is (Ask: "What day is it?"), and much more.

That much more is a folder-full of goodies called the Speakable Items folder. It was installed automatically when you installed the Speech software; you'll find it in your Apple menu, as shown in Figure 30.2.

Each item will perform its namesake action when you speak its name and your iMac or iBook is listening. Note that many of the items require you to select something or have a window active when you say them.

NOTE For example, if you say "Close all windows" when you don't have any windows open, you'll hear the confirming beep but nothing will happen.

FIGURE 30.2 The Speakable Items folder is filled with useful things you can command your iMac or iBook to do for you.

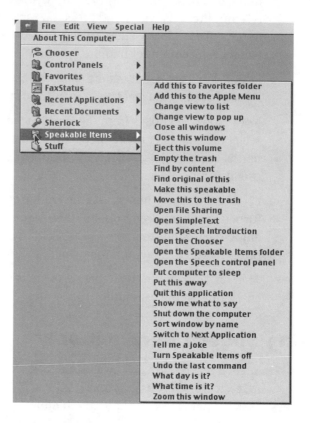

So there you have it. Later this year, Dragon Systems is going to introduce continuous speech recognition for the Mac. It will let you dictate into a word processor. That will be cool. But until then, this freebie from Apple is not too shabby.

NOTE If you find you like Speech Recognition, you might want to buy a headset microphone. Speech Recognition works much better with this type of microphone than with the built-in mic that came with your iMac. Just make sure it's PlainTalk compatible and has the right kind of plug to use with your iMac or iBook. Most online Mac vendors carry one or more models.

31 How to Get Your iMac or iBook to Talk to You

This essay shows you how to have your iMac or iBook speak to you and even read documents to you. It's quick and easy.

Your iMac or iBook can do two things for you. The first is to read the text of alert boxes (e.g., "The Printer is out of paper" or "The Application Microsoft Word has quit unexpectedly") aloud when they appear on your screen. The second is to read you the text of a document. You'll learn how to do both, right now.

Speaking of Alerts...

If you want your iMac or iBook to speak the text of alert boxes, merely open the Speech control panel and choose Talking Alerts from the pop-up Options menu. Now click both checkboxes—Speak the Phrase "Alert" and Speak the Alert Text—and set the wait before speaking to five seconds.

You can have your computer substitute another phrase for "Alert." Use the pop-up menu next to the words "Speak the Phrase" and choose another phrase such as "Rats!" or "It's not my fault." Or, set it to Random from the List to hear a different phrase for each alert box.

OK. Now let's see if it works. Close the Speech control panel and return to the Finder. Create a new, untitled folder (Command+N). Select it and make an alias of it (Command+M). Now throw the original untitled folder in the Trash and empty the Trash. Finally, double-click the alias of the untitled folder and wait five seconds. You should hear a voice say "Alert" (or whatever phrase you chose) and then the text of the alert box: "The alias 'untitled folder alias' could not be opened because the original item could not be found."

If you didn't hear it after five seconds, make sure your iMac or iBook's volume isn't turned down (Control Strip or Monitors & Sound control panel) and that Talking Alerts is turned on in the Speech control panel.

That's it.

NOTE You can, of course, change the voice you hear in the Speech control panel's Voices pane if you wish. Some of the voices are pretty interesting. If you haven't listened to them all, you should.

Read Me

Want your iMac or iBook to read you a story or a letter or a Web page? Guess what? It can. This little-known ability is built into every iMac and iBook in the most unlikely place—in your copy of SimpleText.

To try it out, launch SimpleText. It should be in the Application folder on your hard disk. If you can't find it, use Sherlock (Command+F) to locate it.

Now type, "Hey good looking! What's cooking?"

Finally, choose Sound ➢ Speak All (Command+J). You should hear a voice say "Hey good looking! What's cooking?"

If you didn't hear it, make sure your iMac or iBook's volume isn't turned down (Control Strip or Monitors & Sound control panel).

If you want to have a Web page, AppleWorks, Word, or other type of document read to you, open the document with its parent application, select the text you want to have read, then choose Edit ➢ Copy (Command+C). Now open SimpleText and choose Edit ➢ Paste (Command+V). Choose Sound ➢ Speak All to have the text read to you.

See. I told you it was quick and easy.

32 Turn Your iMac or iBook into a Virtual Sony PlayStation

Here's something else you probably didn't know your iMac or iBook can do: It can run software and play games written for other platforms, including the Sony PlayStation (with Connectix' awesome Virtual Game Station) and to some extent Windows (with Virtual PC or SoftWindows, as described in Chapter 3).

But wait, there's much ore. According to the definitive list on the Emulation Net Web site (`http://www.emulation.net/`), you may be able to find Mac emulators for the following computers, handheld devices, and game consoles: Apple I, II, and III, Atari, Commodore, TI, TRS-80, Colecovision, Intellivision, Nintendo, Sega, Gameboy, Game Gear, Palm Pilot, and TI Calculators, plus some others, too.

What all of these software programs do is *emulate*, or imitate, other hardware devices on your Mac screen. Suffice it to say most of these items are of no use if you don't have some original software for the device. And some of them require the ROM from the original device; others require a ROM image file that may be hard to come by.

But if you have a bunch of software for one of these devices, and you're up for some experimentation, you may be able to get it up and running on your iMac or iBook with an emulator. Better still, if you have PlayStation (awesome) or Windows (usually not-so-awesome) games, you can definitely run them, with varying degrees of success, on your iMac or iBook with the addition of a commercial emulator.

All this and more, when we continue….

Commercial Emulators

There are commercial emulators for Sony PlayStation and Microsoft Windows. Interestingly, one company—Connectix—makes them both. Virtual PC, their Pentium emulator for running Windows software on your Mac, costs about $175 (as does its competitor, Insignia's SoftWindows). Virtual Game Station, Connectix' PlayStation emulator, will run you about $50.

We discussed Virtual PC, and the similar SoftWindows from Insignia, at length in Chapter 3. So I'll keep it brief here: Neither of them is particularly good at playing demanding Windows games. Many games will run, and some will run acceptably. But many or even most will run too slowly to enjoy.

Connectix' Virtual Game Station, on the other hand, lets you run most Sony PlayStation games on your iMac or iBook and plays them near-flawlessly.

Once you install Virtual Game Station—which takes about two minutes—your iMac or iBook can play Crash Bandicoot or many other PlayStation titles, re-creating them faithfully on your iBook oriMac screen.

NOTE You can find a list of PlayStation games Connectix has tested and approved for use with VGS at http://www.virtualgamestation.com/games.html.

I've tried about eight games so far and they've all run pretty much perfectly on my iMac. Virtual Game Station is a very cool hack.

NOTE Since most Blockbuster Video stores rent PlayStation games for a few bucks, Virtual Game Station is a cost-effective way to play a lot of games without paying $30–40 apiece for them.

Joysticks and Other Game Controllers

Of course, if you're going to play PlayStation games on your iMac or iBook, you probably want to use something other than the hockey puck they call the iMac mouse as your input device. Connectix offers the Gravis GamePad Pro USB for $14.99 when you buy Virtual Game Station. If that offer isn't good by the time you read this, you can get one for around $30 from any Mac mail-order house.

Many game pads and joysticks are available for the iMac and iBook and most, like the GamePad Pro USB, configure themselves automatically for use with Virtual Game Station (or other Mac games).

NOTE Check out TheiMac.Com (http://www.theimac.com/imacproducts .shtml), MacBuy (http://www.macbuy.com/) and/or MacInTouch (http://www .macintouch.com/imacusb.html#human) for more information about the wide variety of joysticks and controllers you can buy for your iMac or iBook.

Shareware and Freeware Emulators

I can't be a ton of help here, as I don't have any of these old devices and therefore haven't actually emulated most of them personally. That said, your iMac or iBook can mimic literally dozens of devices if you want to try hard enough.

According to Emulators.net (http://www.emulators.net/), emulators are available that will let your iMac or iBook run software for the following:

Computers Amstrad CPC, Amstrad PCW, Apple I, Apple II, Apple III, Atari 800, Atari ST, BBC Micro, Commodore 64, Commodore Amiga, CP/M, Edsac, IBM PC, IBM Series 1, Macintosh, MIPS R2000, MO5, MSX, Oric, PDP-8/E, SAM Coupé, Sinclair QL, Sinclair ZX81, Sinclair ZX-Spectrum, Thomson TO8, TI99, TRS-80, TRS-80 Color Computer, VAX, and VIC-20

Game consoles Atari 2600, Atari 5200, Colecovision, Intellivision, MESS (multi-console), Nintendo, Nintendo 64, PC Engine/TurboGrafx, Sega Master System, Sega Genesis, Sony Playstation, Super Nintendo, and TB-303/TR-808

Arcade games Z80 Processor, 6502 Processor, 68000 Processor, 6809 Processor, Vector-based, MacMAME, and Space Invaders

Handheld devices Atari Lynx, Nintendo Gameboy, Sega Game Gear, HP 48, Magic Cap, Palm Pilot, and TI Calculators

Another good resource for emulator news is Pete's Computer And Video Game Emulator Page at http://www.netaxis.com/~petebuilt/videogames/emulate.html.

NOTE If the emulator bug bites you hard, use your favorite search engine to find even more emulator Web sites by searching for words or phrases such as "mac emulator," "game emulator," "MacMame," or "emulator and mac."

33 How to Make Most CD-ROMs Run Significantly Faster

This essay discusses just what the name implies. The good news is that this technique can speed up CD-ROMs considerably. The bad news is that it uses up a whole lot of hard disk space for each CD-ROM you want to speed up.

The principle here is that hard disk drives are faster than CD-ROM drives. A lot faster. So accessing images, text, movies, sounds, or whatever from a hard drive is, in most cases, a lot faster than accessing the same files from a CD-ROM.

So we are going to trick your iMac or iBook into using the hard disk in place of the CD-ROM drive by creating an image file of your CD-ROM with Apple's Disk Copy program. Here's how.

How to Do It...

You need Apple's Disk Copy program. It's in the Utilities folder on the Software Install CD that came with your iMac or iBook. So the first thing you need to do is copy the Disk Copy folder from the CD to your hard disk.

Eject the Apple CD and put it away.

There are pretty much two kinds of CD-ROMs—those that require you to install some components on your hard drive before using them and those that run completely from the CD-ROM. This technique will speed up either type. Insert the CD-ROM you want to accelerate in the iMac or iBook's CD-ROM drive and follow any game-specific instructions for installing the game itself on your hard drive. If your disc is one that doesn't require any installation (read the instructions), go ahead with the next step.

Now, here's how to speed up your favorite CD:

1. Launch Disk Copy. (Click Agree if asked.)

2. Choose Image ➢ Create Image From Disk.

3. Locate the CD you want to accelerate (Myth II in Figure 33.1) in the Select the Source Disk dialog box, and click Choose.

FIGURE 33.1 Making my favorite CD, Myth II, faster

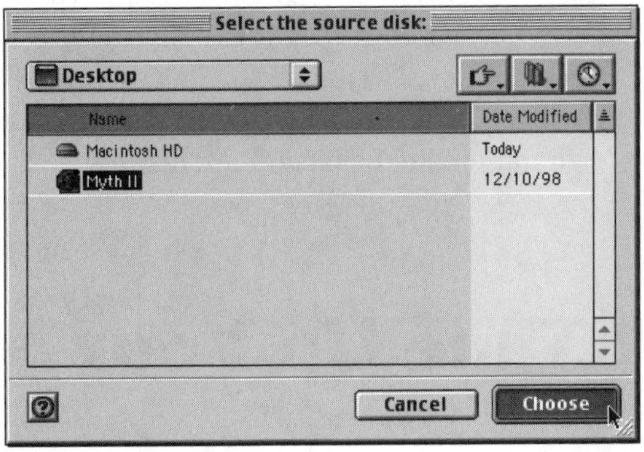

Select the source disk:			
📠 Desktop ⬍		⬆️. 📖. 🕐.	
Name	.	Date Modified	⬆
🖴 Macintosh HD		Today	
💿 Myth II		12/10/98	
ⓘ		Cancel	Choose

4. In the Save File dialog box, choose a destination for your image file, then click Save.

5. Go get a cup of coffee...this will take a while.

Disk Copy is making an image file of the CD. This could take as long as 30 or 40 minutes. But now the hard part is over. All that's left is to show you how to use the .img file in place of the CD.

But first, eject the CD. You won't need it for this next step:

6. Double-click the .img file you just created. A progress bar will appear, as shown in Figure 33.2. (You can press "Skip" if you like to save time.)

FIGURE 33.2 Disk Copy is mounting the disk image of Myth II.

Mounting Image
Verifying checksum for "Myth II.img".
▭▭▭▭▭▭▭▭▭▭▭▭ Cancel / Skip

The CD-ROM image mounts on your desktop just like a real CD would. For all intents and purposes, your iMac or iBook thinks you've inserted a CD. But you haven't. Instead, you've opened an image file of a CD. That image file resides on your hard disk and is thus much faster than a CD.

Now merely launch the software for that CD in the usual way. In other words, if you usually launch an application from your hard disk to use this CD, do that now. Or if you launch a file directly from the CD, launch that file from the CD image you just mounted. Either way, your iMac or iBook will be using the image file on your hard disk instead of the CD. And that's guaranteed to be faster than before!

34 Tune Up Your Monitor

This essay shows you how to change the way things look on your screen, perhaps even for the better....

All the action takes place in your Monitors & Sound control panel, so open that baby up and get ready to rock and roll.

Color Depth, Resolution, Contrast, and Brightness

With the Monitors & Sound control panel open, click the first button, Monitor. This panel manages your monitor's Color Depth, Resolution, Contrast, and Brightness.

Color Depth

Your choices are 256, Thousands, or Millions (of colors); 256 colors will make some games and applications run slightly faster. Millions of colors may make some applications and games run slower. Thousands is a good compromise for most people.

When you choose a lower color depth, you are placing fewer demands on your video card and monitor. So things naturally run a bit faster. My advice is to run at the lowest color depth you can tolerate. Start out with 256. This should be fine for most word processing, Web surfing, and other non-graphics-related activities. If you work with pictures or graphics and find that some images look blocky and poorly defined, try a higher color depth such as Thousands. If you work with photos or video, you'll probably want to choose Millions.

NOTE You can also choose a new color depth from the Control Strip. Click and hold on the icon of a monitor with colored stripes to choose a new color depth from its pop-up menu.

I use the Thousands setting most of the time except when I use Photoshop or other graphics programs. Then I set it to Millions.

Resolution

Your choices are 1,024 × 768, 800 × 600, and 640 × 480 for the iMac and 800 × 600, and 640 × 480 for the iBook. The difference between different resolution settings is how big things appear on your screen. In this case, a picture is worth a thousand words, so Figures 34.1–34.3 show the same Finder and documents at all three resolutions:

FIGURE 34.1 At 1,024 × 768 resolution, everything is quite small on the screen, but you can see a lot of things at once.

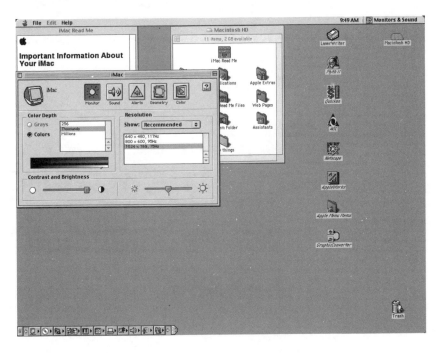

FIGURE 34.2 800 × 600 resolution strikes a good balance—things are neither too small nor too large.

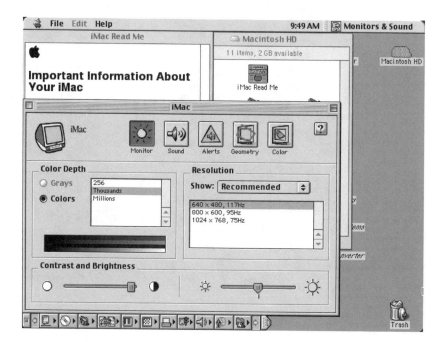

FIGURE 34.3 At 640 × 480 resolution, things appear rather large on screen.

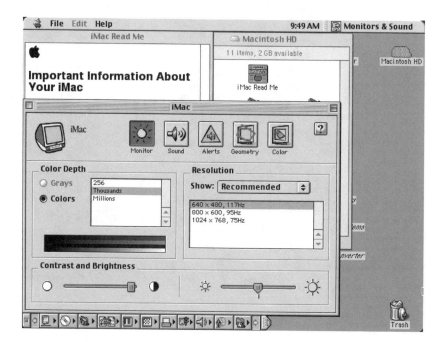

Remember, all three of these images are the same size—13.8 inches measured diagonally. What changes is how much fits in that 13.8-inch area and how big it looks on my screen.

NOTE You can also choose a new resolution from the Control Strip. Click and hold on the icon of a monitor with a gray checkerboard pattern to choose a new resolution from its pop-up menu.

I typically keep my iMac monitor set to 800×600, although for some tasks I switch to $1,024 \times 768$. I rarely use 640×480.

Contrast and Brightness

These settings are purely personal opinion. I keep the contrast cranked almost all the way to the right and the brightness near the middle. Your mileage may vary.

Geometry and Color

There are two other monitor-related buttons at the top of the Monitors & Sound control panel. Those are the Geometry and Color buttons. Geometry manages many aspects of the shape and size of the on-screen image. Color manages color matching—the art of making colors on your screen match their real-world counterparts as closely as possible.

So click the Color button now and take a look. What you should see is that your iMac or iBook is using the iMac ColorSync profile provided by Apple, as shown in Figure 34.4. If the iMac Display profile is not selected, select it now.

NOTE ColorSync is Apple's system for matching what you see on your screen with what you see on another computer screen as well as with printed output.

Chances are the colors are fine if you have iMac's ColorSync profile selected. But if you're adventurous and want to try tweaking the profile yourself, click

FIGURE 34.4 Fine-tuning the ColorSync profile for your iMac

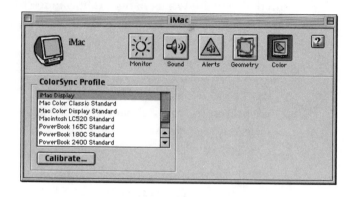

the Calibrate button and follow the instructions. At the end, you can compare your self-made profile with the Apple-supplied iMac profile and use whichever looks better to your eye.

Now click the Geometry button at the top of the Monitors & Sound window. This is where you adjust the image's size, position, and orientation on the screen. Play around with each of the controls. You will find you can make the image slightly bigger with no serious side effects. But it's easy to mess things up and make your screen look worse. If you find you've done just that, don't fret: Click the Factory Settings button to undo all the damage.

Fun and Silliness

This chapter covers a bunch of fun and silly things you might not have known you can do with your iMac or iBook. You can perform all of these things without spending another penny; all are all based upon software that came with your iMac or iBook!

In this thrilling chapter you'll find four frivolous-but-fun essays:

Discovering iMac and iBook Easter Eggs   Reveals a bunch of neat little surprises hidden in the software that came with your iBook or iMac.

How to Create and Install Desktop Background Pictures   Shows you how to do just that.

Icon Mania: Make Your Own Icons   Shows how to create and install any icon on any file.

Making Music Come Out of Your iMac or iBook   Shows several ways to get a song or songs to play from your iMac or iBook, with or without an audio CD in the drive.

So what are you waiting for? Let's go have some fun!

35   Discovering iMac and iBook Easter Eggs

An Easter egg is an unexpected surprise—a message, an image, or a sound— hidden in a Web site, application program, or operating system. In this essay, we'll look at some of the Easter eggs Apple's intrepid programmers have placed in the software you received with your iMac or iBook.

....

NOTE   Some of the eggs don't work with all versions of Mac OS. To find out what version of Mac OS you're using, choose the Apple menu ➢ About This Computer.

Mac OS has been riddled with Easter eggs since time immemorial. Here are a few of the best ones.

About This Computer Easter Eggs

There are at least two Easter eggs in the About This Computer menu item in your Apple menu.

◆ Hold down the Option key and pull down the Apple menu. You'll see that the About This Computer item has changed to About the Finder. Choose this item and you'll see a graphic of a mountain; wait a few seconds and you'll also see a scrolling list of engineering credits. Click anywhere to dismiss it.

NOTE **Little-known fact:** This mountain scene is a colorized reproduction of a picture found in the very first Mac's About Box, circa 1984.

◆ Hold down Command+Option+Ctrl and pull down the Apple menu. You'll see that About This Computer has changed to About the Mac OS 8.5/8.6 Team. Choose this item and you'll see a slide show about the OS engineering team. Click anywhere to dismiss it. This Easter egg does not work with OS 8.1 or below.

Control Panel Easter Eggs

Another classic place for Apple programmers to hide eggs is in control panels. Here are a few of my favorites:

◆ Open the Map control panel, enter **MID** as the city name, then click Find. The map centers on a flashing point in the south Atlantic that represents the Middle of Nowhere. (Works in OS 8.1, 8.5, 8.5.1, and 8.6; you may find the Map control panel in the Apple Extras folder if it's not in your Control Panels folder.)

◆ While you have the Map control panel open, click on the map version number just over the Find button. You'll see the version number and "by Mark Davis" (the programmer of the Map control panel, I would guess) in the City name field until you release the mouse button.

◆ Open the Speech control panel and choose Voice from the pop-up Options menu. Now choose a voice, any voice, then click the speaker icon. Each voice will say something unique and sometimes silly. For example, the Hysterical voice says, "Please stop tickling me," and the

Trinoids voice says, "We cannot communicate with these carbon units." Play them all for a laugh.

◆ Open the ATM control panel. Hold down the Command, Option, and Control keys, then choose About Adobe Type Manager. A picture of the development team appears. Point at any member (don't click!) to see his or her name at the bottom of the window.

Balloon Help Easter Eggs

Balloon Help is another popular repository of interesting Easter eggs. Here are a few I've found:

◆ Turn on Balloon Help (Help ➢ Show Balloons). Open the Extensions folder. Move the cursor directly over the QuickTime extension, as shown in Figure 35.1.

FIGURE 35.1   **Balloon Help on the QuickTime icon provides this treatise on "time."**

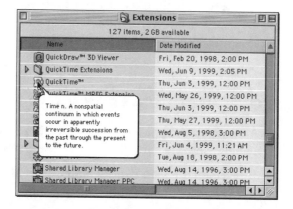

You should see the secret message about time, placed there by (I assume) the QuickTime development team. Cute, huh?

Here are a couple more balloon Easter eggs:

◆ Turn on Balloon Help (Help ➢ Show Balloons). Open the Date & Time control panel and move the cursor directly over the words "Daylight Savings Time is in effect." You should see a reminder to "spring forward and fall back."

◆ Turn on Balloon Help (Help ➢ Show Balloons). Open the Web Sharing control panel. Now choose Apple Menu ➢ About Web Sharing. Finally, point to any of the programmers' names for a balloon comment from them!

More Easter Eggs

I found one more Easter egg in the Script Editor program. To see it, do this:

◆ Open Script Editor (it's probably in the AppleScript folder, which is probably in the Apple Extras folder). Choose Apple menu ➢ About the Script Editor. Now hold down the Control key and click the words Script Editor. They should change to something interesting. Mine says "Dynamic Tofu" but I've heard other people have seen other messages.

For an additional thrill, click the Credits button after doing the Control+click thing. You'll see the "Toy Surprise Alternate Credits."

NOTE If you like Easter eggs, there have been literally hundreds of them in Mac OS software over the past 15 years. And many application programs—Photoshop, Director, etc.—have Easter eggs in them, too. For more information, use your favorite Internet search engine (mine is Ask Jeeves at www.ask.com) to search for "Macintosh Easter egg." You should find a ton of additional information and even more Easter eggs for your enjoyment.

36 How to Create and Install Desktop Background Pictures

Did you know that you can change the pattern of the background in the Finder—usually called the *desktop*—or even replace it with a picture? Well you can.

Which would you prefer? A boring plain background, as shown in Figure 36.1? Or an interesting picture, as shown in Figure 36.2?

All the action takes place in the Appearance control panel (Mac OS 8.5 and above) or Desktop Pictures control panel (Mac OS 8.1).

Here's how to do it yourself.

FIGURE 36.1   Which would you rather have? A boring plain desktop like this…

FIGURE 36.2   …Or a cool picture desktop like this? (That's me and my beloved red Fender Stratocaster, by the way!)

Creating (or Finding) a Desktop Picture

The first thing you need to do is find or create a picture to use.

There are two requirements for this picture. First, it must be a file saved in a format the Appearance or Desktop Pictures control panel can understand: PICT, GIF, or JPEG.

NOTE If you find a picture you like in another format, such as TIFF, BMP, or whatever, you can use GraphicConverter (on the companion CD) to open it, then save it in one of the approved formats.

Second, it should be roughly the same size as your iMac or iBook desktop—640×480, 800×600, or $1{,}024 \times 768$—for the cleanest and best-looking results.

If you have no artistic talent whatsoever, like me, you'll probably want to check out the MacDesktops Web site at www.macdesktops.com/. There you'll find hundreds of gorgeous pre-made Mac desktop pictures in a variety of sizes, all available for downloading at no charge.

NOTE Look for the pictures that match the screen resolution you use most often on your iMac or iBook. I've downloaded a huge collection of pictures from this site in my preferred screen size of 800×600.

Or, if you have the talent, you can create a picture from scratch with Apple-Works or any other graphics program that can save PICT, GIF, or JPEG files.

NOTE For best results, make your page size the same as your screen resolution. So, for example, if you're using AppleWorks, choose Format ➤ Document and set the page size to 800×600 (or whatever).

When you have a picture in the right format and size, here's what to do.

Installing a Desktop Picture (Mac OS 8.5 or 8.6)

Installing a desktop picture under OS 8.5 or 8.6 is a piece of cake. Just follow these steps:

1. Open the Appearance control panel.

2. Click the Desktop tab at the top.

3. Drag your picture onto the rectangle above the word "Pattern," as shown in Figure 36.3.

FIGURE 36.3   Drag your picture onto the rectangle on the left to install it.

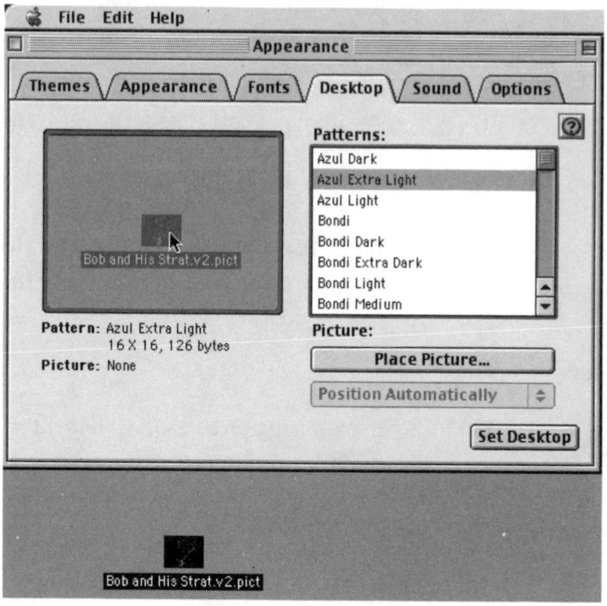

4. Click the Set Desktop button.

That's it! The picture now appears as your desktop picture.

There is one more thing you might want to tinker with, and that's the Position Automatically pop-up menu. This menu governs how the picture is displayed. Just follow along:

Click the Position Automatically pop-up menu and choose one of the options: Position Automatically (usually the best choice), Fill Screen, Scale to Screen, Center on Screen, or Tile on Screen. The little rectangle on the left will show you a miniature version of what your desktop will look like using your selected option. If you like it, click Set Desktop again.

If you'd like a different desktop picture to appear at random each time you restart your iMac or iBook, here's what to do:

1. Create a new folder (I call mine Desktop Pictures).

2. Fill this folder with the PICT, GIF, or JPEG files you want to use as your random desktop pictures.

3. Drag this folder onto the rectangle in the Appearance control panel (instead of dragging a single file onto it).

Now, every time you restart your iMac or iBook, a different picture from this folder will randomly appear as your desktop background.

Installing a Desktop Picture (Mac OS 8.1)

Installing a desktop picture under OS 8.1 is also a piece of cake. Just follow me:

1. Open the Desktop Pictures control panel.

2. Click the Picture button on the left side.

3. Drag your picture onto the rectangle in the middle of the window, as shown in Figure 36.4.

FIGURE 36.4 Drag your picture onto the rectangle to install it.

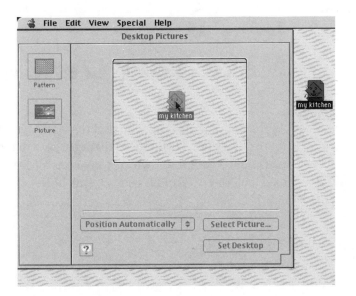

4. Click the Set Desktop button.

Presto! The picture now appears as your desktop picture.

You may want to try out the options on the Position Automatically menu. This menu governs how the picture is displayed. If so, here's what to do:

Click the Position Automatically pop-up menu and choose one of the options: Position Automatically (usually the best choice), Fill Screen, Scale to Screen, Center on Screen, or Tile on Screen. The little rectangle on the left will show you a miniature version of what your desktop will look like using this option. If you like it, choose Set Desktop again.

If you'd like a different desktop picture to randomly appear each time you restart your iMac or iBook, here's what to do:

1. Create a new folder (I call mine Desktop Pictures).

2. Fill this folder with the PICT, GIF, or JPEG files you want to use as your random desktop pictures.

3. Drag this folder onto the rectangle in the Desktop Pictures control panel (instead of dragging a single file onto it).

It's that simple! Now, every time you restart your iMac or iBook, a different picture from this folder appears at random as your desktop background picture.

37 Icon Mania: Make Your Own Icons

As you know, there is an icon that represents every file on your iMac or iBook. Every file on your hard disk comes with one. But did you know that you could create your own custom icons and attach them to any file you like? Well you can, and it's easy. Here's how.

Creating Your Own Icons

It's simple to create your own icons and put them on any file you like. So launch AppleWorks now and let's get started.

N O T E In this tutorial we'll use AppleWorks, 'cause I know you have a copy of it. But rest assured—you can do the same thing in your favorite graphics program (I use Photoshop) if you prefer. I created a template called Icon Template that you'll find on the companion CD-ROM. It will let you skip steps 1 to 4 if you so desire.

1. Launch AppleWorks and create a new Painting document.

2. Choose Format ➢ Document and set the page size to 36 pixels by 36 pixels.

3. Zoom in to 800% to make it easier to work with your picture. (Click and hold on the 100 in the lower left-hand corner of the window until it says 800.)

4. Create a black border 4 pixels wide (as shown in Figure 37.1).

FIGURE 37.1 Your painting should look like this right now. (Or use the template on the CD-ROM.)

NOTE Mac icons are actually 32 × 32 pixels. But the smallest page size AppleWorks allows is 36 × 36. So you'll have to leave a 4-pixel border on all four sides.

5. Draw the picture you want to use as your icon in the white space.

6. Choose the rectangle selection tool and select the area inside the black border, then choose Edit ➢ Copy (or use the keyboard shortcut Command+C).

Your artwork is now on your iMac or iBook's clipboard.

Installing Any Icon on Any File

OK, so now you've created a small picture, 32 × 32 pixels, and copied it to the clipboard. You're ready to install it on any file you like. Here's what to do:

1. Switch to the Finder and find the icon you want to replace. Select that file and choose File ➢ Get Info (or use the keyboard shortcut Command+I).

2. Click once on the icon in the upper left corner of the Get Info window. A black border will appear, as shown in Figure 37.2.

3. Choose Edit ➢ Paste (or use the keyboard shortcut Command+V).

4. Close the Get Info window.

That's it! Your file now sports its new icon, as shown in Figure 37.3 (please excuse my lack of artistic talent).

Copying an Icon from One File to Another

It's also easy to take the icon from one file and copy it to another file. Read on:

1. Select the file with the icon you want to use.

2. Choose File ➢ Get Info (or use the keyboard shortcut Command+I).

3. Click once on the icon in the upper left corner of the Get Info window. A black border will appear.

4. Choose Edit ➢ Copy (or use the keyboard shortcut Command+C).

FIGURE 37.2 The Get Info window is ready to have a new icon pasted in.

FIGURE 37.3 My file now sports a nifty new custom icon.

5. Select the file you want to install the icon on and choose File ➢ Get Info.

6. Click once on the icon in the upper left corner of the Get Info window. A black border will appear.

7. Choose Edit ➢ Paste (or use the keyboard shortcut Command+V).

NOTE If you really like icons, be sure to check out Icon Tools on the companion CD-ROM, which is chock full of nifty icons and special effects you can apply to your icons. Or visit www.iconfactory.com, which is a great place to find pre-made icons. In addition, you can surf the Internet to www.download.com (or your favorite download site) and search for "Mac Icon."

38 Making Music Come Out of Your iMac or iBook

In this essay we'll look at several ways you might get a song or songs to play on your iMac or iBook's speakers, with or without a music CD in the drive.

Using the Apple CD Audio Player

Of course, your iMac or iBook can serve as an audio CD player. But you knew that, didn't you? In case you didn't, here's how to do it:

1. Insert any audio CD into the CD-ROM drive.

2. Launch Apple CD Audio Player (it's in your Apple menu unless you've moved it).

3. Click the Play button.

That's all there is to it. The Apple CD Audio player works pretty much like any audio CD player, with Play, Pause, Fast Forward, Rewind, Next Track, and Previous Track buttons, and so on. Moreover, you can play audio CDs while you're doing something else—like surfing the Internet or using AppleWorks.

WARNING The QuickTime control panel offers an option to auto-play CDs. DO NOT USE IT! There is a nasty Mac virus that depends upon this feature to infect your iMac or iBook. In fact, you should open the QuickTime control panel right now and disable both Enable Audio CD AutoPlay and Enable CD-ROM AutoPlay. There, you've now protected yourself from at least one ugly Mac virus.

So that's one way to make music come out of your iMac or iBook. But what if you are using the CD-ROM drive for something else?

Read on....

How to Play Songs from Audio CDs When the Audio CD Is Not Available

Now here's one trick you probably didn't know: a way to play a song from a CD without having that CD in your CD-ROM drive. This little process depends upon the fact that QuickTime, which comes with your iMac or iBook, can convert audio CD tracks into QuickTime movies, which can then be played any time without the audio CD being present.

Follow along:

1. Insert the audio CD that has the song you want to capture. Note its track number on the CD; you'll need to know that in a moment.

2. Launch MoviePlayer (in the QuickTime folder on your hard disk).

3. Choose File ➤ Open, then navigate to your audio CD and open the track (song) you want to capture to your hard disk.

4. A Save dialog box will appear. Choose an appropriate folder to save the song into and give the song a descriptive name.

5. Click Save.

In a few moments, your song will exist as a QuickTime movie on your hard disk. At this point, you can eject the CD and double-click the song file you just saved. MoviePlayer will open and play your song.

Other Ways to Make Music Come Out of Your iMac or iBook

If you have an Internet connection, you can listen to all sorts of music by installing one of two technologies: RealAudio (www.realaudio.com) or QuickTime 4.0 (www.apple.com/quicktime/).

NOTE If you bought your iMac or iBook after August 1999, there's a good chance it came with QuickTime 4 already installed; if not, you can download it from Apple, for free, at www.apple.com/quicktime/.

At this writing, RealAudio offers a wider selection of "stations," but QuickTime seems to be catching up rapidly.

Both QuickTime and RealAudio are free, but both offer enhanced versions for around $30.

Directions on how to install and configure these technologies are beyond the purview of this book. But rest assured, if you're looking for cool stuff to listen to, you really want to install one or both. (And by the way, they can coexist nicely on the same iMac or iBook, so you don't have to choose one or the other…. Many people, like me, use both.)

Another way to make music come out of your Mac is by downloading and playing MP3 files with MacAMP Lite, covered in Chapter 10.

Things to Keep Your iMac or iBook Running Strong

Let's get this out of the way right up front: There's a good reason for this section of rather more serious subjects in a book otherwise full of flashy and fun stuff. That reason is this: If your iMac or iBook isn't working right, there won't be any flashy fun stuff.

So here are some words of wisdom; a collection of essays for when things go awry:

When Bad Things Happen to Good iMacs and iBooks...   Explains what to do when your iMac or iBook acts up.

How to Resolve Those Vexing Extension and Control Panel Conflicts   Delves into the usually annoying (but-not-anymore) process of diagnosing conflicts on your iMac or iBook.

How to Keep Your iMac oriBook Running Strong   Is about the stuff you should be doing to keep your iMac running at its best.

How to Survive Tech Support   Shows you how to make getting technical support a near-pleasant experience.

Getting Organized with Your iMac or iBook   Is chock full o' tips for organizing your iMac or iBook better.

Back Up, Back Up, and Back Up!   Tells you what you need to know about this important subject.

In other words, this chapter is packed with good, healthy things you need to know to keep that iMac or iBook of yours running strong.

39 When Bad Things Happen to Good iMacs or iBooks...

OK, so your iMac or iBook is crashing, bombing, freezing, or otherwise acting wonky.

NOTE Wonky is a word my friend Andy Ihnatko taught me. It means "funky" or "strange" or "not normal." Or something like that.

Don't worry: 99.9% of problems with iMacs or iBooks can be fixed by their owners.

My first suggestion is that you read the Troubleshooting Handbook or Emergency Handbook, the gold-ish booklet that comes with each and every iMac and iBook. (Which booklet you got—emergency or trouble-shooting—depends on which model iMac or iBook you have.)

It's not a bad little effort and, believe it or not, it offers many useful techniques for getting a wonky iMac or iBook back on track. So your first line of defense should always be that little gold book.

But the Apple booklet fails to make several important things clear—and fails to emphasize a couple of things that I think are important.

WARNING One thing I'd like to point out right up front is that there are only two kinds of iMac and iBook users: those who have lost valuable data and those who will. You must back up your data files or risk losing them. As you might expect, there's an essay on just how to back up files on your iMac or iBook, coming up in a few pages. But please mark my words: If you do not back up your data files, you will someday lose them completely.

So let us look at how to best deal with several ugly scenarios you might experience if your iMac or iBook wonks out on you.

Thawing a Frozen iMac or iBook

If your Mac crashes or freezes every time you do something, the easy answer is "don't do that." If something makes your iMac or iBook crash, don't do it. Unfortunately, that's not always an option. So if you crash, freeze, or other-wise wonk out whenever you do a particular thing, here are some tips and hints to help you get back on track.

NOTE Note that a problem is that much harder to track down if you can't make it manifest itself on demand. Those situations where a program crashes "occasionally," but not "every time I do _____," are near-impossible to troubleshoot. But try the steps in this essay and the next anyway. They may help. If nothing else, the section called "How to Cure Almost Anything Else That Ails Your iMac or iBook" will probably do the trick.

First, open the Extensions Manager control panel and choose the set called iMac Base from the pop-up menu. Close Extensions Manager and restart your iMac or iBook or click the Restart button in Extensions Manager.

The net effect of this process is that your iMac or iBook turns off all but the most essential of your control panels and extensions. This allows you to test whether or not one of them is causing your difficulty. Now try the particular thing that causes you to crash or freeze.

If you still crash or freeze, restart your iMac or iBook while holding down the Shift key. This will start it up without loading any extensions or control panels whatsoever.

If you don't crash or freeze, you can rest assured one of the now-disabled control panels or extensions is causing your problem. Read the next section to discover exactly which one of the little suckers is your culprit.

If you're still having troubles, there are a few more things to try: Apple has released several updates for the iMac and iBook. One is called the iMac Firmware Update 1.0, another is called iMac Update 1.1, and there may be others by the time you read this. Even if you're not having problems now, it would behoove you to visit the Apple update Web page (`http://asu.info.apple.com`) and download and install any updates that are appropriate for your particular model of iMac or iBook.

Here's another idea: If the problem is a program you bought separately from the iMac or iBook that keeps crashing, try reinstalling it.

And another: If a specific program or control panel keeps crashing, try deleting its preference file. You'll find it in the Preferences folder inside the System folder; it will have a name similar to the program or control panel it represents. Move it to the desktop and restart your Mac. If that cures your problem, move the preference file from the desktop to the Trash. If that doesn't cure your problem, move the preference file from the desktop back into the Preferences folder.

If your Mac crashes during the startup process, read the essay "How to Resolve Those Vexing Extension and Control Panel Conflicts," which follows this one.

And finally, if none of those things fixes it, try the technique in "How to Cure Almost Anything Else That Ails Your iMac or iBook" at the end of this essay.

What to Do when Your iMac or iBook Is Hung

You know, hung. Can't do anything. Can't move the cursor. Can't quit or restart. That's hung. Here's what to do:

1. Hold down the Command and Control keys, then press the Power on/off key on the keyboard.

If that doesn't work:

2. Press the Power button on the iMac or iBook itself (not the one on the keyboard). If the dialog box happens to come up, click Restart.

If that doesn't work:

3. Hold down the Command and Ctrl keys and press the Power button on the iMac or iBook itself (not the one on the keyboard).

Believe it or not, one of those three things sometimes lets you restart. Unfortunately, none of them works very often. So when none of them works:

4. Carefully stick a straightened paper clip into the reset hole (Figure 39.1). It's the top one, under the triangle; you'll find it between the Ethernet and modem jacks inside the door on the right side (as you're facing it) of your iMac.

Bingo! This is the million-dollar tip. You can force non-iMacs to reboot, even when they're frozen or crashed, by pressing Command+Ctrl+Power Key. But for reasons beyond the purview of this book, you usually can't force iMacs and iBooks! And that's a bummer. So my advice is to keep a straightened paper clip near your iMac or iBook. You shouldn't have to use it very often but when you do, it's faster and neater than the alternative, which is:

5. Unplug the iMac or iBook and wait 30 seconds before reconnecting and starting it.

FIGURE 39.1 Gently push a straightened paper clip into the little hole under the black triangle.

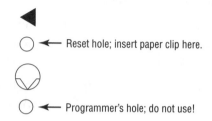

Reset hole; insert paper clip here.

Programmer's hole; do not use!

If your iMac or iBook still crashes or freezes every time you do a particular thing, try the next suggestion.

How to Cure Almost Anything Else That Ails Your iMac or iBook

If you've pored over Apple's handbook, and tried all the tips I've mentioned so far to no avail, here is a last-ditch technique to try before calling tech support. (By the way, there's an essay on tech support coming up soon, so don't call just yet.)

Now this one is sort of a brute-force technique, so be prepared—it may take a while. And you may have to re-enter registration information for some applications and/or some control panel settings, including your Internet settings. You might want to jot that stuff down now while you still can.

1. Insert the iMac or iBook Software Restore CD-ROM in the CD-ROM drive.

2. Restart the iMac or iBook.

3. Hold down the C key on the keyboard so your iMac or iBook will boot from the CD.

4. When the Finder appears, open the Utilities folder on the iMac or iBook Software Restore CD and launch Disk First Aid.

5. Click on your hard disk's name at the top of the window to select it, then click the Repair button.

6. Quit Disk First Aid.

7. Launch the Apple Software Restore program on the iMac or iBook Software Restore CD.

8. Click iMac HD.img at the top left of the window to choose the proper disk image for the restore operation.

9. Click the checkbox for Restore in Place.

WARNING If you don't click this checkbox or you choose "Erase Hard Disk before Restoring," you will lose everything on your hard disk. I mean it. Since that's not your intention, just check Restore in Place and everything will be just peachy.

10. Click the Restore button.

The wonderful and oft-overlooked Restore in Place command replaces only Apple System Software and other applications and factory settings that came with your iMac or iBook, leaving all your other files untouched. It's a bit drastic, but it is truly the cure for almost anything that ails your iMac or iBook.

If nothing in this essay or the next one (and nothing in Apple's booklet) cured your ailment, you probably have a serious problem with your iMac or iBook. Read the essay on tech support coming up in a few pages, then call Apple or your Apple dealer.

40 How to Resolve Those Vexing Extension and Control Panel Conflicts

Perhaps the most disturbing and annoying thing that can go wrong with an iMac or iBook is when an extension or control panel conflict, sometimes called a *startup conflict*, occurs.

N O T E Extensions and control panels that load code into your iMac or iBook's memory at startup time are usually represented by those little icons that march across the bottom of your screen when your iMac or iBook boots.

If you're like me and add functionality to your iMac or iBook by installing third-party extensions and control panels—GoMac, Action Files, QuicKeys, and so on—or even if you don't, it's only a matter of time before something that loads at startup conflicts with something else.

How Do I Know when I Have a Startup Conflict?

The easy way to know is if your Mac is crashing or freezing during the startup process. Restart while holding down the Shift key, which disables all of your extensions and control panels. If things start up normally with the Shift key held down, you have a conflict involving one or more of your extensions or control panels. See the next section for instructions on resolving it.

The harder way is when a program, control panel, or even the Finder crashes or freezes whenever you perform a specific action. This *could* be the result of a conflict. But it could also be something else—like a messed-up preference file (see previous section) or a defective program (try reinstalling it). The "How to Cure Almost Anything Else That Ails Your iMac or iBook" tutorial in the previous essay may help you out if nothing else has. As may reinstalling the software if it didn't come with your iMac or iBook.

But first, find out if a conflict is to blame by restarting while holding down the Shift key, which disables all of your extensions and control panels. Try to perform the specific action. If you crash, it's not a startup conflict; it's something else. Try the techniques earlier in this chapter and in Apple's gold booklet.

If you don't crash, it's almost certainly a conflict involving one or more of your extensions or control panels. See the next section for instructions on resolving it.

You may find that you need a particular extension or control panel to re-create the specific action. For example, if the problem has to do with a CD-ROM, you'd need to enable the extensions required for CD-ROM access.

NOTE If you're interested, those extensions would be the Apple CD/DVD Driver, Apple Photo Access, Audio CD Access, Foreign File Access, High Sierra File Access, ISO 9660 File Access, and UDF Volume Access.

Or, if your problem requires dial-up Internet access, you'd need to enable all the OpenTpt extensions, the Remote Only extension, plus the Modem and Remote Access control panels.

If that's the case, do this:

1. Open the Extensions Manager control panel.

2. Create a new set. (Choose New Set from the File menu or use the keyboard shortcut Command+N).

3. Name the set **AllOffButNeeded**.

4. Choose All Off from the Edit menu.

5. Click the On/Off checkbox to turn on the extensions or control panels you need to perform the test.

6. Click the Restart button.

7. Perform the specific action that causes the crash.

If you crash now, with only your most essential control panels and extensions enabled, it's not a conflict, it's something else. Try the techniques in the first section and Apple's gold booklet. If, on the other hand, you don't crash, it's a conflict involving one or more of your extensions or control panels. See the next section for instructions on resolving it.

NOTE You can make Extensions Manager appear at startup if you like by pressing and holding the spacebar after you power up or restart your computer. Hold the spacebar until the Extensions Manager window appears.

OK, How Do I Fix It?

So you've established through one of the aforementioned methods that you are indeed experiencing a conflict that involves one or more of your extensions or control panels.

The gold troubleshooting or emergency handbook that came with your iMac or iBook has a page-and-a-half-long method for resolving conflicts. That method will work, but it will take a long time and cause you much grief. I have a much better way for you, one that is faster and easier and almost painless.

On your companion CD-ROM you'll find the Conflict Catcher 8 Demo in the Utilities folder. Run the CC Demo Installer to install Conflict Catcher 8 on your hard disk, then restart your iMac or iBook.

NOTE This will install a seven-day demo of Conflict Catcher 8, a utility from Casady & Greene that I recommend highly if you run many third-party extensions and control panels like I do. It's like Extensions Manager, only much better. Among its many tricks, it can automatically diagnose startup conflicts.

After you restart, you'll see a demo screen (the nag notice) for Conflict Catcher 8. Read it, then click Continue. (Always click Continue when you see this screen, unless, of course, you want to purchase a copy of Conflict Catcher 8 online. In that case, click the Purchase Online button.)

A Conflict Catcher tip-of-the-day will appear. Read it, then click OK.

NOTE When you get a chance, read the tips. Conflict Catcher 8 has many unique capabilities besides being the easiest way to track down elusive conflicts.

The main Conflict Catcher 8 window appears. Now the fun begins. Basically, Conflict Catcher 8 is going to manage the process of trying all different combinations of extensions and control panels turned on and off, to determine which one (or, occasionally, more than one) is causing your difficulty. Now follow these steps:

1. Choose Start Conflict Test (Command+T) from the Special menu. A dialog box will appear asking permission to scan your System files. Click OK.

If the scan discovers any damage, a dialog box will tell you which file(s) were involved. Follow the instructions in the dialog box.

If no damage is found, a dialog box will say so. Click OK.

2. A new dialog box will ask if you're currently experiencing a problem. You are. Click Yes.

3. Yet another dialog box will appear. Type a brief description of the problem here. Don't change the selection on the Conflict Test menu; it should remain set to System Folder Items. Click OK.

4. The Conflict Test Summary window appears. If you know you need a file(s) turned on, click the Needed Files button and select the file(s) you need turned on. If you have a suspicion that a particular file is part of your problem (some recently installed control panel or extension, for example), click the Intuition button and select the file you suspect.

5. Once you've done all that, click the Start Conflict Test button. The main Conflict Test window appears; click Continue Startup to get on with the test.

Your iMac or iBook will restart. When the desktop appears, you'll see a dialog box reminding you that a conflict test is in progress. Click OK to dismiss it. Now perform the specific action that causes the crash. Note whether the problem occurs, then open Conflict Catcher. (Hint: There is now a Conflict Catcher menu to the right side of your menu bar for your convenience, as shown in Figure 40.1.)

FIGURE 40.1 **You now have a handy Conflict Catcher menu on the right side of your menu bar. It lets you open Conflict Catcher or change sets without opening Conflict Catcher. Very neat.**

If doing the specific action caused a crash or freeze, don't worry; reboot your iMac or iBook using the techniques in the first essay in this chapter and follow along.

Either way, the next thing you'll see is a dialog box with four choices:

◆ Problem Gone

◆ Problem Exists

◆ I Forgot, Repeat Test

◆ Stop Test

Click the appropriate choice.

NOTE This first time you should choose Problem Gone, as Conflict Catcher has cleverly turned off all your extensions and control panels that load at startup. In fact, if the problem still occurs, it isn't due to a startup conflict at all and Conflict Catcher will tell you so at this point (if you click Problem Exists). If that's the case, try the techniques in the first essay in this chapter and Apple's gold booklet before you start tearing out your hair.

Click Problem Gone, and the main Conflict Catcher window will appear. Click Restart.

Your iMac or iBook will reboot, and Conflict Catcher will activate some of your extensions and control panels. When the desktop appears, you'll see a dialog box reminding you that a conflict test is in progress. Click OK to dismiss it. Now perform the specific action that causes the crash. Note whether the problem occurs, then open Conflict Catcher again or reboot if you crashed.

Click Continue when you see the nag notice, then go through the Problem Gone, Problem Exists, I Forgot, Repeat Test, or Stop Test routine again. This time it's OK if the problem is gone; that's part of Conflict Catcher's process of elimination. Choose the appropriate item—gone, exists, forgot—then click Restart.

Keep going through this process—reboot, see if problem exists or not, tell Conflict Catcher the answer, reboot, see if problem exists or not, and so on—until Conflict Catcher finally tells you which one of your control panels or extensions is causing your heartache. Or, occasionally which two of your control panels or extensions are causing your heartache. Then disable that puppy (or puppies) and be on your merry way.

Once You've Identified the Culprit

Once Conflict Catcher 8 has told you which extension or control panel is to blame for the problem, it will offer to disable the recalcitrant extension or control panel for you.

But what if you want or need that extension or control panel?

The first thing to do is delete the culprit file and any preference file by dragging them to the Trash (look in the System folder for the Preferences folder; if the extension or control panel left behind a preference file, it'll be in there).

Then, you can try reinstalling the extension or control panel. If it's part of the Mac OS, use the Customized Installation feature of the Mac OS Install program (on your iMac or iBook Software Install CD-ROM). If it's a third-party extension or control panel, try reinstalling it from the master CD-ROM or downloading a fresh copy.

If the freshly installed copy also causes the problem, there's one more thing you can try: changing the order in which the extension or control panel loads. Sometimes an extension or control panel works better if it loads earlier or later in the startup process. Here's how to do it:

Open Conflict Catcher 8 and drag the suspect file as far up or down the list as you can. That will cause it to load either earlier or later in the startup process. Reboot.

If the problem still exists, open Conflict Catcher 8 and try dragging the suspect file the opposite direction. So, if you dragged it up before (so it loaded earlier), try dragging it down this time (so it loads later). Drag it as far up or down as you can.

If you're still having the problem after all of this, you're going to have to learn to live without the extension or control panel that causes the problem. It's not compatible with your iMac or iBook. Contact the company's tech support people for information on what (if anything) you can do next.

Other Good Features of Conflict Catcher 8

Conflict Catcher 8 has lots of other great features, and I give it my highest recommendation. Aside from being the only easy way I know to get to the bottom of tough conflicts, it also gives you many other useful capabilities. For example, I have a Game set of extensions and control panels. Conflict Catcher 8 loads only the files I need for my games and doesn't load a bunch of other things I don't need when I'm playing. I crash less and have more memory available for games this way.

But wait, there's more. Conflict Catcher 8 can also give you lots of information about which extension or control panel does what from its database of over 4,100 extensions and control panels, if that kind of thing interests you. And it can scan the System folder for damaged or corrupted files, a handy thing indeed. Finally, it lets you choose a startup set by holding down a single key at boot time. So if I hold down the G key, my Games set loads! Neat!

Once you've used the demo for seven days, you'll know whether it's worth $80 to keep; I think many of you will find it is.

41 How to Keep Your iMac or iBook Running Strong

You can do a few things to keep your iMac or iBook in tip-top shape. Some are plain common sense:

◆ Don't put your iMac or iBook where it's likely to be jarred while it's in use. A good bump while it's running can cause your hard disk to crash.

◆ Allow room on all sides of your iMac or iBook. It needs adequate ventilation.

◆ Don't allow massive quantities of dust to accumulate on your iMac or iBook. Dust can affect proper ventilation, too.

◆ Never force the CD-ROM tray in. If it's not going in easily, there's something wrong. Stop and check it out.

◆ Back up important files. (This one is so important it gets its own essay in a few pages.)

But a few may not be as obvious.

For example, you need to occasionally rebuild your iMac or iBook's invisible desktop files. And you should run Apple's Disk First Aid periodically to avoid problems with your hard disk. Not to mention that you need to clean your mouse to get rid of accumulated schmutz every so often.

Read on.

Rebuild Your Desktop Once a Month

If you've owned a Mac for a while, you probably know that you should rebuild your Desktop every so often.

The invisible Desktop files keep track of which application goes with which document and other mundane disk-related housekeeping information. Because invisible Desktop files take so much abuse—files being saved and deleted all the time—they are subject to corruption or damage or even bloating if left to their own devices. Rebuilding your Desktop once a month is good for your iMac or iBook.

Even Apple agrees. Though I couldn't find any mention of Desktop rebuilding in my iMac materials, an Apple technical note dated March 1999 says, "It is generally a good idea to rebuild your Desktop file once a month or so."

A tip-off that your Desktop needs rebuilding is when you see "an application can't be found for this document" warning or a dialog box offering to open a document with a program other than the correct program (assuming the correct program is still on your hard disk, of course). Another tip-off is when icons lose their identity and become generic looking. If any of that happens to you, rebuild your Desktop. And even if none of it happens, you should rebuild your Desktop about once a month.

Here's how:

1. Restart your iMac or iBook.

2. Before the Desktop appears, press both the Command and Option keys and keep holding them down until you see a dialog box that says, "Are you sure you want to rebuild the Desktop on the disk 'your disk's name here'?"

3. You do, so click OK.

That's it. Your iMac or iBook will whir and click a bit, and then things will be hunky-dory for your invisible Desktop files. At least until next month.

If you use a calendar program like the excellent Consultant (demo included on the companion CD-ROM), why not create a repeating event to remind you once a month to rebuild your iMac or iBook's desktop? Your iMac or iBook will thank you for it.

Run Disk First Aid Once a Month

Disk First Aid is the Apple-supplied program that repairs damage to your hard-disk directories. Like rebuilding your Desktop, you should probably use Disk First Aid's repair feature about once a month to keep your iMac or iBook healthy and happy.

Running Disk First Aid is kind of like rebuilding your Desktop, only more comprehensive. Again, since your hard disk is in constant use, there is a good chance that at some point its invisible files—known as the Desktop and the directories—will become damaged or corrupted. Rebuilding the Desktop fixes most problems with the invisible Desktop files; using Disk First Aid's Repair function fixes most problems with the invisible directory files.

Again Apple agrees. In fact, with Mac OS 8.5 (which many iMacs and iBooks came with), Disk First Aid runs automatically after a crash or freeze.

Even so, it's a good idea to run it once a month anyway, just in case. It should be on your hard disk already in the Utilities folder, but if it's not, you can find it in the Utilities folder on your iMac or iBook Software Install CD. Copy Disk First Aid from there to the Utilities folder on your iMac or iBook.

Now launch Disk First Aid. At the top of the window you'll see your hard disk's name under the heading Select Volumes to Verify. Click your hard disk to select it. Then click the Repair button, as shown in Figure 41.1.

You may receive a warning that Disk First Aid can't do its thing while other applications are open. Click Continue. If you have unsaved documents in open applications, you'll be given a chance to save them.

Now just sit and watch for a minute or two. With any luck, the next thing you'll see is a message that says, "The volume 'your disk's name here' appears to be OK" or "The volume 'your disk's name here' was repaired successfully."

FIGURE 41.1 Click your hard disk (Macintosh HD), then click Repair and all will be well. Probably.

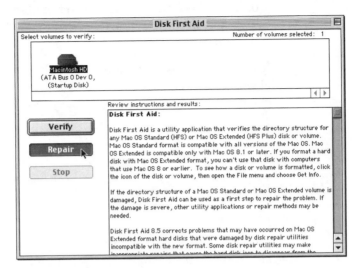

If it says anything other than that, you might want to back up important documents as soon as possible. It could be nothing, but it could also indicate an accident waiting to happen to your hard disk.

NOTE If this ever happens and you own a disk-repair program such as Norton Utilities, TechTool Pro, or DiskWarrior, it would probably be a good idea to try it now. These programs can often repair disk damage that Disk First Aid can't.

If Disk First Aid encounters problems it can't repair and your iMac or iBook is still under warranty, contact Apple for advice on what to do next. If it's not under warranty, you might want to consider backing up your hard disk, then erasing and reformatting it. This is a huge hassle, but it usually cures all but the most permanent hardware-based hard-disk damage.

WARNING This means you are about to erase your entire hard disk. Anything and everything on it is about to be deleted and rendered irretrievable.

To initialize (reformat or erase) your hard disk, you must boot from the iMac or iBook Software Install CD. Insert it in the CD-ROM drive, then restart while holding down the C key. Now launch Drive Setup (from the Utilities folder).

In Drive Setup, choose Functions ➤ Initialization Options and click Low Level Format in the dialog box. This ensures your hard disk will be reformatted as completely as possible. Now go ahead and initialize.

WARNING Once again let me remind you that this technique will erase everything on your hard disk. Forever.

Once the initialization is complete, reinstall your software from your backup or the Apple Restore CD-ROM or both.

If Disk First Aid still finds problems, your hard disk is probably defective.

Clean Your Mouse Occasionally (iMac only)

It's not a joke. Mouse balls need cleaning occasionally.

If you turn your mouse upside down, you will see that there is a small ball inside it. This ball will eventually become quite dirty. And when it does, your cursor may skip across the screen or not move smoothly.

First and foremost, use your mouse on a clean and lint-free surface. If your mousing surface is dusty, dirty, or grimy, it won't be long before the insides of your mouse are dusty, dirty, or grimy, too.

But eventually, no matter what you do, it will get dusty. And dirty. And even a little grimy. So here's what to do to clean the little sucker:

1. Turn off your iMac.

2. Turn your mouse upside down and rotate the plastic retaining ring on the bottom counter-clockwise.

3. Turn the mouse right side up with one hand and catch the ring and ball with your other hand.

4. Set the ring in a safe place. This is important; without the ring the mouse ball will fall out.

5. Turn the mouse upside down. Gently blow into the mouse ball hole to remove any dust that has accumulated there.

6. There are three small rollers inside the mouse ball hole. Clean them with a cotton swab moistened with water. Resist the temptation to use anything stronger.

Be sure you get all the rollers' surfaces clean. Rotate them with your fingers so you can clean the back sides. And if they're particularly scummy, you can scour them gently with your fingernail.

7. Wash the mouse ball with warm soapy water. Again resist the temptation to use anything stronger than mild, well-diluted, dish detergent.

8. Dry the mouse ball thoroughly with a clean and lint-free cloth.

9. Reinstall the mouse ball and retaining ring.

You probably don't have to do this as often as rebuilding your Desktop or running Disk First Aid. But you should probably do it at least once or twice a year to keep your iMac or iBook running at its best.

42 How to Survive Tech Support

Every so often, something breaks on your iMac or iBook. A piece of software mysteriously stops working and you're baffled as to why. Or the CD-ROM drive stops mounting CDs. You've tried the fixes in Apple's booklet—and in the preceding sections—and still, nada.

It's time to call tech support, at either Apple or the maker of the program that's broken.

You've heard the stories of hour-long waits—often listening to elevator music—on many popular software and hardware vendors' tech support lines. Or computer store personnel who obviously know less than you do. Relax. Take a deep breath. It's doesn't have to be that bad. If you need to call tech support, here are some tips and techniques for making the experience as painless as possible.

Relax and Stay Calm

By the time you're ready to call for technical support, chances are you're mad as heck. I know what you want to do is scream at the top of your lungs, "YOUR DARN SOFTWARE STINKS!"

Don't. Take some deep breaths. Walk around. Do not under any circumstances begin your phone call to tech support while you are angry. Trust me, that will only make it worse.

There is an old saying, "You catch more flies with honey than vinegar." It really applies to tech support. If you're cranky and teed-off, you will probably not get what you need from the tech support rep. (And you'll probably get crankier and more teed-off in the process.) If, on the other hand, you're polite and well informed, you'll have a much better chance of that person on the other end of the phone taking a genuine interest in helping you out.

So calm down, read the rest of this section, and don't make that call until you're relaxed and ready.

Use Online Support If You Can

Sometimes your problem is not that severe. If you are able to access the Internet or even America Online, you may be able to get help that way without the time or expense of a phone call.

Apple in particular has many resources online for iMac and iBook users. The main iMac support Web page can be found at: `http://www.info.apple.com/support/index.taf?product=imac`. The iBook support page wasn't up when I wrote this, but if you go to `http://www.apple.com` and look around, you should be able to find it.

From there you can get help solving problems, visit the Tech Exchange—a chat board for problem solving—download iMac and iBook updates, and find lots of useful information about iMacs and iBooks.

Another good Apple page to know is the Tech Information Library, Apple's knowledge base with product information, technical specifications, and troubleshooting information about Mac OS and your iMac or iBook. It's searchable and easy to use. You'll find it at `http://til.info.apple.com/`.

If you use America Online or UseNet news groups, consider posting a message describing your problem in the appropriate area and asking if anyone knows a fix. This method often works better than contacting the manufacturer. Don't forget to check back for replies over the next few days.

If your problem is with a non-Apple product, check the documentation. It often includes an e-mail address where you can write with questions. And most software vendors offer some type of tech support on their Web site. That address should also be in the documentation.

NOTE If you don't have the documentation, you can sometimes find out more about a program by choosing About This Program from the Apple menu. The program needs to be open and active (frontmost), of course. You can often find Web addresses in this About box.

Know the Answers before They Ask

When you do make a phone call to tech support, they're going to want a lot of information from you—what model, how much memory, what version of Mac OS, virtual memory on or off, and so on. Be prepared; gather the information before you make the call.

Here's a quick way to find and gather everything they're likely to ask and more. In your Apple menu you will find a program called Apple System Profiler. If it's not in your Apple menu, use Find or Sherlock to search for it. Now launch it.

Click the first tab at the top, System Profile. This tells you what version of Mac OS you're running and a whole lot more. It's a really good idea to have all this information handy before you need to call tech support. If you want to print a copy, here's how:

1. Choose File ➤ New Report (Command+N).

2. Click the checkboxes for everything you see in the next window. You want the most complete report possible.

3. Click OK.

4. You will see View Report As at the top of the next window, with radio buttons for choosing either Apple System Profiler document or Text document. Click one, then the other, and take a look at the results in the window below. Choose the one that you prefer.

5. Choose File ➤ Print (Command+P).

If you don't feel like printing it, leave this program open when you call so you'll have the answers handy.

Be at Your Computer when You Call

This one seems like common sense, but I still hear about people calling tech support from work when their computer problem is at home. Trust me on this one: It won't work. You'll just waste your time and the support technician's time as well. Be seated in front of the problem computer, with the computer turned on (if possible), before you make the call.

Have Good Answers

Your friendly tech support rep will have lots of questions for you. Try to explain what is happening on your computer screen clearly and succinctly. You will have a much better chance of getting your problem solved if the technician understands exactly what the problem is.

And be ready with good answers to their questions. "It doesn't work," is not a good answer. "It freezes right after I choose Print," on the other hand, is a very good answer.

Finally, if you see a particular error message every time you do something, write it down. The tech support person will almost certainly want to know exactly what the error message said.

43 Getting Organized with Your iMac or iBook

You can do a lot of quick and easy things to make using your iMac or iBook easier.

The second half of the book is about the programs and files on the companion CD-ROM. It has lots of information about things that will make using your iMac or iBook easier. But you have to install the items and learn how to use them.

This little essay, on the other hand, is dedicated to a few cool tips that won't require you to install anything extra or learn anything new. The tips you're about to read just make things faster and easier, for free.

You gotta like that!

Use Aliases

Aliases are one of the greatest organizational tools your iMac or iBook offers. Learn to use them.

Basically, an *alias* is a little file that opens another file. This has enormous implications for your iMac or iBook. It means you can have a file appear to be in more than one place at a time without having multiple copies of the file taking up space on your hard disk. Aliases are great.

NOTE If you don't know what aliases are or how they work, open Mac OS Help and search for "alias." There you'll find a bunch of useful information about creating and using aliases. If you don't use aliases often, I recommend it highly.

This essay deals mostly with using aliases to make life with your iMac or iBook easier. If you've never given aliases much thought, now is the time to give them a try!

Streamline Your Apple Menu

The Apple menu is a very handy thing. But you'd hardly know that, the way Apple has packed the darn thing full of stuff you'll hardly ever use. So I like to streamline mine, stashing the things I don't use very often in a subfolder I call Stuff. It's faster, easier, and cleaner than the way Apple ships it.

The tutorial you're about to see has two purposes. The first is to make your Apple menu more useful immediately on the assumption that shorter is better, as shown in Figures 43.1 and 43.2.

The second purpose, though, is more important. That is to teach you how to customize your Apple menu yourself. Once you've learned how to modify yours, you'll be amazed at how useful you can make it. And amazed at the

FIGURE 43.1 A stock iMac Apple menu—look at all that stuff you'll hardly ever use!

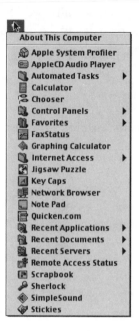

FIGURE 43.2 My shorter, sweeter, more useful Apple menu, after performing steps 1–3 below.

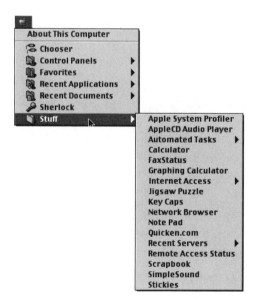

changes you'll find yourself making to it to make using your iMac or iBook easier.

OK, here's what to do:

1. Open the System folder. Locate your Apple Menu Items folder. Open it.

2. Create a new folder inside the Apple Menu Items folder. I named mine Stuff. You can name yours whatever you like.

3. Select all the items in this folder that you don't use very often and drag them into your new folder (the Stuff folder, for me).

For me, this consisted of Apple System Profiler, AppleCD Audio Player, Automated Tasks, Calculator, FaxStatus, Graphing Calculator, Internet Access, Jigsaw Puzzle, Key Caps, Network Browser, Note Pad, Quicken.com, Recent Servers, Remote Access Status, Scrapbook, SimpleSound, and Stickies.

4. Take a gander at your new, streamlined Apple menu (it should look like Figure 43.2).

A Few More Apple Menu Hints...

Now that you've shortened and sweetened your Apple menu, here are a few more tips for its efficient and effective use.

You Can Stash an Alias of Anything You Use Often in Your Apple Menu

In the end, your Apple menu should be personalized to suit your needs. A month from now it should not look much like Figure 43.2. In other words, if you use Apple/ClarisWorks (or any program or document) frequently, make an alias of it and put it in your Apple menu for gosh sakes.

You Can Stash an Alias of the Apple Menu Items Folder Right in the Apple Menu

You can even put an alias of the Apple Menu Items folder right in your Apple Menu Items folder. It sounds weird, but it lets you quickly open your Apple menu items to add or delete aliases. Give it a try.

You Can Have More Recent Applications and Recent Documents If You Want Them

I love the Recent Applications and Recent Documents features. That's why I left them in my Apple menu rather than moving them into the Stuff sub-folder. But they remember only the last 10 items you used, at least they do if you haven't changed the way they were configured at the factory.

In my humble opinion, 10 isn't enough. I want them to remember 30 items. Or 40.

If you'd like your Recent Applications, Recent Documents, and/or Recent Servers folders to remember more than 10 items, open your Apple Menu Options control panel and adjust the settings for the number of recently used items you want your iMac or iBook to remember, as shown in Figure 43.3.

FIGURE 43.3 Here's how to make your iMac or iBook remember more recently used items.

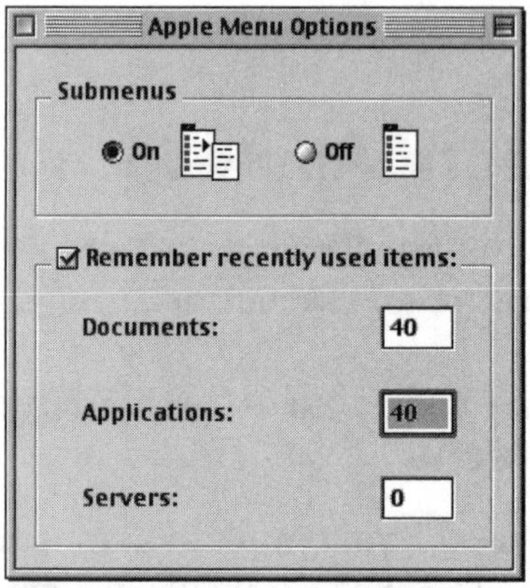

You Can Stash an Alias of the Apple Menu Items Folder on the Desktop

If you really like the Apple menu and get into customizing it regularly, con-sider making an alias of it and leaving that alias right on the Desktop, where it's easy to get at.

Which brings us nicely to the next point I'd like to make, which is…

The Desktop Is Another Great Place for Aliases

The Desktop—the backdrop that lives behind windows in the Finder—is another great place for frequently used stuff. In some ways it's even handier than the Apple menu.

I have aliases for AppleWorks, Quicken, America Online, Netscape Navigator, Myth II, and my Apple Menu Items folder on my desktop. Those are the things I use the most.

This technique is handy, it's free, it's quick, and it allows you to drag documents right onto programs to launch them, something you can't do with the Apple menu.

So get in the habit of putting aliases for your frequently accessed items right out there on the Desktop. I keep mine up on the right near my hard disk icon, as shown in Figure 43.4. But you can keep yours anywhere you like.

FIGURE 43.4   The Desktop is another great place for aliases of frequently used items.

NOTE   To make an alias of any item quickly and easily, select the original item, hold down Command and Option, then drag into another window or onto the Desktop. An alias of the original item is created automatically. Neat, huh?

If You Have Mac OS 8.5, Check Out Favorites

A new feature Apple added with OS 8.5 is the concept of favorites. *Favorites* are merely aliases of frequently used files that appear in a special Favorites folder in the Apple menu.

To create a favorite:

1. Find the item you want to make a favorite in the Finder.

2. Click it once to select it.

3. Choose File ➤ Add to Favorites.

Or:

1. Find the item you want to make a favorite in the Finder.

2. Hold down the Control key and click and hold on it.

3. Choose Add to Favorites from the pop-up contextual menu.

That's all there is to it. Now if you look in the Favorites submenu on your Apple menu, you'll see that an alias of the item now appears there.

To remove a favorite:

1. Open the Favorites folder (there's an alias of it in the Apple Menu Items folder; the original is in your System folder).

2. Drag the item you want to remove to the Trash.

Favorites are yet another way aliases can be useful to you. Give them a try if your iMac or iBook came with OS 8.5 or you've upgraded to it.

44 Back Up, Back Up, and Back Up!

I said it before and I'll say it again (but this is the last time, I promise):

There are only two kinds of iMac and iBook users—those who have lost valuable data, and those who will. If you don't back it up, you will lose it someday, guaranteed.

If it matters to you, you better back it up. If you don't, you run the very real risk of losing it forever.

Hard disks crash and die. Every single one of them will, someday. Files become corrupted, damaged, and/or unusable. This is a fact of computing.

If you only have one copy of a file, someday that file will be lost to you with potentially catastrophic results.

You must back up any file you wish to use in the future. It's that simple.

Don't Ignore My Advice Or...

For those of you about to ignore my advice and not back up, allow me to introduce you to the nice folks at DriveSavers. If your hard disk crashes and you haven't backed it up, they're your best shot.

Here's the deal: If you don't back up and something goes wrong with the only copy of that important file, or your entire hard disk, you're going to have to call them. And it's going to cost you a lot more than a good backup solution would have.

That is the bottom line.

DriveSavers charges a lot to recover your data from crashed and otherwise damaged hard disks (hundreds to thousands of dollars). And, although they're mostly successful, they can't guarantee that they can save any single file. You pay your money and you take your chances. Oh yeah, and since your iMac or iBook has its hard disk inside, you'll have to ship the whole shebang to them for anywhere from a couple of days to several weeks.

So there you have it. You can choose to adopt good backup habits now, or you can spend even more money with DriveSavers later. Because you are going to lose a file or files someday.

I know some of you will still ignore my advice. For you, here's DriveSavers' phone number: 415-382-2000.

Finally, though chances are good you won't be able to do much Web surfing if you need it, here is the URL for DriveSavers' Web site: http://www.drivesavers.com.

Hardware Considerations for Backing Up

The object of backing up is to make copies of important files and stash them somewhere other than your hard disk. Since iMacs and iBooks don't come with floppy disk drives, this will require the addition of a hardware device.

Which one you choose is a function of how much you're willing to spend, how much data you have to back up, and how much time you want to devote to swapping disks or cartridges.

Though a detailed discussion of backup hardware choices is beyond the purview of this book, I will say that I've had excellent luck with DAT (Digital AudioTape), CD-R (CD-Recordable), MO (magneto-optical), and Super-Disk drives in the past. All of these devices are now available for the iMac and the iBook and its USB bus; you will need one to back up your data.

For what it's worth, I have had bad luck with Iomega Jaz and Zip drives. I don't think they're reliable and I don't recommend them for something as critical as backing up your important files.

Software Considerations for Backing Up

This one is easy. Unless you only need to back up a couple of files, you need a copy of Retrospect or Retrospect Express from Dantz Development (`http://www.dantz.com`). There are few other backup software programs available and none that I trust like the offerings from Dantz.

Both programs can back up an entire disk, a folder, or a group of selected files. Both programs can do complete and incremental backups. Both programs can back up your files to an Internet location off-site (more on this in a moment).

Retrospect is more expensive, has better filtering (called *selectors*), and supports tape drives. Retrospect Express is significantly less expensive, is simpler and easier to use than Retrospect, but works only with disks and cartridges (not tape).

You need one or the other. Period.

How Much of My Stuff Should I Back Up?

Only you can determine your backup needs. How much of your stuff can you afford to lose? Moreover, how long can you spare to make things "like they were" again?

Here's something to think about—everything that came on your iMac or iBook's hard disk can be restored from one of the CD-ROMs that came with it. That means none of this stuff—AppleWorks/ClarisWorks, America Online, Internet Explorer, the System folder, etc.—needs to be backed up. If any of it gets damaged or destroyed, you can easily restore it from the CD.

But (isn't there always a "but?") you probably do want to back up more than just documents you create. There are other important files you should back up, like your AOL Online Files folder, or your browser's bookmark file, or the entire Preferences folder inside the System folder.

Then there's the question whether to backup the System folder. I modify mine often, so I do back it up every day. It adds a few minutes and a few megabytes a day to my incremental backups but I think it's worth it. If something goes wrong today, I can make things just the way they were yesterday in just a few minutes.

You may choose not to back up your System folder (you can reinstall it from the CD-ROM), but the Preferences folder should always be backed up. It contains the settings for your control panels and applications, among other things. If you have to restore your System folder from the CD, having these preferences afterwards can save you hours of tweaking.

NOTE Personally, I believe you should back up your entire hard disk. Even though it wastes a lot of space backing up stuff you could restore from CD, I think it's better. For me, it means that if anything happens and I have to erase/reformat my hard drive—always a possibility with any computer—I can quickly make things "just like they were yesterday" by restoring from my full backup. For the price of a few blank CD-R disks or DAT tapes, I sleep better at night knowing I could be back up and running in a couple of hours even if my hard disk dies.

On the other hand, if you have little worth preserving on your hard disk, you can just drag important documents to a SuperDisk, CD-R disk, the Web, or whatever, and that'll be enough for you.

Whatever you choose, a little or a lot, just remember that if it's not backed up, you're likely to lose it. And if it's not backed up, it will take you longer to restore it if a catastrophe does occur.

How Many Backups Are Enough?

To be as safe as possible, you need three backups of whatever you decide to back up. Here's why. If you only have one backup, and a file becomes damaged on your hard disk, then you back it up, you now have two damaged files and no undamaged ones. Or say, unbeknownst to you, your Mac catches a virus, then you back up your hard disk. Now your backups are infected. That's bad.

So you need three backups, with one of them stored offsite, somewhere other than the building that your iMac or iBook is in. Why is this? Because if your only backups are in the same building or room as the iMac or iBook and disaster strikes—fire, theft, earthquake, flood, or whatever—you'll be out of luck if you don't have a backup offsite.

You need to rotate among three backup sets and store one of them offsite. Here's how I do it:

On Sunday I back up to Set A and store it offsite.

On Monday, Wednesday, and Friday I back up to Set B.

On Tuesday, Thursday, and Saturday I back up to Set C.

On Sunday I back up to Set B and store it offsite, bringing Set A back into rotation.

On Monday, Wednesday, and Friday I back up to Set A.

On Tuesday, Thursday, and Saturday I back up to Set C.

On Sunday I back up to Set C and store it offsite, bringing Set B back into rotation.

And so on....

Backing Up to the Web

There are actually three ways you can back up your files over the Internet.

First and foremost, either flavor of Retrospect will let you back up over the Internet (assuming you have an Internet connection, of course) to Dantz Certified Internet Backup Site.

Dantz Certified Internet Backup Site (IBS) promises to:

1. Maintain high standards of quality, security, and customer service.

2. Maintain an Internet connection fast enough to service all their customers.

3. Maintain a backup plan that includes daily, rotating, off-site backups.

4. Keep servers in secure locations with limited access and alarm systems.

5. Develop a disaster recovery plan.

6. Monitor servers all day, every day, for downtime and problems.

7. Maintain UPS systems for continued service during power interruptions.

8. Use server software and configurations tested and certified by DantzLab.

I have tried them and they deliver what they promise—safe, secure, offsite backup. This would be my choice if I were going to back up over the Internet.

A second choice is the iMac floppy Web site, which offers 3 megabytes of free virtual storage at `http://imacfloppy.com/`. This is a pretty good deal if you have only one or two small documents to back up.

The final choice is the BackJack Internet backup service at `http://www` `.backjack.com/`. They offer their own software and secure servers and charge a setup fee plus a monthly charge.

The main problem with all these methods of backing up to the Web is that it is slow—40 megabytes of files could take more than an hour to back up.

And the other problem with backing up to the Web is that it gets quite expensive quite quickly.

For these reasons I don't really recommend backing up to the Web for most iMac and iBook users. For what you'll spend in a year or two, you could buy a hardware device and a pile of disks, cartridges, or tapes.

But I wanted you to know the option exists. Still, for most of you, a good hardware device and a copy of Retrospect or Retrospect Express will make the best backup solution.

Software on the CD-ROM

This part of the book is dedicated to the cool software provided on the companion CD-ROM. There's software that will improve your productivity. There's software to make using your iMac or iBook better and easier. There's software to make using the Web better. And, of course, there are even some excellent games and game demos.

NOTE The software on this companion CD-ROM has been scanned with the latest version of Norton Anti-Virus and was found to be free from infection.

I've handpicked nearly 70 freeware and shareware programs for your enjoyment, subdivided them into seven categories for your convenience, and placed each category in its own folder on the CD. Of course, each category has its own chapter:

◆ Chapter 8: Utilities

◆ Chapter 9: Graphics

◆ Chapter 10: Audio and Sound

◆ Chapter 11: Web and Online Stuff

◆ Chapter 12: Business-like things

◆ Chapter 13: Games and Game Demos

◆ Chapter 14: More Cool Stuff

Three other things you'll find on the CD are the AppleWorks Templates covered in Chapter 1 and a pair of bookmark files—one for Microsoft Internet Explorer and one for Netscape browsers—with every URL mentioned in the book.

NOTE Don't you wish every book had this?

Most of the files on the CD are StuffIt archives—the ones with the `.sit` suffix. These files need to be decompressed before you can use them. (The other files are either installers or self-extracting archives that don't need to be decompressed with StuffIt Expander.) Since your iMac or iBook came with StuffIt Expander installed, the `.sit` files should decompress when you double-click them. If they don't, run the Aladdin Expander 5.1.3 Install program in the Utilities folder to install StuffIt Expander on your hard disk. Then drag any `.sit` file you want to decompress onto the StuffIt Expander icon (or the alias of it the installer placed on your desktop).

Also, since this book and CD were finished in the summer of 1999, there may be newer versions of some of the programs available by the time you read it. So, before you install any of these programs, read the documentation and visit their Web site. You may discover that a later, greater, better version is available. And if you're really into it, also visit `http://www.download.com` (or your favorite Mac shareware/freeware site) and poke around among the Mac software every so often.

Finally, visit the Mac-oriented Web sites, such as MacIn Touch and MacNN, which announce new Mac products—including freeware and shareware—on a regular basis.

WARNING   One last thing: Any time you install new software, you run the risk of incompatibilities and/or crashes. If you don't back up your hard disk, or at least your important files, you run a very real risk of losing them. See Chapter 7 for details, but heed this warning: Do not install any new software if you don't have a current backup of at least your most important files.

About Shareware

Many of the files on the companion CD are distributed as "shareware." If you're not familiar with the concept, it's "try-before-you-buy" software. You can install and test the software at no charge, but after the free-trial period expires you are honor-bound to either throw the software in the Trash or send the author a check (or pay online).

Please remember this: You are obliged to pay for any shareware program you continue to use beyond the trial period. The fact that you paid for this book DOES NOT relieve you of that obligation. The authors of these programs were kind enough to grant me permission to include their works on this CD. I am begging you—please—pay for any program you continue to use.

Shareware is a wonderful thing. There are literally thousands of useful and unique programs available via this extremely desirable method of software distribution. But it all depends on us. If we don't pay for shareware we use, the authors will lose their incentive to create new programs. And that would be a horrible loss. So, if you use a shareware program regularly, please pay your dues.

End of sermon.

Utilities

This is a very long chapter. That's because there are so many excellent Mac utilities available and I didn't want to leave any of the great ones out!

Rather than waste a bunch of space telling you what I'm going to tell you in the coming pages, let's just dive right in to the best-ever utilities for your iMac or iBook, presented in alphabetical order (the same order they appear in the folder on your CD).

NOTE What Is a Utility? I define a utility as "a program that makes using your Mac better, faster, or more elegant." Compare this to an application program, which I define as, "a computer program that mimics something you do without a computer—write, draw, edit, read, etc." So Microsoft Word, Simple-Text, AppleWorks, Adobe Photoshop, etc. are application programs. And Sherlock, Apple Menu Options, the Control Strip, and everything in this chapter are utilities.

45   ACTION GoMac

ACTION GoMac makes using your iMac or iBook easier by adding a Windows-like Task Bar and a Start menu. It also includes the ability to replace the Control Strip, more elegant keyboard program switching than Mac OS 8.5, and a host of helpful features that aim to let you control your Mac with stunning efficiency.

In this case, a picture is definitely worth a thousand words, so Figure 45.1 shows what GoMac looks like.

It would behoove you to read the brief 41-page manual in the ACTION GoMac 2.0 folder. But since I'm sure you're in a hurry to get started, here's a quick introduction to the power of GoMac.

FIGURE 45.1   GoMac gives you a Start menu and a multipurpose Task Bar.

How to Use It...

Decompress the file ACTION GoMac 2.0.sit, then open the ACTION GoMac 2.0 folder, run the ACTION GoMac 2.0.Installer, and restart your iMac or iBook. When your iMac or iBook returns to action, you'll see an ACTION GoMac welcome screen. Read it, then click the Let's Go! Button.

The first thing you will notice is that you now have a Start menu and Task Bar at the bottom of your screen. This is GoMac. From left to right you'll see the Start menu, the QuickLaunch items, buttons for all currently open applications, and a clock.

The Start menu is kind of the heart of GoMac, and, of course, you can customize it to your heart's content. Let's start with something simple: adding or removing an item from the Start menu.

To add or remove items from your Start menu:

1. Click the Start menu and choose Settings ➤ Start Menu Items. The Start Menu Items folder (it's in your System folder) will open.

2. To add an item, put an alias of it in the Start Menu Items folder.

3. To remove an item, drag its alias from the Start Menu Items folder to the Trash.

You can customize lots of other aspects of this menu. To check them out, either click the Start menu and choose Settings ➤ ACTION GoMac or open the ACTION Utilities control panel. Either way, you'll see the GoMac Preferences dialog box. Click the Start Menu tab to change the appearance of the Start menu itself, choose which special items GoMac displays automatically, and even change the name of the Start menu.

Just to the right of the Start menu, you'll see several small icons (there are five of them in Figure 45.1. These are my QuickLaunch items. Clicking any of these icons launches the associated program immediately or switches to that program if it's already open.

To add or remove QuickLaunch items:

1. Click the Start menu and choose Settings ➢ QuickLaunch Items. The QuickLaunch Items folder (it's in your System folder) will open.

2. To add an item, put an alias of it in the QuickLaunch Items folder.

3. To remove an item, drag its alias from the QuickLaunch Items folder to the Trash.

Since it's using valuable screen real estate, GoMac provides a mechanism for using Control Strip modules. You need only install them and they'll appear in the Task Bar on the right side, next to the clock. I've installed five—CD-ROM, monitor bit-depth, speaker volume, monitor resolution, and file sharing—as you can see in Figure 45.1.

To install a Control Strip module in the Task Bar:

1. Ctrl+click the clock in the Task Bar.

2. Choose Install Module from the pop-up menu.

3. Choose the control panel module you wish to install.

To remove a Control Strip module from the Task Bar:

1. Ctrl+click the clock in the Task Bar.

2. Choose Remove Module from the pop-up menu.

3. Choose the control panel module you wish to remove.

The last feature I want to point out is the task switcher. To see it in action, launch at least one program, then press Command+Tab. Before you installed GoMac, that would have switched you from one program (or the Finder) to the next (Command+Tab application-switching is built into Mac OS 8.5 and later). With GoMac, as long as you keep the Command key depressed, you can cycle through your open applications by pressing the Tab key again and again. When you release the Command key, the highlighted program (AppleWorks in Figure 45.2) will become active.

If you don't care for this feature (I can't imagine anyone not liking it, but who knows…) or want to change the keys it uses, open the Action Utilities control panel and click the Task Bar tab.

FIGURE 45.2 The task switcher appears when you press Command+Tab and remains on screen until you release the Command key.

My Two Cents...

I wouldn't be without GoMac. The Command+Tab feature alone is worth the $30. And the Task Bar, Start menu, QuickLaunch, and Control Strip functions can't be beat. GoMac is a keeper in my book.

N O T E ACTION GoMac 2.0 is commercial software available from Power On Software, Inc. (http://www.actionutilities.com/ and http://www.poweronsoftware.com/) and at the time of this printing costs approximately $29.95.

46 ACTION Files

ACTION Files makes using your iMac or iBook easier by adding a menu of commands at the top of every Open and Save window. These menus contain commands that help you get more information, create new folders, make aliases, duplicate files and folders, rename items, navigate to recently used folders or files instantly, or move any item to the Trash.

ACTION Files' powerful Find command helps you find files quickly and easily without closing the Open or Save dialog box. And you can view information about each file, including a file's size, date, label, and kind, using any font. Oh, and did I mention that you can sort the list by name, size, date, kind, and label in either ascending or descending order?

But wait, there's more: You can even move formerly immobile Open and Save windows whenever you need to see what is behind them, and you can resize them, too.

Once again a picture is worth a thousand words, so here is a before and after shot of AppleWorks' Open dialog box, as shown in Figure 46.1.

FIGURE 46.1   The AppleWorks Open File dialog box before (top) and after (below) ACTION Files

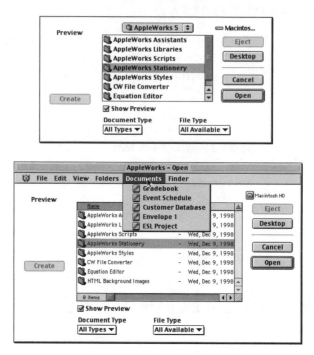

How to Use It...

Decompress the file ACTIONFiles1.2.sit, then open the ACTIONFiles1.2 folder, run the ACTION Files 1.2 Installer, and restart your iMac or iBook.

To see it in action, launch your favorite program, then choose File ➢ Open or File ➢ Save. See that menu bar in the dialog box? Notice that it's now a real Mac window with a title bar and everything? That's ACTION Files in action.

Suffice it to say you need do nothing more to begin enjoying ACTION Files. But if you want to customize almost any aspect of it, you can. Just open the

ACTION Utilities control panel, make sure the ACTION Files icon is selected at the bottom of the window, then choose the appropriate tab at the top—Intro, Menus, List, General, or Compatibility.

One thing I would do is click the Menus tab and increase the number of folders and files ACTION Files keeps track of—in other words, how many items show up in ACTION Files' Documents and Folders menus. The default is 10 and to me, that's not enough. I have all of mine set to 40 items and it works great that way.

My four favorite features are:

1. The movable and resizable ACTION Files Open and Save windows.

2. The Documents and Folders menus.

3. The Find command.

4. The ability to click any file or folder you can see behind the Open or Save window and have the List window instantly show that file or folder. Give it a try—click on a file or folder in the Finder behind an Open or Save window and watch what happens to the list in the window.

NOTE It's always a good idea to read the readme file that comes with any new program.

My Two Cents...

Holy cow! This is another fine program I wouldn't dream of being without. I can't imagine anyone trying it and then going back to the old way.

Try it—you'll like it!

NOTE ACTION Files 1.2 is commercial software available from Power On Software, Inc. (http://www.actionutilities.com/ and http://www.poweronsoftware.com/) and at the time of this printing costs approximately $29.95.

47 **Aladdin DropStuff**

To understand why you might need DropStuff, I have to start out with a little background. StuffIt archives are the Mac industry standard for compressed files. The main reason you might want to compress a file or folder is that compressed files and folders use up less disk space—anywhere from 0% to as much as 60% less, depending on the type of files you're attempting to compress.

NOTE If you use America Online, you probably don't need to install DropStuff, as it can compress your files automatically. Just click the Compress Attachments checkbox when you attach files.

You can fit more files on a floppy (or Zip or SuperDisk or even on your hard disk) if you compress them. And if you're sending files electronically, as attachments to e-mail, compressing the files will make them upload and download faster.

WARNING Most Microsoft Windows users cannot decompress StuffIt files. So if you know you are sending a file to a Windows user, do not compress it. If you feel you must compress the files (for size reasons), use the shareware program ZipIt or have the Windows user obtain StuffIt Expander for Windows, then use DropStuff on your end.

Having said all of that, Aladdin DropStuff does two things:

1. Creates StuffIt archives quickly and efficiently
2. Enhances StuffIt Expander (if installed), so it can expand more formats

How to Use It...

Run the Aladdin DropStuff 5.1 Installer to install DropStuff on your hard disk.

To create a StuffIt archive, simply drag the file(s) or folder(s) onto the Drop-Stuff icon (or an alias of the DropStuff icon; one was placed on your desktop automatically when you installed DropStuff). DropStuff then compresses the file(s)/folder(s) into a StuffIt archive and puts the archive in the same folder that you dragged from, using the name of the file or folder as the name of the archive. Your original files, of course, are not deleted when you do this. If you don't want them around, drag them to the Trash.

You can also create a self-extracting archive that any Mac OS user can decompress, even without a StuffIt product:

1. Double-click the DropStuff icon.

2. Choose File ➢ Preferences.

3. Click the Make Self-Extracting checkbox.

4. Click OK.

If you have installed StuffIt Expander (also included on the CD), installing DropStuff gives it the ability to expand just about any file format you might encounter. These include formats from Macintosh, Unix, and IBM-PCs and compatible machines like Mime/Base64, TAR (.tar), and Unix Compress (.Z). StuffIt Expander will also be able to expand StuffIt SpaceSaver files and join StuffIt segmented files.

NOTE It wouldn't kill you to read the DropStuff readme file if you want to know more....

My Two Cents...

If you send e-mail enclosures and don't use America Online, DropStuff can save you (and your e-mail recipients) time. Or, if you're having trouble fitting files on a single disk or cartridge, or your hard disk is getting full, Drop-Stuff can make those files and folders smaller.

Otherwise, you probably don't need it.

NOTE Aladdin DropStuff 5.1 is shareware available from Aladdin Systems, Inc. (http://www.aladdinsys.com/) and currently costs approximately $30. On the other hand, if you do a lot of compressing and decompressing (see the next essay), you may be interested in DropStuff's more powerful big brother, the commercial utility StuffIt Deluxe. You'll find details on the Aladdin Web site.

48 Aladdin Expander (a.k.a. StuffIt Expander)

StuffIt Expander is the simplest, most efficient way to expand compressed and/or encoded files that you may have received from the Internet, an online information service, bulletin board system, over a network, or from a co-worker. It handles the four most common compression and encoding formats: StuffIt and Zip archives (.sit, .sea, and .zip), BinHex (.hqx), MacBinary (.bin), and UUencode (.uu). ShrinkWrap disk image files and Private File security-encrypted (.pf) files are also accessible via StuffIt Expander.

NOTE Don't forget that if you install DropStuff, you'll be able to decode several additional formats including Mime/Base64, TAR (.tar), and Unix Compress (.Z).

In other words, StuffIt Expander decodes the most commonly used compression and encoding file formats used on Macs as well as PCs.

How to Use It...

Run the Aladdin Expander 5.1.3 Install to install StuffIt Expander on your hard disk.

> **NOTE** Chances are you have a copy of StuffIt Expander on your hard disk since it comes with all iMacs and iBooks. But the version on the companion CD is 5.1.3, which is more than likely a more recent version than yours (unless you bought your iMac or iBook in September 1999 or after). Version 5.1.3 has some features and capabilities older versions don't have and can decode some files earlier versions can't. Since StuffIt Expander is freeware, I recommend you get rid of your older version and install 5.1.3 instead.

StuffIt Expander is a breeze to use. To expand an item, drag its icon onto the StuffIt Expander icon (or an alias of the StuffIt Expander icon; one was placed on your desktop automatically when you installed StuffIt Expander). You may also drag multiple icons, a folder, or a disk icon onto StuffIt Expander, and it will expand any compressed or encoded files within the folder or disk.

In other words, to expand or decode a file or files:

1. In the Finder, select one or more icons that you want expanded.

2. Drag them onto the StuffIt Expander icon until it is highlighted.

3. Let go of the mouse button.

StuffIt Expander will open, and you'll see a progress dialog. It will expand each archive into a new folder, located in the same folder as the archive. When everything is expanded, StuffIt Expander automatically quits.

There are also several shortcuts you might want to take advantage of:

◆ If you hold down the Option key when dropping files on the icon, or when choosing Expand from the File menu, you can choose preferences that will apply only that one time to file expansion; after that, StuffIt Expander will go back to using your previously set preferences.

◆ If you hold down the Command key when choosing Expand from the File menu, you will be able to select a folder (or entire disk) to expand, instead of a single file. Normally, you would just drop a folder or disk onto StuffIt Expander to accomplish this.

◆ If you hold down the Shift key when choosing Expand from the File menu, and a Watch folder has been defined, the Watch folder is scanned for new files to expand.

NOTE To learn more about the useful Watch Folder feature, check out the StuffIt Expander readme file.

My Two Cents...

Being a frequent Internet user, I wouldn't dream of being without the latest StuffIt Expander. And you can't beat the price—free!

NOTE Aladdin StuffIt Expander 5.1.3 is freeware available from Aladdin Systems, Inc. (http://www.aladdinsys.com/).

49 CatFinder

CatFinder is "The Intuitive Disk Cataloging Utility By Keith Turner." Which is to say that it's a disk-management tool that catalogs your disks. It can catalog floppies, hard disks, CD-ROMs, Zip disks, SuperDisks, or virtually any disk. Once you've cataloged a disk, you can browse its contents without having the disk mounted, then use CatFinder's powerful find and report features to help you search for files and create printed reports. Furthermore, CatFinder can catalog the contents of StuffIt archive files (.sit files) automatically. Finally, CatFinder can print diskette labels.

How to Use It...

Decompress the file CatFinder 2.1.2.sit. This will create the CatFinder 2.1.2 folder, which contains the program and support files.

Launch CatFinder 2.1.2, then click the Try It button. The first time you run CatFinder, you'll see a dialog box telling you that you have no disks cataloged and asking if you'd like to catalog one now. Click OK. Select a disk to catalog (usually your hard disk, but if you have another disk mounted you can catalog it instead) and click OK. In a few seconds your catalog appears onscreen.

Once you've cataloged a disk you can:

◆ Create a report on the files it contains by choosing Catalog ➤ File Report (or using the keyboard shortcut Command+R). This report can include your choice of Name, Kind, Size, Label, Creator, Type, Creation Date, and/or Modification Date. You can sort the report by any of these items.

◆ Create a report on the catalog and the media it represents by choosing Catalog ➤ Catalog Report (or using the keyboard shortcut Command+C). This report can include your choice of Name, Total Size, Free Space, Media Type, Creation Date, Modification Date, Number of Files, and/or Number of Folders. You can sort the report by any of these items.

◆ Create a label by choosing Catalog ➤ Labels (or using the keyboard shortcut Command+B).

◆ Search for a file by choosing Catalog ➤ Find (or using the keyboard shortcut Command+F).

◆ Search for duplicate files by choosing Catalog ➤ Find Duplicates (or using the keyboard shortcut Command+D).

My Two Cents...

CatFinder is great for obsessive people who have to know the exact contents of each and every disk on their shelf as well as for compulsive label printers. Since I'm neither, I have no use for CatFinder. But others have told me they swear by it. So it's here if you want it or need it.

If you like CatFinder, check out DiskTracker, also on the companion CD. It does everything CatFinder does and has better label-making capabilities.

NOTE CatFinder 2.1.2 is shareware available from Keith Turner (http://www.mindspring.com/~shdtree/) and at the time of this printing costs approximately $25.

50   CMTools

CMTools makes your iMac or iBook's contextual menu more useful. In programs that support the contextual menu, such as the Finder, it provides the following functions:

- ◆ Launch applications, files, and folders
- ◆ Create aliases directly in your designated folders
- ◆ Decompress files
- ◆ Compress any items
- ◆ Copy files and folders
- ◆ Move files and folders
- ◆ Change the creator and type codes of files
- ◆ Lock/unlock files
- ◆ Open files directly with your preferred applications
- ◆ Access the Application menu via the contextual menu

Since we've already established that a picture is worth a thousand words, let's take a look at the contextual menu before and after CMTools, as shown in Figure 50.1.

Note the four new commands CMTools added—Copy To, Make Alias In, Move To, and Refresh Menus.

Here's how it works.

FIGURE 50.1   The contextual menu before CMTools (left) and after CMTools (right)

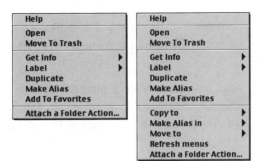

How to Use It...

Decompress the file CMTools3.0.sit, then open the CMTools3.0 folder and launch CMTools Helper & Installer. Click the Install CMTools button, then, after the installer does its thing, restart your computer. When your iMac or iBook returns to action, your contextual menu will be enhanced.

Here's how it actually works: When you install it, CMTools creates a folder named CMTools Configuration (located in the Contextual Menu Items folder of your System folder). This folder is organized in 14 sub-folders, each dedicated to a separate function of CMTools, as shown in Figure 50.2.

FIGURE 50.2   CMTools offers 14 separate functions; the CMTools Helper & Installer program lets you turn them on or off.

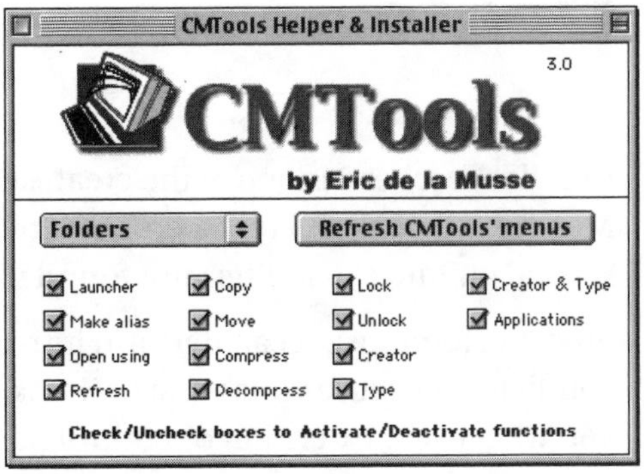

NOTE Don't change the names of these folders or CMTools will be unable to find them and will create new folders automatically.

Explaining how to configure each of the 14 functions is beyond the scope of this essay. Suffice it to say that the readme file contains everything you'll ever need to know about setting up and using CMTools and a lot more.

My Two Cents...

I'm a big fan of using the contextual menu to save time and effort. Therefore, I'm a big fan of CMTools. It takes a little fooling around with the special folders to get them set up just the way you like them. But it's worth it. And hey, you can't beat the price! Free is always good.

NOTE CMTools 3.0 is freeware available from Eric de la Musse (http://perso.cybercable.fr/edlm10//US/index.html).

51 Conflict Catcher 8 Demo

Conflict Catcher 8 is one of the greatest and most useful utilities of all time. Mostly it's a powerful replacement for Extensions Manager, but it also has several unique capabilities not found in any other utility I know of.

First and foremost, it can perform its namesake function: It can track down conflicts that cause your iMac or iBook to crash or freeze. It can also tell you what every extension or control panel does, allow you to create powerful links between extensions and control panels (see next section), and much more.

How to Use It...

Decompress the `conflictcatcher805demo.sit` file. Open the Conflict Catcher 8 Demo folder, then run the CC Installer program, click Continue, click Install, then click Restart.

The first time you restart your iMac or iBook after installation, Conflict Catcher will stop the startup process and show you its stuff. Click Continue in the first window you see, and the Conflict Catcher Tips window will appear.

NOTE If I were you, I'd click the Next button 30 times to read all the tips immediately. But that's not mandatory.

When you're finished reading tips, click OK, and the main Conflict Catcher window will appear. Take a look at it, then click Continue Startup.

NOTE During the startup process, click any of the icons at the bottom of the screen to see what they do. To continue starting up, press the spacebar.

When the Finder appears, notice the new Conflict Catcher menu on the right side of the menu bar. Choose Open Conflict Catcher. (You can also launch Conflict Catcher by opening its icon in the Control Panels folder.) Click Continue to dismiss the "nag" screen. The Tip window appears. Read the tip, then click OK.

NOTE To make Conflict Catcher appear at the beginning of the startup process, hold down the spacebar or press Caps Lock once.

In the main window, you can click any file's name to turn it on or off. Highlighted files are on; un-highlighted ones are off.

To learn more about a file, click once in the white area to the left of any file's name, and a magnifying glass icon appears, as shown in Figure 51.1.

FIGURE 51.1 Conflict Catcher shows you the details for the QuickTime extension.

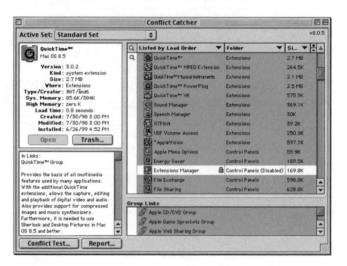

This feature alone might be worth the price of admission, but wait, there's more.

Another excellent feature of Conflict Catcher is *links*. Links allow you to create link extensions and control panels three ways. First, Grouped links let you turn on or off several extensions or control panels simultaneously.

NOTE To see this in action, click the QuickTime extension. You'll see that six extensions are turned off when you turn it off. That's because there are six items in the QuickTime Group link.

The second type of link is Incompatible, which you would use for extensions or control panels that can't be used together. With an Incompatible link, if you turn one item on, the incompatible item is turned off automatically.

Finally, Forced Order links allow you to specify that one extension or control panel should always load before (or after) another, which is sometimes necessary if you have a conflict.

Speaking of conflicts, if you ever have one—a crash or freeze during startup or a reproducible crash or freeze in an application or the Finder—Conflict

Catcher 8 can resolve it for you. Just click the Conflict Test button and follow the instructions.

Conflict Catcher 8 is a deep and sophisticated utility, so there's no way I can tell you everything about it in the three pages I'm allotted. Fortunately, the demo includes an excellent help system (choose Help ➢ Conflict Catcher Help or use the keyboard shortcut Command+?). Better still, the commercial version comes with an excellent and informative 200-page manual written by David Pogue.

My Two Cents...

I have a copy for every one of my Macs and wouldn't be without it under any circumstances. It's worth every penny.

NOTE Conflict Catcher 8 is commercial software available from Casady & Greene, Inc. (http://www.casadyg.com) and at the time of this printing costs approximately $70 (to download) or $80 (boxed copy delivered).

52 CopyPaste

CopyPaste improves your iMac or iBook's built-in copy and paste mechanism by offering you *ten* clipboards instead of the *one* you're used to. Once it's installed, you can copy up to ten items to the clipboard, then selectively paste them wherever you like.

CopyPaste also lets you modify text on the clipboard. Among the options are: Upper Case—converts the text to upper case; Lower Case—converts the text to lower case; Word Caps—starts each word with a capital; Sentence Caps—starts each sentence with a capital, if the text is already in lower case; Text Analyser—counts characters, words, sentences, and paragraphs; and much more.

How to Use It...

Decompress the file `CopyPaste folder.sit`. Open the CopyPaste 4.3.1 folder and drag the file `CopyPaste 4.3.1` onto the System Folder icon. Your iMac or iBook will tell you it needs to go in the Extensions folder. Click OK. Now open the CopyPaste Drag&Drop Helper.*f* folder and drag the file `CopyPaste Drag&Drop Helper` into the Startup Items folder (it's inside your System folder). Finally, restart your iMac or iBook to use CopyPaste.

CopyPaste gives you ten clipboards instead of just one! And it's easy as pie to use:

1. Select an object (picture, text, sound...).

2. Hold down the Command key.

3. Press C (to copy), X (to cut), or V (to paste).

4. Type a number between 1 and 9 without releasing the Command key.

5. Release the command key.

In other words, just type the usual keyboard command for copy (Command+C), cut (Command+X), or paste (Command+V) and then any number between 1 and 9 before releasing the Command key. The addition of a number to the usual commands gives you ten clipboards.

In case you've forgotten which clipboard goes with which number, or you prefer the mouse to the keyboard, you'll find each clipboard listed in submenus in the Edit menu of every application, as shown in Figure 52.1.

FIGURE 52.1 Ten clipboards are way better than one.

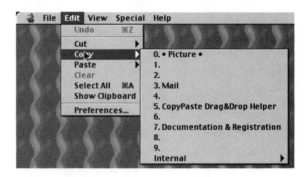

If you forget what is on your clipboards, CopyPaste offers a palette for managing your clips, as shown in Figure 52.2.

FIGURE 52.2   The CopyPaste palette lets you easily manage your clipboards.

You can show or hide this palette in three ways:

◆ Hold down the Command key while pressing first the C key, then the P key. (i.e., Command+C, then Command+P).

◆ Select Palette from the CopyPaste Utilities menu (found in the Internal submenu in the Edit menu's Cut, Copy, or Paste submenus).

◆ Type Command+C, then click anywhere while continuing to hold down the Command key.

NOTE   When you use this technique, the palette will appear right under your cursor.

CopyPaste also offers a Clip Recorder that remembers and records the last ten items copied with Command+C. You can save any set of ten clips for reuse at another time. And you can automatically force a clipboard or clipboards to be written to a file if you wish.

Once again, there's way more to CopyPaste than I can show you here in these few pages. So please take a few minutes to read the CopyPaste 4.3 manual.srd file, which you'll find in the Documentation & Registration folder.

My Two Cents...

CopyPaste is an incredibly useful utility. Once you get used to it, you'll wonder how you ever lived without it.

NOTE CopyPaste is shareware available from Julian Miller/Script Software (http://www.scriptsoftware.com/) and at the time of this printing costs approximately $20.

53 Default Folder

Default Folder is a control panel that enhances Open and Save dialog boxes to make it easier for you to manage files. With it you can:

◆ Set up a default folder for any or all applications.

◆ Switch among recently used folders from a pop-up menu.

◆ Easily navigate to your favorite folders.

◆ Share common sets of recent and favorite folders between all Open and Save dialogs, including Mac OS 8.5's Navigation Services dialogs.

◆ Click on a Finder window to list its contents in an Open or Save dialog.

◆ See available disk space and switch between disks from a pop-up menu.

◆ Open the folder shown in an Open or Save dialog in the Finder.

◆ Create folders, get information (including changing name, type, and creator), and move items to the Trash from within file dialogs.

◆ Rebound to the last file you used.

◆ Click on grayed-out filenames to enter a name in Save dialogs.

◆ Make "Replace" the default option instead of "Cancel" when saving a file with the same name as an existing file.

◆ Speed up the display of Open and Save dialogs by turning off custom color icons in the file list.

NOTE If it sounds like Default Folder is a lot like ACTION Files, you're right. They're two different programs that do pretty much the same thing. While it's possible to install and run both, I'd recommend choosing one or the other. Each one has things the other doesn't and you might prefer the interface of one over the other. So my advice is to try them both, then decide which one you prefer.

WARNING If you install ACTION Files after installing Default Folder, it may incorrectly tell you that Default Folder is not compatible and ask you to disable it. Default Folder and ACTION Files can be used together, if you wish. With ACTION Files installed, you must hold down the Command key to access Default Folder's pop-up menus. You can also fix this problem by reordering your extensions so that Default Folder loads before ACTION Files at startup. (You can do this with a startup manager such as Conflict Catcher, or by renaming the ACTION Files Extension so it comes alphabetically after Default Folder and moving it to the Control Panels folder.) Note that Default Folder and ACTION Files must both load after the Appearance extension.

How to Use It...

Run the Default Folder 3.0.2 Installer, then restart your iMac or iBook.

To see Default Folder in action, launch any application that has an Open or Save command, then choose Open or Save. Default Folder adds four icons to your Open and Save dialog boxes, as shown in Figure 53.1.

Default Folder lets you store groups of default folder settings, so you can use different setups for different people or tasks. These groups are called *folder sets* because they keep track of groups of folders. You must have at least one folder set defined in order to use most of Default Folder's features. To get you up and running quickly, Default Folder automatically chooses preferences and creates one folder set for you. This feature allows you to immediately start using Default Folder without even looking at the control

FIGURE 53.1 Default Folder adds four icons to your Open and Save dialog boxes—(l. to r.) Utility (pulled down), Disks, Favorites, and Recent.

panel. You can then use the icons in your Open and Save dialogs to add folders to the menus.

To add a new default folder without using the control panel, simply select the Use "current folder" as the Default Folder item from Default Folder's pop-up menus in an Open or Save dialog box ("current folder" will be replaced by the name of the folder whose contents is currently displayed).

Default Folder is even more customizable than ACTION Files. To modify its settings or keyboard shortcuts, open the Default Folder control panel and click the Prefs button.

As usual, there's more to Default Folder than I have space to explain. Fortunately, the Default Folder User's Guide and the control panel's online help are both excellent, so please use them.

My Two Cents...

I happen to prefer ACTION Files to Default Folder, but you may not. Give it a try. I will say that everyone should probably be using either Default Folder or ACTION Files. Either one makes using Open and Save dialog boxes better, faster, and easier.

NOTE Default Folder is shareware available from St. Clair Software (http://www.stclairsoft.com) and at the time of this printing costs approximately $25.

54 Desktop Resetter

Desktop Resetter is a one-trick pony that's worth its weight in gold if you need it. To need it, you must meet two criteria:

1. You must change your monitor's resolution occasionally (or play games that change it automatically for you).

2. You must keep more than a couple of icons on the Finder's desktop.

If you meet those two criteria, you're going to love this program. Here's what it does—if you change monitor resolutions and have a lot of icons on your desktop, the icons get messed up and rearranged. This is usually undesirable, requiring you to manually move every icon back where you like it.

Desktop Resetter remembers how you like your icons arranged on the desktop, then puts them back just that way any time they get messed up.

How to Use It...

Decompress the file `Desktop Resetter 1.1.1.sit`.

NOTE You can throw the Desktop Resetter 1.1.1 68K program away—it's only for older Macs and you don't need it.

First, set your icons to the way you would like them to be positioned, so when you reset them, they go back to this position.

Open the Desktop Resetter 1.1.1 folder and launch Desktop Resetter 1.1.1 PPC. Click the Remember button.

That's it. Your icons are remembered and ready to be reset whenever their positions get messed up.

NOTE The icons can always be re-remembered if you don't like your current setup.

The next time your desktop icons get out of order, run Desktop Resetter 1.1.1 PPC, but this time click the Reset button and wait a few seconds. Once it's finished, the icons that you had remembered previously will be reset to your preferred positions.

There is also a Settings dialog, where you can set hotkeys for Desktop Resetter. Click the Settings button to turn them on if you like.

My Two Cents...

You either need it or you don't. If you do, send Nick his $10. He deserves it.

NOTE Desktop Resetter is shareware available from Nick D'Amato (http://members.home.net/goddfadda/) and at the time of this printing costs approximately $10.

55 DiskTracker

DiskTracker is another disk cataloger, similar in scope to CatFinder. Like CatFinder, it makes it easy to search for files on multiple floppy disks, CD-ROMs, SuperDisks, Zip disks, or other storage media.

Like CatFinder, it has powerful searching and reporting features. And, like CatFinder, it can catalog the contents of StuffIt archive files (.sit files) automatically. One thing that's different is the label-printing feature—Disk-Tracker's is better (see next section).

How to Use It...

Decompress the file DiskTracker 1.1.4.sit. Open the DiskTracker 1.1.4 folder, launch the DiskTracker 1.1.4 application, and click the Not Yet button.

To catalog a volume, choose Scan ➤ Online Volume (or use the keyboard shortcut Command+M). Select a volume, then click the Scan button.

To search a catalog, you can use either of two Find functions. The first, just called Find (Search ➤ Find or Command+F), is similar to Sherlock's Find and lets you search by name, size, or other attribute. The second Find function, Find Using Filter (Search ➤ Find Using Filter or Command+E), is more unique and lets you search for files and folders such as: empty folders, major applications, or icon files using pre-built filters, or using a filter you built yourself, as shown in Figure 55.1.

FIGURE 55.1 **This filter I built finds only files and folders that are bigger than 3,000K and did not come with my iMac.**

```
┌─────────────────── Edit Item Filter ───────────────────┐
│ Find items whose:                                      │
│ ┌────────────────────────────────────┐   ┌─────────┐  │
│ │ Size is greater than 3,000K AND    │   │ AND   ▲▼│  │
│ │ Label is not 'Came with iMac'      │   └─────────┘  │
│ │                                    │   ┌─────────┐  │
│ │                                    │   │ Edit... │  │
│ │                                    │   └─────────┘  │
│ │                                    │   ┌─────────┐  │
│ │                                    │   │ Insert..│  │
│ │                                  ▲ │   └─────────┘  │
│ │                                  ▼ │   │ Delete  │  │
│ └────────────────────────────────────┘   └─────────┘  │
│ ┌───────┐ ┌─────────┐       ┌────────┐ ┌──────────┐   │
│ │ Group │ │ Ungroup │       │ Cancel │ │    OK    │   │
│ └───────┘ └─────────┘       └────────┘ └──────────┘   │
└────────────────────────────────────────────────────────┘
```

NOTE The day I got my iMac, before I installed a single item, I set the label of every file on my hard disk to "Came with iMac." This lets me know quickly if any file came with my computer (label = Came with iMac) or if it was added later (label ≠ Came with iMac).

DiskTracker's extensive label-making capabilities may be its best feature. To create a label, choose Label ➤ Template Editor. Using the Template Editor is a lot like working with a drawing program or AppleWorks' Draw module. Figure 55.2 shows a picture of a CD label I created in about two minutes.

FIGURE 55.2 A CD label I created in about two minutes

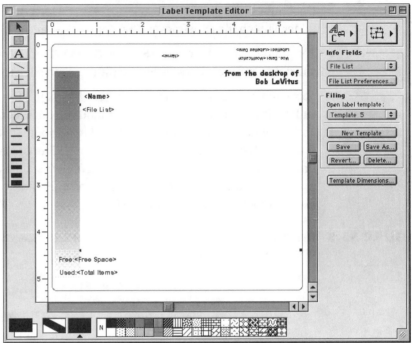

As usual, I don't have the space to show you all of the things DiskTracker can do. Fortunately, the 62-page DiskTracker user manual (in the Disk-Tracker 1.1.4 folder) is quite comprehensive.

My Two Cents...

As I said before, I'm not compulsive about cataloging or labeling disks, so I don't use either one (CatFinder or DiskTracker). I guess if I were only going to pay for one, DiskTracker is the one I'd pay for, mostly because of its better label-making capabilities (and it's $5 cheaper).

NOTE So why even include CatFinder? I dunno. Because there was enough space on the CD for both and some of you may choose it (over DiskTracker) for whatever reason.

NOTE DiskTracker is shareware available from Mark N. Pirri (TheVortex @kagi.com [e-mail; the Web site was not functional at press time]) and at the time of this printing costs approximately $20.

56 Drag'nBack

Drag'nBack is a simple backup program that lets you devise a backup strategy that suits your particular needs.

The author explains it better than I could:

"You can think of Drag'nBack as a container—it remembers files that are dropped over it. It remembers the backup disks it used. If you have new files or folders to back up, drag and drop them over Drag'nBack. If you double-click on Drag'nBack's icon to open it, Drag'nBack will back up the files it remembers. Drag'nBack only backs up files that have changed since the last backup. It will prompt you for the backup disks that are needed."

NOTE A backup disk can be any Finder-mountable storage device—floppy disk, Zip disk, CD-RW, or whatever. The location and label of each file is preserved. Thus, the backup file is ready to use with most application programs without decoding, decompressing, or restoring.

Drag'nBack can also find files, open a document or application, delete unwanted older files, defragment a disk, synchronize files, open a folder window on the desktop, get Finder Info, make an alias file, and more.

How to Use It...

Decompress the file `DragnBack2.9.6.sit`. Now launch the Drag'nBack User's Guide and choose Topics ➤ Quick Start, and read the section that begins "Try This Exercise First" and go through the 15-step exercise.

NOTE Hey, there's no point in my wasting space in the book repeating this stuff. The tutorial in the User's Guide is first rate. I couldn't have done better. So work through it, and you'll not only have learned how to use Drag'nBack but you'll have made your first backup.

My Two Cents...

As you know from Chapter 7, I'm a nut about backing up your files. And Drag'nBack can make it almost painless. Still, for my $50, I prefer Retrospect Express, a commercial program from Dantz Development (`http://www.dantz.com/dantz_products/express.html`). On the other hand, if you can't be bothered with buying commercial backup software, you should definitely adopt Drag'nBack. (Don't forget to pay the shareware fee.)

WARNING My point is that you absolutely must back up important files. Use Drag'nBack, Retrospect Express, or something. But for gosh sakes, back up your stuff. I promise you this: If you don't back up, you will someday lose important files. I guarantee it.

NOTE Drag'nBack is shareware from Enterprise Software (`http://members.aol.com/RealIP/index.html`) and at the time of this printing costs approximately $50.

57 EZNote

Have you ever needed to jot down a note quickly and be able to easily find it later? Or wanted to copy some text while Web browsing without copying and pasting between applications or saving the text to a file? Or needed to jot down a phone number quickly without launching a program? EZNote is a control panel that can do these things and more at the touch of a hotkey (which will instantly bring up its built-in text editor) and do them without leaving the application you are in and without having to open another program.

Another hotkey brings up a list of all your notes, which you can edit, delete, search, replace, print, and move from category to category (and, of course, you can create as many categories as you like).

Plus, EZNote lets you do all kinds of text editing including changing fonts, styles, sizes, all caps, all lower case, smarten quotes, stupify quotes, etc.

Some uses for EZNote (from its readme file) are:

◆ Bring up a text editor instantly with one keypress.

◆ Quickly edit text on the clipboard (edit, change it to all upper case or lower case, remove line feeds, etc.).

◆ Copy selected text from any application with one keystroke and store it for later reading or editing.

◆ Keep an online journal of daily activities.

◆ Keep a to-do list.

◆ Keep commonly used text clippings for pasting into any application.

◆ Grab a note or selection of text from any category without having to leave the application you're in.

◆ Maintain a simple and easy-to-access address book and phone number list.

◆ Collect and organize the information from those scattered text document and clipping files.

How to Use It...

First, double-click the file EZNote(1.41).sea, click Continue, and save the folder to your hard disk. Then, drop the EZNote file and EZNote Plugins folder onto your System folder and restart your iMac or iBook.

EZNote's default hotkeys are:

◆ Ctrl+F13 for a blank note

◆ Ctrl+F14 to copy any selected text and paste it into an EZNote

◆ Ctrl+F15 to get/edit any notes you have created

◆ Command+Option+click to get the EZNote pop-up menu, as shown in Figure 57.1

FIGURE 57.1   **Command+Option+click anywhere to bring up the EZNote menu.**

Using either your hotkeys or the EZNote pop-up menu, you can quickly:

◆ Open a new, blank note (Ctrl+F13).

◆ Copy any selected text to an EZNote (Ctrl+F14).

◆ Open the EZNote text editor (Ctrl+F15).

Give it a try.

> **NOTE**   You can change any of the hotkeys by opening the **EZNote** control panel (from the **Control Panels** menu of your **Apple** menu).

EZNote stores your notes in categories. You can add, delete, and/or rename categories in the EZNote text editor (Ctrl+F15). You'll find these commands in the File menu.

Once you've copied a note (any text) to EZNote, you can move it to a different category, rename it, delete it, copy it to the clipboard, edit it, and more, again using the EZNote text editor's File, Edit, and Plugins menus.

N O T E   There's much, much more that this program can do, but I have many more utilities to cover and only so many pages to do it in. So once again, I'm going to refer you to the (excellent) user's manual, called "EZNote Documentation."

My Two Cents...

This is a very cool utility. I learned about it only recently and am giving it a try. So far I like it a lot. I expect I'll be sending John a check for $20 when my trial period expires.

N O T E   EZNote is shareware available from John V. Holder (`http://www.northcoast.com/~jvholder/`) and at the time of this printing costs approximately $20.

58   File Buddy

File Buddy is a powerful utility for managing files and folders. I think of it as the Swiss Army Knife of utility applications, because it can do so many different things. Here are just some of the things File Buddy can do (from the File Buddy 5 readme):

◆ View and edit a wide range of file and folder information.

◆ Create droplets that automatically apply changes to items dropped on them, even recursively within folders.

◆ Find files using an extensive set of search criteria, which can be expanded using plug-ins for such tasks as finding files containing specific resources.

◆ Modify the name of multiple items, e.g., remove ".txt" from several filenames at once.

◆ Rename a group of files sequentially.

◆ Create custom icons from PICTs on the clipboard; from other icons; for folders; with blank icons; using only small icons.

◆ Create aliases easily in your favorite places.

◆ Create volume and folder inventories that can be compared to report new, deleted, and modified files and folders.

◆ Find empty files and folders, duplicate files, broken aliases, and unused preference files.

◆ Automatically repair broken aliases.

◆ Rebuild desktops, even on floppies.

◆ Move files and folders.

◆ Copy files and folders, even invisible files on CDs.

◆ Delete resource forks and data forks of files.

WARNING File Buddy is a powerful program capable of wreaking major havoc on your hard disk. Many of its functions can damage files irreparably. So, I recommend it only if you are extremely comfortable with the workings of your iMac or iBook. If you consider yourself a novice or beginner, you're probably better off not messing with it.

How to Use It...

Run the File Buddy 5.0.2 Installer to install the File Buddy 5.0.2 folder on your hard drive. Once it's installed, you need to rebuild your iMac or iBook's desktop by restarting, then holding down Command and Option until the Are You Sure You Want to Rebuild the Desktop File? dialog box appears. Click OK and wait a minute or two. Now File Buddy is ready to use. Double-click the File Buddy 5.0.2 icon to launch File Buddy.

NOTE You ought to rebuild your iMac or iBook's Desktop every month or two anyway. It won't hurt anything and can improve performance and keep your hard disk running smoothly.

My gosh, there's so much to File Buddy, I don't know where to start. So I'll just give you a quick demo and then you're on your own.

Here's how to see File Buddy in action for yourself:

1. Open the File Buddy 5.0.2 folder.

2. Drag the file Viewing the Online Help onto the File Buddy 5.0.2 icon.

File Buddy will open and show you its information window for the Viewing the Online Help file, as shown in Figure 58.1.

FIGURE 58.1 **The File Buddy information window for the document "Viewing the Online Help"**

```
┌──────────────────────────────────────────────────────────────┐
│ ☐  ══════ Info for: Viewing the Online Help ══════          ▤ │
│                          ⟨🔥⟩⟨📋⟩⟨📁⟩ ⟨📂📂📂⟩⟨📤⟩⟨🗑⟩  ⟨⁇⟩ │
│   ┌──┐                                                        │
│   │::│  Viewing the Online Help                              │
│   └──┘                                    Label: None  ⬍  ⬍  │
│   ┌Standard Finder Info──────────────────────────────────┐  │
│   │   Kind: SimpleText document      Resource Fork: 372 bytes│
│   │   Size: 8 K on disk, (1,156 bytes used)  Data Fork: 784 bytes│
│   │                                                        │  │
│   │  Where: Macintosh HD:my stuff: iMac I Didn't Know Software:Utilities:File Buddy 5.0.2:│
│   │                                                        │  │
│   │  Created: Fri, May 29, 1998, 9:52:41 AM  ⬍           │  │
│   │  Modified: Wed, Dec 23, 1998, 4:40:40 AM  ⬍          │  │
│   │  Version:                                             │  │
│   └───────────────────────────────────────────────────────┘  │
│   ┌File and Folder Flags──┐ ┌Type and Creator Signature───┐  │
│   │ ☐ Invisible  ☐ Use Custom Icon│ Type: TEXT ⬍  Creator: ttxt ⬍  Copy ⬍│
│   │ ☑ Inited     ☐ Name Locked   │                       │  │
│   ┌File Flags─────────────┐ Comments: ● Finder ○ Attached │  │
│   │ ☐ Alias    ☐ Has Bundle │ ┌───────────────────────┐   │  │
│   │ ☐ Stationery ☐ File Locked│ │                       │   │  │
│   │ ☐ Shared   ☐ No INITs    │ (Revert)(Change All)(Cancel)(Save)│
│   └───────────────────────┘ └───────────────────────────┘  │
└──────────────────────────────────────────────────────────────┘
```

This window offers you many options. You can modify the file's flags, type, creator, and comments using the controls at the bottom of the screen. You can change the file's label using the label pop-up menu. You can reveal the file in the Finder, create an alias for it, copy it, move it to another disk or folder, or move it to the Trash using the buttons at the top right of the window. You can even change the creation or modification dates by clicking the double-headed arrows next to these items.

WARNING I strongly recommend you click the Cancel button now. If you make modifications to this file—like turning on its invisible flag—you may render it unusable.

To get at File Buddy's other features—finding duplicates, empty folders, or unused icons, or erasing free disk space, for example—just launch File Buddy by double-clicking it.

One other feature bears mentioning and that is File Buddy's Drop Keys. If you hold down certain keys as you drag a file onto File Buddy, you can invoke different options, as shown in Figure 58.2.

FIGURE 58.2 **File Buddy's Drop Keys**

Edit Drop Keys		
Click a button to set the drop keys for that action.		
Ask First Dialog Command	**Move/Copy** Control	
Get Finder's Info Option+Shift	**Make Alias** Command+Option+Shift	
Get App's Info Option	**FB Get Info** Command+'i'	
Move to Desktop Command+Shift	**Group Info** Shift	
Find Original Command+Option	**Find App** Shift+Control	
View in List Command+'l'	**Find Similar** Command+'s'	
Rebuild Desktop Command+'d'		
Use Defaults	**Cancel** **Save**	

So, for example, dragging a file onto File Buddy while holding down Option and Shift will get you the file's Finder Info (as if you had selected the file and chosen File ➢ Get Info or used the shortcut Command+I). Or, if you hold down the Command key as you drag a file onto File Buddy, you'll get the "Ask" dialog, as shown in Figure 58.3.

FIGURE 58.3 Hold down the Command key when you drag a file onto File Buddy and you'll get this dialog box. Click any button to invoke that action.

NOTE To change the Drop Keys, choose Edit ➢ Drop Keys.

WARNING I feel obligated to mention again that File Buddy is capable of really messing up your hard disk and the files it contains. Be sure you completely understand what you're doing before you use it.

Perhaps the best way to learn more about File Buddy is to launch it and open its online help by choosing Help ➢ File Buddy Help or using the shortcut Command+H. There's a lot more to this program than I have space for, so I strongly recommend you spend time with the online help and read the File Buddy 5 readme and Read These FAQs documents (in the Important Things to Read folder).

My Two Cents...

If you're a power user, you'll find some (or all) of File Buddy's functions invaluable. But it's important to remember that File Buddy can be extremely destructive to files or disks.

I recommend this program for only those of you who are comfortable using a program that could render files or disks unusable. And, of course, I don't recommend using it unless you back up religiously.

N O T E File Buddy is commercial software (according to the File Buddy 5 readme file, though it's distributed as if it were shareware) available from Laurence Harris/SkyTag Software (`http://www.skytag.com/FileBuddy .stuff/FB_home_page.shtml`) and at the time of this printing costs approximately $40.

59 FinderPop

FinderPop is a control panel that makes your contextual menus better and more powerful. Its features include:

◆ User-selectable contextual menu font/size/icon size

◆ Automatic contextual menu pop-up by clicking and holding without having to press the Ctrl key

◆ Fast, easy disk, folder, and StuffIt archive navigation

◆ A number of optional submenus—including Processes, Contents of Selected Folder, Finder windows, FinderPop, and Desktop, as you can see in Figure 59.1.

FIGURE 59.1 **A normal contextual menu (left) and one enhanced by FinderPop (right)**

Help
Open
Move To Trash
Get Info ▶
Label ▶
Duplicate
Make Alias
Add To Favorites

Help
🪨 Set File Type ▶
🗔 Applications ▶
🗂 Finder Windows ▶
🖥 Desktop ▶
Open
Move To Trash
Get Info ▶
Label ▶
Duplicate
Make Alias
Add To Favorites

In addition, FinderPop enhances navigation via the standard File dialogs, as shown in Figure 59.2.

FIGURE 59.2 Click on a folder, and FinderPop "pops up" its contents! Slick!

FinderPop's motto is "click different." And once you've tried it, you surely will click differently.

How to Use It...

Decompress the file FinderPop180.sit. Drag the FinderPop control panel and FinderPop Extensions icons onto your System folder. A dialog box will alert you that FinderPop needs to be stored in the Control Panels folder. Click OK. Now restart your iMac or iBook to enable FinderPop.

There are two places you can see FinderPop in action: The first is anywhere in the Finder. Just click and hold down the mouse button anywhere—in a window, on any icon, or on the desktop background—and the FinderPop menu will appear, as shown in Figure 59.1, bottom. (You can also hold down the Ctrl key and click any of those places.)

The second is in any Open or Save dialog box. Just click and continue to hold down the mouse button on any folder in the file list. A pop-up menu displaying its contents will appear, as shown in Figure 59.2.

My favorite feature is the FinderPop folder. Much as the Apple menu displays the contents of the Apple Menu Items folder, so too does FinderPop display the contents of its own special folder, the FinderPop Items folder. Again like with the Apple menu, you can extend the FinderPop submenu by adding items (documents, applications, folders, or aliases to anything) to the FinderPop

Items folder. The big difference between the FinderPop menu and the Apple menu is that by Ctrl+clicking an icon in the Finder and selecting an item from the FinderPop submenu, you achieve the same effect as if you'd dropped the Finder icon on the item you chose from the FinderPop menu! So, by having appropriate aliases in your FinderPop items folder, you can quickly and easily open a Finder icon using a particular application, or move it to another folder, or copy it, or make an alias of it....

For example, if you add an alias of Aladdin's popular DropStuff compression program to your FinderPop Items folder, you can instantly compress a bunch of files in the Finder by selecting them, bringing up the contextual menu, and choosing DropStuff from the FinderPop menu. And so on.

A wealth of other useful options are available once you've installed FinderPop. If you just want to dive in, open the FinderPop control panel and have at it. But, at risk of sounding like a broken record, I'm going to have to refer you to the FinderPop Manual if you want to know more about these options and how they work.

My Two Cents...

FinderPop is another utility I have installed on all my Macs and wouldn't want to be without. Try it for a few days and I think you'll agree.

N O T E FinderPop is freeware from Turlough (Turly) O'Connor (`http://www.finderpop.com`).

60 HelpLess

HelpLess is a system extension and control panel that helps people with extended keyboards avoid the annoying delay that occurs when they accidentally hit the Help key instead of the Delete key.

Without HelpLess installed, you can experience quite a long delay while the current application launches its help system in response to the Help key being pressed. For example, in the Finder there is a delay while Apple Guide is launched.

With HelpLess installed, hitting the Help key causes nothing more than a simple beep to be played. This alerts the user to their mistake, and they can then just carry on typing without waiting for the help system to swing into action. If you want to bring up the help system, then you just need to press a modifier key and HelpLess will tell the system that you pressed the Help key, thus activating the available help.

How to Use It...

Decompress the file HelpLess-112.sit. Now drag the file called HelpLess Extension from the HelpLess-112 folder onto your System folder. A dialog box will alert you that HelpLess Extension needs to be stored in the Extensions folder. Click OK, then restart your iMac or iBook.

NOTE The file called HelpLess Control is actually an application and can live anywhere on your hard disk. However, the author suggests that the best place to put it is in the Control Panels folder. Because it is an application, you will need to place it there yourself. (In other words, you can't just drag it onto your System folder and have it go into the Control Panels folder automatically.)

Open HelpLess Control to configure the program. First, click the Active button in the upper right corner to turn HelpLess on. Then, choose On or Off for the warning sound and choose a modifier key (Command, Shift, Ctrl, or Option). Finally, if you want the Help menu to appear in the right side of the menu bar as it used to under Mac OS 7, click the System 7 Position checkbox (this option requires you to restart your iMac or iBook).

That's it. From now on if you accidentally press the Help key on your keyboard, nothing will happen. (Of course, you'll hear a beep if you enabled that option. Otherwise, nothing.) To access Help, hold down the modifier key you selected in HelpLess Control previously and press the Help key.

My Two Cents...

It's a one-trick pony, but if you find yourself pressing that Help key too often, it's probably worth the $10.

NOTE HelpLess is shareware from Peter Hardman/Redpoint Software (`http://sodium.ch.man.ac.uk/pages/redpoint.html`) and at the time of this printing costs approximately $10.

61 QuicKeys Demo

QuicKeys is a multi-purpose macro program that (according to the box) "automates and customizes your Mac so it does what you want when you want it, without a lot of frustration or hassle." I couldn't have said it better myself. QuicKeys is one of the most useful Mac utilities ever invented. It can take care of almost any boring, redundant, or time-consuming task by recording your keystrokes and mouse clicks, then playing them back when you need them.

NOTE In QuicKeys parlance, these macros are called *shortcuts*.

Here are just some of the things I use QuicKeys for:

◆ Launch (or switch to) programs by pressing one of the F-keys on my keyboard. Microsoft Word is F1, Consultant is F2, Internet Explorer is F3, and so on.

◆ Insert the date and/or time automatically when I'm typing (my QuicKey for this is Ctrl+`).

◆ Insert boilerplate text automatically when I'm typing. For example, if I type Ctrl+L, QuicKeys inserts the text "Very Truly Yours, (carriage return, carriage return) Bob LeVitus (carriage return) Author, Raconteur, and Consultant." Or if I type Ctrl+A, it types my complete address.

◆ Create keyboard shortcuts for any menu item that doesn't have one already, in any program or the Finder. For example, Ctrl+Tab is the QuicKey shortcut I use for "Empty Trash."

How to Use It...

Decompress the file QuicKeys Demo.sit, then open the QuicKeys 4.0 Demo folder and launch qkmac40demo. Click Continue, click Continue again, click Agree, type your name and company if you like, choose Install 30-Day Demo, then click OK. Finally, click Install. A dialog box will warn you that your Mac needs to be restarted after installation. Click Yes. Wait for the installation to finish, then click Restart.

When your iMac or iBook comes back to life, you'll notice some new stuff on your desktop: a floating toolbar, a new menu (the QuicKeys menu) at top right next to the Application menu, and a QuicKeys demo reminder window (which you can close by clicking its close box). The installer also places a QuicKeys folder at root level on your hard disk and installs the QuicKeys control panel in your Control Panels folder.

Due to the usual space considerations, I am unable to show very much of QuicKeys' remarkable power. But let's, very quickly, make the program instantly useful to you. To do this, we're going to run a program called QuicKeys Setup Assistant. You can launch it by choosing it in the QuicKeys menu, by clicking the star (leftmost button) in the QuicKeys floating toolbar, or by double-clicking the QuicKeys Setup Assistant icon in the QuicKeys folder on your hard disk. Do that.

When the QuicKeys Setup Assistant appears, click the right arrow to begin. On the second screen you see, click the File Tools button, then click the right arrow again. On the next screen, choose File Launch, then click the right arrow again.

We're going to create a shortcut that launches AppleWorks when you press the F12 key. So click the Choose button and locate the AppleWorks program, then click the right arrow again.

Now click the Keystroke field and press F12. If you want to be able to trigger this shortcut by choosing it from the QuicKeys menu, click the Show in QuicKeys menu checkbox. If you want the shortcut to appear as a button in the QuicKeys toolbar, click that checkbox. Click the right arrow again, then click Create Shortcut.

If you want to create more shortcuts, click Continue. If you want to quit, click Quit.

To see your shortcut in action, press F12. AppleWorks should launch immediately.

NOTE This time I really feel terrible. QuicKeys is a rich and rewarding program and I have barely scratched the surface of all the great things it can do to save you time and effort.

I urge you to spend some time reading QKMac.pdf, the online manual for QuicKeys. After you get some of your own shortcuts set up, I know you'll be as addicted to QuicKeys as I am.

My Two Cents...

The bottom line is that QuicKeys can automate almost any Mac task and makes using a Mac so much better I'm amazed Apple doesn't include it with every Mac they sell.

I have not used a Mac without QuicKeys in at least eight years and I would dread ever having to do so. If I were stranded on a desert island with a Mac and could only take one utility, this would be the one.

So try it—I know you'll learn to love it as much as I do.

NOTE QuicKeys is a commercial software demo available from CE Software (http://www.cesoft.com) and at the time of this printing costs approximately $100.

62 Snitch

Snitch is a control panel that extends the Get Info command (File ≻ Get Info or Command+I), allowing you to view and edit a variety of different information about a file, alias, folder, or disk.

Let's do that "picture is worth a thousand words" thing again; Figure 62.1 shows a Get Info window before and after Snitch.

FIGURE 62.1 The Get Info window for the Snitch control panel, with (bottom) and without (top) Snitch

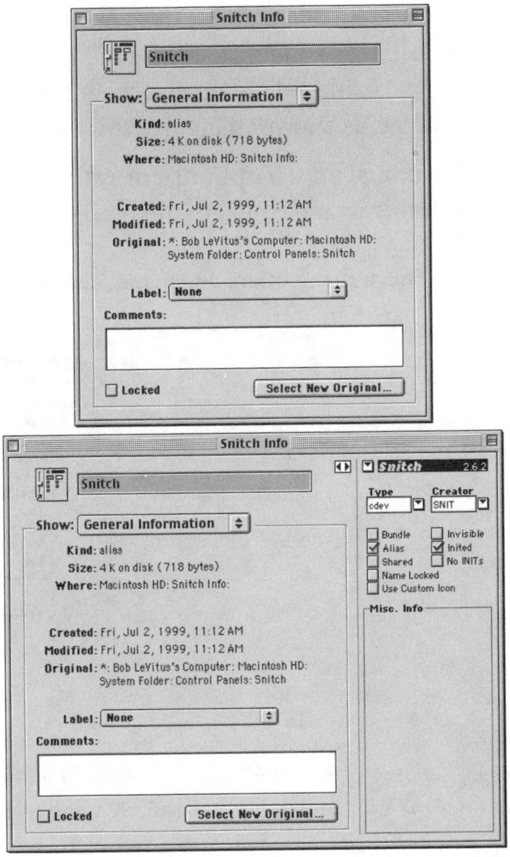

WARNING Snitch is useful but can make permanent changes to files that can render them useless. So if you're going to use it, do so with caution.

How to Use It...

The Snitch installer will automatically install everything you need to use Snitch.

To turn Snitch on and off, or configure its options, open the Snitch control panel.

Once it's installed and turned on, select any icon on your hard disk, then choose File ➢ Get Info or use the keyboard shortcut Command+I. Snitch will be displayed along with the information that is normally in a Get Info window, as shown in Figure 62.1.

Additional Snitch options are available by clicking the little downward-pointing triangle next to the name Snitch, as shown in Figure 62.2.

FIGURE 62.2 The Snitch menu offers additional options.

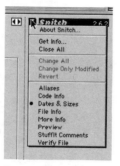

NOTE Snitch has particularly good hypertext documentation. Open the file `Snitch_Documentation.html` with your favorite browser.

My Two Cents...

I suppose some people will find Snitch's capabilities invaluable, but I haven't really found much use for it.

NOTE Snitch is shareware available from Mitch Jones (http://www .niftyneato.com/) and at the time of this printing costs approximately $20.

63 T-Minus Ten

T-Minus Ten is another automation utility that can do some (but not nearly all) of what QuicKeys does and for a lot less money. T-Minus Ten lets you configure hotkeys and hot spots to launch applications, scripts, and documents. With it you can set up a schedule to provide an off-hours autopilot for running back-up scripts or downloading stock quotes. Finally, T-Minus Ten lets you create reminders of important events, such as birthdays and anniversaries.

In fact, anything you can open or script can be automated with T-Minus Ten.

How to Use It...

Decompress the file T-Minus Ten 2.1.sit, then launch the T-Minus Ten program. The first time you launch it, you will see a window informing you that T-Minus Ten needs to install the T-Minus Ten extension. Click the Install button.

That's it. After installation, the main T-Minus Ten window will be displayed. It has four tabs: Start/Stop, Tasks, Activity Log, and Preferences.

The Start/Stop panel indicates whether or not T-Minus Ten is active. Tasks will automatically run only when the system is active. The system should already be on. If not, press the Start button to enable the system.

The Tasks panel is where most of the action takes place. You can turn any file or AppleScript into a task. If the file is an application or document, the task automatically opens the file. If the file is an AppleScript, it runs the script.

Let's create a task that does the same thing as the shortcut we created with QuicKeys in the previous essay—launch AppleWorks when you press F12. To create a task, do one of the following:

1. Select New Task from the File menu.

2. Click the New Task button in the Tasks panel.

3. Drag a file into the Tasks panel.

The easiest way is the third way, so drag the AppleWorks icon onto the Tasks panel now. A new AppleWorks Task window appears. Type in a name (**AppleWorks F12**), then click the Trigger tab. Choose When a Hotkey Is Pressed from the Run This Task pop-up menu. Now press the F12 key and click the Save button.

That's all there is to it. Now whenever you press F12, AppleWorks will launch.

In addition to using a hotkey for your trigger, you can also trigger a task at startup, at shutdown, after so many minutes of idle time, or by clicking a hot spot on the screen.

N O T E   Choose Help ➤ T-Minus Ten Guide to read the online manual.

My Two Cents...

I don't use it because QuicKeys can do everything it can do and much more. But although QuicKeys is much more powerful, it's also much more expensive and somewhat more complicated.

The bottom line is that if all you need is the kind of simple automation T-Minus Ten offers, it's a great value at $20.

N O T E T-Minus Ten is shareware available from Mark Krenek (mk@kagi.com) and at the time of this printing costs approximately $20.

64 TechTool

TechTool is a utility that solves many difficult problems that elude other utilities. TechTool lets you:

◆ Analyze your U.S. and International System file for damage.

◆ View devices on your LAN.

◆ Save file comments before rebuilding a desktop database.

◆ Zap your PRAM (Parameter RAM).

◆ Delete the Desktop file (a better alternative than rebuilding).

◆ Clean your floppy drive (when used with a drive-cleaning disk).

◆ See the date your computer was manufactured and how many hours of use it has had.

N O T E I don't trust this feature—it says my iMac, which I've used for months, has zero hours of use and was manufactured yesterday.

◆ View, print, and save a multitude of information about your Mac.

In other words, TechTool is a handy way to find out a lot of things about your iMac or iBook that you would have a hard time discovering any other way. And it offers better mechanisms for zapping your PRAM and rebuilding your Desktop than Mac OS.

How to Use It...

Decompress the file TechTool 1.1.8.sit, then launch TechTool v1.1.8. Click once to dismiss the splash screen and you're ready to rock and roll.

WARNING The first thing you should do is choose Info ➢ Read Me/ Instructions (or use the keyboard shortcut Command+H) and read the entire thing. TechTool is powerful medicine for your iMac or iBook and can cause severe problems if misused. And, of course, it's always a good idea to have a backup of your data before using a program that messes with your iMac or iBook's internal workings, such as the desktop and PRAM. The readme explains these things in full detail, and you'd be making a huge mistake to try to use TechTool without reading it.

Since I insist you read the documentation before attempting to rebuild your Desktop or zap your PRAM, I won't cover those features here. What I will do is show you how to gather and read all sorts of information about your iMac or iBook and how to analyze your System file for hidden damage.

In fact, let's do that first. Click the System Analyze button. Now wait a few minutes. If there is any damage, TechTool will report it and tell you what you should do to correct it. If everything is hunky-dory, you'll see a cheerful message like the one shown in Figure 64.1.

FIGURE 64.1   TechTool gave my System file a clean bill of health!

To learn more about your iMac or iBook, click any of the buttons at the bottom right:

◆ The Hardware button displays information about your iMac or iBook, such as how much RAM you have installed, what type of PowerPC processor you have, and so on.

◆ The Extensions button lists all your installed extensions and tells you the filename, type, creator, version, creation date, and modification date for each one.

◆ The CDEVS button lists all your installed control panels and tells you the filename, type, creator, version, creation date, and modification date for each one.

◆ The General button displays more information about your iMac or iBook, such as what version of Mac OS is installed, plus lots of stuff you probably don't care much about (version numbers for Open Transport, AppleTalk, etc., and lots of other stuff only useful to programmers).

◆ The Network button lists all devices available on your network.

◆ The Print Info button prints the information currently being displayed (based upon which button you've pressed).

◆ The Save Info button saves the information currently being displayed (based upon which button you've pressed) as a SimpleText file.

◆ The Help button brings up the same Help screen as Info ➢ Read Me/ Instructions (or Command+H).

◆ The Register, Personalize, and Special buttons show you propaganda from TechTool's maker, Micromat.

NOTE Micromat also makes a more powerful commercial repair and recovery program, TechTool Pro, that sells for around $150 and is considered by many—including me—to be a fine alternative to Norton Utilities.

My Two Cents...

Hey, it's free and it's useful. What more can you ask for? Unless you own a copy of TechTool Pro, TechTool is well worth keeping around if only for its improved Desktop and PRAM tools.

NOTE TechTool is freeware available from Micromat, Inc. (`http://www.micromat.com`).

65 TypeIt4Me

TypeIt4Me is a tool to speed up typing. First you define a set of abbreviations and the full-text entries that they represent, then you watch TypeIt4Me expand them on the fly, even as you continue typing!

Abbreviations can represent any text you like, such as:

◆ A long, hard-to-type word like *benzo-methyl-tricarbo-something-or-other*

◆ Your name and address

◆ A standard end-of-letter closing such as Very Truly Yours, (carriage return) Bob LeVitus (carriage return), Author, Raconteur, and Consultant

◆ An entire paragraph of text

◆ A short word that you often misspell (such as *teh* instead of *the* or *taht* instead of *that*)

◆ Your e-mail signature

◆ HTML tags for Web pages

In short, TypeIt4Me can type just about anything you need to type often faster than you could type it yourself.

How to Use It...

Run the TypeIt4Me installer and restart your iMac or iBook.

The first thing you'll notice is the new TypeIt4Me menu in the upper left-hand corner of the menu bar. TypeIt4Me stores its information in a file you create. So pull down the TypeIt4Me menu and choose New File, as shown in Figure 65.1.

FIGURE 65.1 Start by creating a new TypeIt4Me file.

Click Save.

Now launch a program you can type text in, such as SimpleText or Apple-Works. Type the text you use to end a letter or an e-mail. For example, I generally use:

Regards,

Bob LeVitus

Wordsmith, Raconteur, Author of 33 books including

Mac OS 9 For Dummies and *Mac Answers: Certified Tech Support,*

and columnist for *MacCentral* and the *Houston Chronicle*

Boblevitus@boblevitus.com

http://www.boblevitus.com

When you finish typing, select your text and copy it to the clipboard (Edit ➤ Copy or Command+C).

Now pull down the TypeIt4Me menu and choose Add an Entry. The Enter Your Abbreviation window will appear. Type two or three letters to use as your trigger for this chunk of text (I used *rega*, which are the first letters in *regards*), then click OK.

To trigger the automatic typing of the text represented by an abbreviation, you can either type the abbreviation or select the abbreviation from TypeIt4Me's pop-up menu.

To see TypeIt4Me in action, type your abbreviation followed by a space. Presto. TypeIt4Me types the whole thing instantly!

Once you define an abbreviation, it is available at all times, anywhere text can be typed, no matter if you are using your word processor, paint program, Finder, address book, Web browser, or any application at all!

That, in a nutshell, is how it works.

NOTE TypeIt4Me will not bother me when I type *regards* or *regal*, since it looks for the letters *rega* as a separate word, i.e., preceded and followed by spaces or by the punctuation marks of my choice.

NOTE The TypeIt4Me User Manual is excellent and detailed. Be sure to read it if you want to really harness the power of TypeIt4Me.

My Two Cents...

Simply awesome! Another must-have utility. Try it for a week, and you'll be absolutely convinced it's one of the greatest Mac utilities of all time.

NOTE TypeIt4Me is shareware available from Riccardo Ettore (http://www .r-ettore.dircon.co.uk/) and at the time of this printing costs approximately $27.

66 ZipIt

ZipIt is a Macintosh program to zip and unzip files. That's all it does.

NOTE Zip is the PC/DOS/Windows equivalent of StuffIt, which compresses files to save space on disks and time when sending via e-mail.

How to Use It...

Decompress the file ZipIt 1.3.8.sit, then launch the ZipIt application. The "nag" window appears; click Not Yet to try ZipIt.

An untitled ZipIt window appears. To compress a file, drag it onto this window then choose File ➤ Save.

To decompress a .zip file, drag it onto the ZipIt icon.

That's about it.

My Two Cents...

If you often receive or download .zip files, or need to create .zip files for your less-fortunate (read: PC-using) friends or associates, ZipIt may be just the ticket.

NOTE StuffIt Expander can expand (but not create) most `.zip` files. But, in my experience, some `.zip` files can't be decompressed with StuffIt Expander. ZipIt can usually decompress these files. So, if you deal with many `.zip` files, it's probably a good program to keep handy.

NOTE ZipIt is shareware available from Tom Brown (`zipit@softlock .com`) and at the time of this printing costs approximately $15.

Graphics

This is a chapter about the graphics and graphics-related software on the companion CD-ROM. There aren't nearly as many of these programs as there were utilities in Chapter 8, but the four programs described herein are all very cool nonetheless.

So, without further ado, let's take a look:

67 GraphicConverter

GraphicConverter converts the most common ATARI, Amiga, and IBM graphics (picture) formats to Macintosh formats and back again, if desired. It also lets you do some types of image editing—cropping, resizing, etc.— and generate lists that include information about each picture. Graphic-Converter offers superior viewing capabilities with its Slide Show and Browse Folder features, both of which come in handy if you want to view the latest family photos or need to look at some graphics files from work. GraphicConverter is also great for prepping scans of photos that you want to put up on the Web.

From the readme file:

> GraphicConverter imports PICT, Startup-Screen, MacPaint, TIFF (uncompressed, packbits, CCITT3/4 and lzw), RIFF, PICS, 8BIM, 8BPS/ PSD, JPEG/JFIF, GIF, PCX/SCR, GEM-IMG/-XIMG, BMP (RLE compressed BMPs also), ICO/ICN, PIC (16 bit), FLI/FLC, TGA, MSP, PIC (PC Paint), SCX (ColoRIX), SHP, WPG, PBM/PGM/PPM, CGM (only binary), SUN, RLE, XBM, PM, IFF/LBM, PAC, Degas, TINY, NeoChrome, PIC (ATARI), SPU/ SPC, GEM-Metafile, Animated NeoChrome, Imagic, ImageLab/Print Technic, HP-GL/2, FITS, SGI, DL, XWD, WMF, Scitex-CT, DCX, KONTRON, Lotus-PIC, Dr. Halo, GRP, VFF, Apple IIgs, AMBER, TRS-80, VB HB600, ppat, QDV, CLP, IPLab, SOFTIMAGE, GATAN, CVG, MSX, PNG, ART, RAW, PSION, SIXEL, PCD, ST-X, ALIAS pix, MAG, VITRONIC, CAM, PORST, NIF, TIM, AFP, BLD, GFX, FAX, SFW, PSION 5, BioRad, JBI, QNT, DICOM, KDC, FAXstf, CALS, Sketch, qtif, ElectricImage, X-Face, DJ1000, NASA Raster Metafile, Acorn Sprite, HSI-BUF, FlashPix (with QuickTime 4).

GraphicConverter exports PICT, Startup-Screen, MacPaint, TIFF (uncompressed, packbits and lzw), GIF, PCX, GEM-IMG/-XIMG, BMP, IFF/LBM, TGA, PSD, JPEG/JFIF, HP-GL/2, EPSF, Movie (QuickTime), SUN, PICS, PICT in Resource, PBM/PGM/PPM, SGI, TRS-80, ppat, SOFTIMAGE, PNG, PSION, RAW, WMF, XWD, XBM, XPM, System 7 Clip, PAC, Icon, RTF, VPB, Psion, X-Face.

And last but not least GraphicConverter has the special feature to convert complete folders or a set of pictures from one format to another format.

How to Use It...

Launch the GraphicConverter 3.6.2US file and click Install. That's it. GraphicConverter is now installed. Open the GraphicConverter 3.6.2 (US) *f* folder (at root level on your hard disk) and launch the GraphicConverter program. Wait a few seconds, then click Try It.

Since GraphicConverter doesn't come with any sample files, let's create one we can use for this demonstration. Press Command+Shift+3. This creates a file called Picture 1 at root level on your hard disk. Switch back to Graphic-Converter, choose File ➤ Open, and open this file.

NOTE If you have Mac OS 8.5 or later, the first time you use Graphic-Converter's Open or Save command, you'll see a dialog box asking if you want to use old or new Open and Save dialog boxes. For the sake of this tutorial, it doesn't matter which you choose. You can always change this setting in GraphicConverter's Preferences (on the General tab) later if you so desire.

Now let's assume, for the sake of this quick demonstration, that you want to crop the image (eliminate part of it) and save it as a JPEG file, so you can use it on your Web page. Here's how:

1. Click the selection rectangle tool if it's not selected already, as shown in Figure 67.1.

FIGURE 67.1   Begin by selecting the selection rectangle tool (circled—top right).

NOTE   If a dialog box appears, that means the selection rectangle tool was already selected. Just click OK and continue.

2. Click and drag a selection rectangle onto your picture, selecting the part of the picture you want to use.

3. Choose Edit ➤ Trim Selection, or use the keyboard shortcut Command+Y.

4. Choose File ➤ Save As.

5. Choose JPEG/JFIF from the pop-up Format menu.

At this point, you could just click Save and be done with it. Or you can click the Options button and change the JPEG quality setting before you click Save.

NOTE As usual, I don't have nearly enough space to tell you about all the cool stuff GraphicConverter can do. Fortunately, the documentation file—Documentation (US).srd—while lacking a tutorial, is fairly comprehensive. If you plan to use this program much, it's worth reading the whole thing.

My Two Cents...

Well heck, if you need a tool to view graphics files or convert graphics files from one format to another, you can use either the $35 GraphicConverter or a much more expensive program such as Adobe Photoshop or Corel-Draw. If you typically work with graphics, and particularly if those graphics originated on a computer other than a Mac, this is one heck of a handy program.

NOTE GraphicConverter 3.6.2 is shareware available from Lemke Software (100102.1304@compuserve.com or lemkesoft@aol.com) and at the time of this printing costs approximately $35.

68 Icon Tools

Icon Tools is a complete icon factory and more. It lets you modify any file's icon with a single click, add special effects, rotate, flip, and much more.

Icon Tools also has a unique Icon Stamps feature that lets you instantly mark your documents and applications with tags, symbols, markers, labels, or widgets of any kind. You can make your own stamps, too.

It also features Icon Frames, which lets you add your own backgrounds to icons or make custom folder (or disk, CD-ROM, or Zip) icons for your favorite applications.

Finally, Icon Tools lets you create preview icons for pictures and movies of any kind.

How to Use It...

Run the Icon Tools 1.6 Installer, then restart your iMac or iBook. Once it comes back to life, you can access Icon Tools by Ctrl+clicking any icon. When you do, you'll see a contextual menu that looks like Figure 68.1.

FIGURE 68.1   Icon Tools adds six items to your contextual (Ctrl+click) menu: Copy Icon, Paste Icon, Reset Icon, Icon Tools, Icon Stamps, and Icon Frames.

Help
Open
Move To Trash
Get Info ▶
Label ▶
Duplicate
Make Alias
Add To Favorites
Copy Icon
Paste Icon
Reset Icon
Icon Tools ▶
Icon Stamps ▶
Icon Frames ▶

The Copy Icon, Paste Icon, and Reset Icon commands do just what you might expect. Use the Copy Icon command to copy the selected icon to the clipboard and the Paste Icon command to paste it into another file or folder. The Reset Icon command changes the icon back to the way it was before you messed with it.

The Icon Tools menu item offers six submenus—Effects, Move To, Rotate, Make, Stamps, and Advanced, plus the Preferences command. The Icon Stamps item offers immediate access to several dozen stamps.

NOTE   Ctrl+click any icon, then choose Icon Tools ➢ Stamps ➢ Show Icon Stamps Folder to see them all.

Finally, the Icon Frames menu item offers immediate access to several dozen frames.

NOTE Ctrl+click any icon, then choose Icon Tools ➢ Frames ➢ Show Icon Frames Folder to see them all.

The best way to get to know Icon Tools is to just play around with it. Try some stamps, some frames, and some of the effects. It's fun, and if you are unhappy with the results, you can simply Ctrl+click and choose Reset Icon to make things just like they were.

NOTE To learn more about how to use Icon Tools, read the Icon Tools readme file. It's pretty good.

My Two Cents...

This is pretty cool program if you like to diddle with icons. Don't forget that you can create your own icons from scratch, as explained in Chapter 6.

NOTE Icon Tools 1.6 is shareware available from Alessandro Levi Montalcini and Riccisoft (http://www.riccisoft.com/icontools/) and at the time of this printing costs approximately $15.

69 Kaleidoscope

Kaleidoscope is a complete makeover for your iMac or iBook. Kind of like the Appearance control panel on steroids, Kaleidoscope changes the way your iMac or iBook's Desktop, menu bar, and menus look. Each look is known, in Kaleidoscope parlance, as a *scheme*.

NOTE Kaleidoscope comes with seven schemes, but thousands more are available at `http://www.kaleidoscope.net/schemes/`.

In this case, a picture is worth a million words, so take a gander at Figure 69.1, which shows my iMac before and after Kaleidoscope.

NOTE The scheme shown at the bottom of Figure 69.1 is called Scherzo! and it is one of the seven schemes included with Kaleidoscope.

How to Use It...

Run the Kaleidoscope 2.1.2 Installer-US program, then restart your iMac or iBook. When it comes back to life, open the Kaleidoscope control panel and click Select Scheme. Choose a scheme and click Choose. That's it. Your iMac or iBook's look will change instantly.

Another way to change schemes is to go to the Apple menu and select one of the choices from the Kaleidoscope Schemes submenu. If the Finder says it cannot find an application to open the scheme, try rebuilding the desktop by restarting your iMac or iBook, then holding down the Command and Option keys until a dialog box asks you if you want to rebuild the desktop. You do.

NOTE The Kaleidoscope Schemes submenu in the Apple menu is an alias to a folder inside the Kaleidoscope Goodies folder. You can actually put your schemes anywhere you want; they do not need to stay in this folder. To select a scheme, just open it in the Finder by double-clicking its icon, as if it were a normal document. You can also switch schemes by dragging a scheme and dropping it on the open Kaleidoscope control panel window.

That's pretty much it. If you want to know more about Kaleidoscope, read the readme file. If you want to learn how to create your own schemes, read

FIGURE 69.1 My iMac before (top) and after (bottom) Kaleidoscope

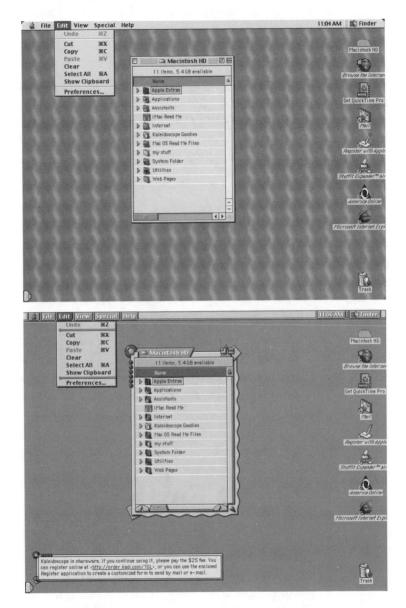

Creating K1 Schemes and K2 Scheme Reference. All of these files can be found in the Kaleidoscope Goodies folder, which you'll find at root level on your hard disk.

WARNING Creating your own Kaleidoscope themes is extremely geeky and requires Apple's ResEdit resource editor. Warning: ResEdit is powerful juju. Never use it on any file without making multiple backups of the file first.

My Two Cents...

It's up to you. If you want your iMac or iBook to sport a unique look and feel, you're going to love Kaleidoscope. If you're a purist, you'll probably hate it. Personally, I think it's a very clever hack, though I choose not to use it myself. (I guess that makes me a purist!)

NOTE Kaleidoscope 2.1.2 is a shareware available from Greg Landweber and Arlo Rose (http://www.kaleidoscope.net/) and at the time of this printing costs approximately $25.

70 Planet Earth

Planet Earth is a real-time 3-D model of the Earth with continuously changing night shadows and clouds. It produces an extremely accurate picture of the Earth. You can easily rotate and magnify the globe to see a distant or close-up view of the Earth from space.

The clouds are updated four times daily and are automatically downloaded and displayed when an Internet connection is active .

NOTE The cloud images are provided by the University of Wisconsin-Madison Space Science and Engineering Center (http://www.ssec.wisc.edu).

How to Use It...

There's not much to it. Decompress the file Planet Earth 2.0.4.sit, then open the Planet Earth folder and launch the Planet Earth PPC application.

The first thing you'll see is a window asking you to drag the city closest to you from the list into the box. Once you do that, click OK.

NOTE You can click the Go Away box of the little nag notice window to make it go away.

To make the Earth fill your screen, choose Control ➤ Full Screen or use the keyboard shortcut Command+F. To make the globe center on your city, choose Control ➤ Center on My City or use the keyboard shortcut Command+M. To retrieve the latest cloud information over the Internet, choose Control ➤ Force Cloud Data Download or use the keyboard shortcut Command+R.

The tool palette, shown in Figure 70.1, has five tools and an expansion triangle.

FIGURE 70.1 **Planet Earth's tool palette**

◆ Click the triangle on the left to expand the tool palette to show more information about your current view—the time, latitude, longitude, and time of last cloud update.

◆ The Hand tool lets you rotate the Earth by clicking and dragging.

◆ The Zoom tools let you zoom in or out.

- ◆ The Cloud button turns the clouds on or off.
- ◆ The Sun button turns the shadows on or off.

That's pretty much it. If you like the image, you can turn it into a screen saver by choosing Edit ➤ Preferences or using the keyboard shortcut Command+;. Click the Control tab at the top to set your screen saver options.

N O T E   Planet Earth's online help (Help ➤ Planet Earth Help) will tell you anything else you might want to know about the program and its operation.

My Two Cents...

I don't know…. It doesn't do much for me, but maybe it will for you. So go for it—you can try it for two weeks at no charge. You might as well give it a shot.

N O T E   Planet Earth 2.0.4 is shareware available from Lunar Software (http://www.lunarsoft.com/register) and at the time of this printing cost approximately $30.

Audio and Sound

This chapter is about the audio and sound-related software on the companion CD-ROM. Again, there aren't nearly as many as there were utilities in Chapter 8, but the three programs in this chapter are all very cool nonetheless. If you like the way your iMac or iBook can play sound, you're going to love these programs.

So, without further ado, let's take a listen.

71 Agent Audio

Agent Audio is a very cool sound-resource customization program that lets you locate the available sounds embedded within programs and files and replace them with your favorite sound files. You can also "rip" a sound out of any file that contains sounds and use it as your beep (alert) sound. You can do this through an attractive, easy-to-use interface that provides you instant access to everything you need for full sound customization.

With Agent Audio you can:

◆ View and play sounds embedded within programs and files.

◆ Replace a program's sounds with your own Macintosh sound files.

◆ Save a program's sound resources to individual Macintosh sound files.

◆ Create archives of sound settings for backup or reverting to them later.

How to Use It...

Decompress the file agent_audio-PPC.sit, then open the agent_audio-PPC folder and launch the Agent Audio v1.2 (PPC) program.

To begin customizing, you must first select the program or file you intend to customize. This program or file is referred to as the *Destination File*, because it is the file to which you will be installing your sounds. The Destination File will appear on the left side of the Agent Audio window and will have its available sounds displayed in the Destination List.

Your Destination File must be a program or file that contains sounds. Agent Audio will not accept files that do not contain sound resources. There are three ways to open a Destination File:

◆ Click on the Open Destination File button, located at the upper-left corner of the Destination List area of the Agent Audio window and denoted with a plus sign.

◆ Choose File ➢ Open Destination File, or use the keyboard shortcut Command+O.

◆ Drag a program or file with sound resources right into the Destination List.

Upon opening your Destination File, Agent Audio will automatically display the available sound files it contains in the Destination List. The list will display each sound resource's name (if available) and resource identification number. You can customize any sound listed in the Destination List with your own sounds.

Since I lack the space to explain all of what Agent Audio can do, let's just do one thing—extract a sound from the Nanosaur program that came with your iMac or iBook and install it as an iMac or iBook beep (alert) sound. Here's how:

1. Open the Nanosaur folder, open the Data folder, open the Audio folder, and drag the file `Main.sounds` onto Agent Audio's Destination List (see Figure 71.1).

FIGURE 71.1 **Drag Nanosaur's Main.sounds file onto Agent Audio's Destination List.**

2. Listen to some of the sounds by either double-clicking them or pressing the Play button—the right-facing triangle on the left side of the Destination List. When you find one you'd like to use as a beep sound on your iMac or iBook, select it by clicking it once.

3. Click the Create Sound Archive button—the second button from the left on the bottom of the Audio Agent window.

4. Click the System 7 Sound File radio button in the Save dialog box and save the file to your hard disk.

5. Quit Agent Audio, then switch to the Finder and locate the file you just created.

NOTE To hear the file, double-click it in the Finder.

6. Drag the newly created System 7 Sound file onto your System folder. A dialog box will ask you if you want to put this sound into your System file. You do, so click OK.

NOTE If any other programs are running, you'll have to quit them before this step will work.

7. To make this sound your beep sound, open the Monitors & Sound control panel, click the Alerts button, then choose its filename from the list of Alert Sounds.

That's it. The sound you ripped off from Nanosaur is now your beep (alert) sound.

NOTE As usual, there's more to this program than I have space for here. So check out the Agent Audio Manual. It's pretty darn good.

My Two Cents...

If you deal with sounds, or would like to rip sounds out of your games and other programs, Agent Audio is just the ticket.

N O T E Agent Audio 1.2 is shareware available from Clixsounds (http://www.clixsounds.com) and at the time of this printing costs approximately $12.

72 MacAMP Lite

MacAMP Lite is a program that can play various popular sound file formats, such as MPEG Layer II and III (MP3), CD Audio, .MOD, and .S3M.

N O T E Those formats are, more precisely: 669, .AMF, CD Audio, .DSM, .FAR, .IT, .M15, .MED, .MOD, .MP1, .MP2, .MP3, .MTM, .S3M, .STM, .ULT, and XM. MacAMP Lite supports the sound formats listed with its default engines. However, you can easily expand this list of sound formats by adding other engines to the Plugins folder. Visit http://www.macamp.net/addons/index.shtml for info.

How to Use It...

Decompress the file macamp-lite-152.sit, then open the MacAMP Lite *f* folder and launch the program MacAMP Lite. You will see a MacAMP Lite window thumb in the top-right corner of the screen, as shown in Figure 72.1.

When you click on the thumb, a windoid pops open, giving access to MacAMP Lite's controls, as shown in Figure 72.2.

FIGURE 72.1 MacAmp Lite's "thumb"—Click it once to make the whole MacAMP Lite window appear.

FIGURE 72.2 MacAMP Lite's controls

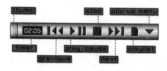

To see how it works, do this:

1. Insert an audio CD in your iMac or iBook's CD ROM drive.

2. Drag one of the songs (tracks) onto the MacAMP Lite icon.

NOTE The song should start playing immediately. If it doesn't, click the Play/Pause button.

That's pretty much it. You drag almost any audio file onto the MacAMP Lite icon and it will play.

NOTE As you've seen, MacAMP Lite can play CD Audio files. But its best feature is its ability to play MP3 audio files. It is one of a very few Mac programs that do that. But alas, it doesn't come with any MP3 sample files. So, if you'd like to try MP3, surf to http://www.mp3.com, where you can download thousands upon thousands of MP3 files.

You can find out more about the program and its features by reading the Documentation file in the MacAMP Lite folder.

My Two Cents...

Well, if you like MP3, this is pretty much the only game in town, at least at this writing. Try it. You'll probably like it.

NOTE MacAMP Lite 1.5.2 is shareware available from @Soft (http://www.at-soft.net/) and at the time of this printing costs approximately $10.

73 SoundMachine

SoundMachine is another sound file player for common audio formats such as m-law (mu-law), AIFF, SDII, and WAVE. It has a clean, simple interface and is well suited to be a helper application for Web browsers. Or, you can use it as a stand-alone application.

How to Use It...

Run the SoundMachine Installer program, then open the SoundMachine 2.7.1*f* folder and launch the SoundMachine 2.7.1 application.

Since SoundMachine doesn't come with any sample sound files, we'll demonstrate how it works by playing the title song from the game Nanosaur, which happens to be an AIFF sound file. Here's how:

1. Launch SoundMachine if it's not already running.

2. Choose File ➤ Open and navigate to Nanosaur's Audio folder. (The path to it is Applications ➤ Nanosaur ➤ Data ➤ Audio.)

3. Open the file called TitleSong.aiff.

4. Click the Play button (the left-facing triangle).

Ta da! The song plays.

If you open the file using SoundMachine's Open command, you can probably listen to it.

My Two Cents...

SoundMachine can play some sound file formats other players can't. For example, MacAMP can't play AIFF or WAV files, but SoundMachine can. So if you're a big sound fan, you'll probably find a use for it.

NOTE SoundMachine 2.7.1 is shareware available from Rod Kennedy (rod@kagi.com) and at the time of this printing costs approximately $10.

Web and Online Stuff

Here is a chapter about programs that make using the Web and other Internet stuff better. Each of these six programs on the companion CD has something great to be said for it. If you use your iMac or iBook to access the Internet, you're going to love them all.

So let's log on.

74 Banish AOL Involuntary Disconnects with AlwaysONline

If you use America Online and you've ever been logged off involuntarily due to inactivity, you're going to love AlwaysONline. That's because Always-ONline recognizes and dismisses all of AOL's different types of timer messages that, if unanswered, could cause you to be logged off AOL.

AlwaysONline can be set to do everything from playing a sound when a timer message is detected to switching AOL to the front whenever AOL creates any type of window in the background.

How to Use It...

Decompress the file `AlwaysONline 2.05b1 Folder.sit`. Open the Always-ONline 2.05b1 folder and drag the AlwaysONline 2.05b1 icon onto your System folder. Your iMac or iBook will tell you it's going to put it in the Control Panels folder. That's what you want. Click OK. Now restart your iMac or iBook. Once it comes back to life, AlwaysONline will start working whenever you're logged on to AOL.

If you do nothing more, AlwaysONline will keep you from being automatically logged off of America Online even if your computer sits idle for a long time.

But AlwaysONline has features you can select manually to make sure that it does exactly what you want. To do so, open the AlwaysONline 2.05b1 control panel, shown in Figure 74.1. When the shareware nag screen appears, click Later.

NOTE Every time you open the control panel, you will encounter the nag screen, reminding you to pay for AlwaysONline 2.05b1. You'll be sent a special code that makes this nag screen and all the others like it go away if you pay. Personally, I think this is lousy. I wouldn't mind if the nag screen started showing up after the 15-day trial period was up. But to have to see it every time you use the control panel, and another when you reboot your iMac or iBook, is a bit too much.

FIGURE 74.1   You can change AlwaysONline's options in the AlwaysONline 2.05b1 control panel.

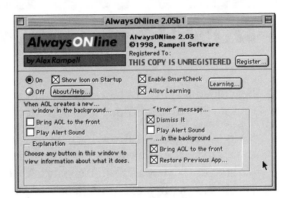

NOTE Click on any checkbox to read more about it in the Explanation portion of the window at lower left. Or, click the About/Help button for even more extensive help.

My Two Cents...

If you need it, it's worth every penny. Fortunately, I have a cable modem and can, for the most part, avoid AOL completely.

NOTE AlwaysONline 2.05b1 is shareware available from Rampell Software (http://www.rampell.com/software) and at the time of this printing costs approximately $15.

75 Downloads by the Batch: Now or Later with Download Deputy

Download Deputy is a batch-downloading utility. It lets you create lists of remote files to batch-download at a later time.

If you frequently download bunches of files, it lets you use your Mac time more efficiently. You can even use Download Deputy to download large batches of HTML files from Web sites. In addition, the registered version of Download Deputy lets you schedule separate batch lists to start separate batch downloads at specified times.

You can trigger the batches to download while you're at lunch or after you leave for the night—when it won't interfere with your using your iMac or iBook.

How to Use It...

Decompress the file Download Deputy PPC 3.1.sit, open the DD PPC 3.1 folder, and launch the application Download Deputy PPC 3. Click anywhere to make the splash screen go away.

You'll then see Download Deputy's main window.

NOTE I know what you're thinking…. You don't want to have to type the URL of every file you want to download. Don't worry. You won't have to.

To add files to its queue, drag them from your browser onto the Download Deputy window, as shown in Figure 75.1.

FIGURE 75.1   **Drag a file's link from your browser to Download Deputy's window to add it to the queue.**

NOTE Sadly, the unpaid version included here allows you to have only two items in your queue, making it virtually worthless unless you pay the $21 shareware fee.

My Two Cents...

I am fortunate and have a cable modem. It's roughly ten times faster than the internal modem on your iMac or iBook. So I have no need to queue up my downloads. Just today I downloaded more than 100 megabytes in about an hour.

Anyway, I don't use Download Deputy, but if you download a lot of files each day, you might find it useful.

N O T E Download Deputy 3.1 is shareware available from Silesa Software (`http://www.ilesa.com/`) and at the time of this printing costs approximately $21.

76 ircle Is "the" Chat Client for IRC

ircle (rhymes with *circle*) is a Macintosh program to use IRC (Internet Relay Chat). IRC enables you to talk (actually, type), in real time, to other Internet users around the world. IRC is organized in channels on a specific topic. You can also talk privately with someone. It's a lot like AOL's Chat feature, but it's available to anyone on the Internet instead of just to AOL members.

N O T E According to the ircle readme file, there are about 50,000 users and 20,000 channels on IRC worldwide.

WARNING IRC can be politically incorrect. In fact, it can sometimes be downright pornographic. Like the Internet itself, IRC is largely unregulated. So you might, at any time, find channels devoted to things you'd rather not have your kids see. Or that you'd rather not see yourself. In other words, IRC can often be NC-17 or worse. Forewarned is forearmed.

How to Use It...

NOTE You have to be connected to the Internet or ircle won't work.

Decompress the file ircle 3.0.4 US.sit, open the ircle 3.0.4 US folder, then launch the application, ircle 3.0.4 US. To try the program, click Not Yet.

Now, assuming you have an active Internet connection, you can find a chat to join. The first thing to do is click one of the connections in the Connections window list, then click the Connect button (as shown in Figure 76.1).

FIGURE 76.1 Choose a connection from the list, then click Connect to get connected to that IRC server.

This connects you to that particular IRC server. You'll probably be asked to use a nickname other than *ircleuser*. If so, type a new "handle" and click OK.

That's it. You're connected. You type your input into the Inputline window and press Return to send it. You see other people's responses (and what you type) in the large window.

NOTE ircle arbitrarily dumps you into a chat room at random. There may be no other users there. If there are none, read on:

To see a list of channels for the server you're currently connected to, choose Windows ➤ Channel List or use the shortcut Command+L. When the Channel List appears, click the Refresh button. To change channels, click the channel in the list you want to join, then click Join.

NOTE Alas, there isn't much in the way of documentation, just a vague reference in the readme file to the manual: "The ircle manual can be downloaded (soon!) from http://www.ircle.com/reference/." It wasn't there the last time I checked.

My Two Cents...

If you like to chat, and you have some reason not to want to chat on AOL, IRC is just the ticket. And ircle is a very fine Mac IRC client.

NOTE ircle is shareware available from Onno Tijdgat (http://www .ircle.com) and at the time of this printing costs approximately $15.

77 Clean Up Text with textSOAP

textSOAP is a utility to clean up text taken from the Internet—Web sites or e-mail. If you've ever had to clean up Internet text by hand, you'll be pleased to learn that textSOAP:

◆ Removes extra spaces

◆ Removes hard carriage returns

◆ Removes forwarding characters

◆ Removes angle brackets

◆ And more

How to Use It...

Run the textSOAP 2.0.1 Installer and restart your iMac or iBook. Locate the textSOAP 2.0 *f* folder (it's probably in your Applications folder) and launch the textSOAP application.

First you need some text that needs cleaning. So either copy a bunch of text onto the clipboard, then switch to textSOAP and paste the text into the Workspace window, or choose File ➢ Open and open a text file.

textSOAP uses "cleaners" to clean up your text; they are available from the quickClean palette, as shown in Figure 77.1.

The SCRUB cleaner is probably the one you'll use most often. It is actually a multi-cleaner, performing multiple "cleans" at once. It will strip spaces, forwarding characters, %Hex, =Hex (MIME encoding), line feeds, and paragraphs in one shot.

NOTE Order is important, and SCRUB calls the cleaners in the proper order to get you the results you want. If it doesn't do what you expect or want, choose Edit ➢ Undo or use the shortcut Command+Z.

FIGURE 77.1 The quickClean palette offers 20 different "cleaners;" click any one to apply it to the text in the main window.

The other cleaners do pretty much what you'd expect. Experiment with them and don't forget Undo if you need it (Command+Z).

When you're finished, either copy your cleaned-up text back to the clipboard and then paste it into another document, or choose File ➤ Save As (or its shortcut, Command+S), to save it as a text file.

My Two Cents...

The more text you mangle, the more likely you are to need a program like textSOAP. If you have ever searched and replaced quote marks, carriage returns, and such manually, this program is just what the doctor ordered.

N O T E textSOAP 2.0.1 is shareware available from Unmarked Software (http://www.unmarked.com/) and at the time of this printing costs approximately $20.

78 URL Manager Pro Lets You Manage Your URLs Better

URL Manager is the best URL (bookmark) manager in the world. It allows you to organize and collect URLs. It's powerful, easy to use, and fully Drag-and-Drop aware.

URL Manager Pro works closely with Navigator, Explorer, Anarchie, Fetch, Net-Finder, Claris Emailer, and Eudora and can add bookmark menus to the menu bar of these applications. It also adds the URL Manager shared icon menu to the menu bar, which lets you create bookmarks for Web pages from within Navigator/Explorer, add notes, grab all URLs on a Web page or in an e-mail message, or explore the Internet with a predefined set of search engines.

In addition:

- ◆ URL Manager Pro remembers the last 1,000 Web pages you visited.
- ◆ URL Manager Pro can validate the URLs of your bookmarks.
- ◆ URL Manager Pro can find and delete duplicate bookmarks.
- ◆ URL Manager Pro can store and read bookmark files to FTP servers.

The more time you spend on the Internet, the more useful you'll find URL Manager Pro.

How to Use It...

Run the URL Manager Pro Installer program. Open the URL Manager Pro 2.5 folder and launch the URL Manager Pro application. Wait a few seconds, then click the Not Yet button.

URL Manager Pro opens and displays the sample bookmark file. Take a look at it. You'll be seeing it again in just a second, in a menu working with your browser. To see this file in action, connect to the Internet, then open your favorite browser.

And there you have it. In the menu bar of your favorite browser you will see the two new menus: one with a diamond icon (the URL Manager Pro shared icon menu) and another entitled Sample. Pull down the Sample menu. If you choose an item from this menu, your browser will take you to that URL instantly.

To add a bookmark to URL Manager Pro, merely choose Sample ➤ Add Bookmark or use the shortcut Command+B. Or, you can drag any link from your browser onto URL ManagerPro.

One of my favorite features is Mondriaan, a control strip module that lets me launch my browser and have it create a new window for each of my favorite sites with one click. So every morning I click the Mondriaan control strip module, and my browser launches and opens a separate window for each of my favorite "daily" Web sites:

- ◆ http://www.macosrumors.com/
- ◆ http://www.macintouch.com/
- ◆ http://www.macfixit.com/
- ◆ http://www.maccentral.com/
- ◆ http://www.macnn.com/
- ◆ http://www.macsurfer.com/

It's sweet.

NOTE Of course, there's a lot more URL Manager Pro can do. Check out the documentation. It's pretty good.

My Two Cents...

Best darn URL manager ever made. I wouldn't surf without it, and neither will you. Give it a try, then send Alco his money. It's worth it.

NOTE URL Manager Pro 2.5 is shareware available from Alco Blom (http://www.url-manager.com/) and at the time of this printing costs approximately $25.

Business-like Things

This chapter is about the business-like software on the companion CD-ROM—programs that will help you manage your business better using your iMac or iBook. If you use your iMac or iBook productively, you are going to love these six great programs.

79 Simple and Swift: Address Book

Address Book is an easy-to-use program that manages lists of names, addresses, and phone numbers.

NOTE I use another program, Consultant (coming up soon in this chapter), but many people have told me they love Address Book.

According to the Address Book Getting Started file, it offers:

◆ Preset fields for easy set-up and data entry

◆ A memory-resident list for fast finding and sorting

◆ Multiple sort capabilities

◆ Utilities that allow importing from other databases, word processing programs, and personal information managers

◆ Exports to mail merge, databases, word processors, spreadsheets, and palmtop computers, including Newton, Psion 3A, Sharp Wizard, and HP95LX

◆ Printing on envelopes, labels, business cards, postcards, rolodex, standard and custom address books, and lists, in color if your printer supports it

◆ Printing of postal bar codes

◆ Phone-dialing through modems, the Mac speaker, hyperdialer™, and Desktop Dialer™

- ◆ A log file for logging calls and taking notes
- ◆ A call timer
- ◆ Templates
- ◆ On-line help
- ◆ Multiple-language capability
- ◆ Password protection
- ◆ Regular updates on the Internet from regular download sites

Address Book is a bit rough around the edges in some places, and its interface will never win any beauty contests, but it's a capable performer that does a few things quite well.

How to Use It...

Run the AddressBook4.0.8.Install application to install the Address Book folder on your hard disk. Open the Address Book folder and launch the Address Book application.

You'll be asked to save your Preference file. Once you do that, you'll be asked if you have an Address Book List file. You don't, so click No. You'll then be asked to create a new List file. Create the file and save it to your hard disk. Finally, the Address Book Edit Record window appears, as shown in Figure 79.1.

FIGURE 79.1 **Address Book: A simple, fast program for managing names and addresses**

Edit Record (Auto Capitalize Is Off ⌘J)
Cray Research
655A Lone Oak Dr. Eagan, MN 55121
Upgrades from Macintosh
612 452 6650 — Category ⌘K
Prev — Revert
Next — Done

Fill in the blanks to create a record. When you're finished, click Done.

Once you've played with the program a little, open the Sample List file of 75 records and experiment further. To view any record, double-click it in the list.

NOTE The sample list brought back memories. It's obviously more than 10 years old, listing long-forgotten Mac entities such as SuperMac, OLDUVAI, MAUG, Smethers-Barnes, Software Supply (original Suitcase and Pyro), and more. What a blast from the past!

One nice feature is that Address Book can dial the phone for you using its built-in speaker or modem. Click the Dial button next to any phone number in the list and hold the phone up to the speaker on your iMac or iBook to dial using the speaker. To dial using your modem, choose Prefs & Help ➤ Dialing Setup.

Address Book's Find mechanism is lightning fast. Click the Find button or use the shortcut Command+F. Search for *Apple*. Quick as a flash, the first record to match your request appears. Click the Prev and Next button to see other records that contain the word *Apple*.

Address Book also offers categories for your records, several sorting options, and various printing options: Print Envelopes, Print Rolodex Cards, Print Labels, and Print Phone Book, all of which can be found in the File menu.

Anyway, there's a lot more to Address Book than I have space to list. Check out the Getting Started document for details.

My Two Cents...

Personally, I use Consultant, which we'll talk about in a few pages. But in its defense, Address Book is fast, easy to learn, and does what it does pretty well.

That said, I hate the old and ugly interface. And I hate its "modal-ness," where it doesn't let me use other programs and such. However, it could very well serve your needs—thus its inclusion here.

NOTE Address Book 4.0.8 is shareware available from Jim Smith (http://www.jimsmithsoft.com)and at the time of this printing costs approximately $30.

80 The Text Editor of Champions: BBEdit Lite

BBEdit Lite is the greatest text-editing program of all time. I mean that. It's so good I once wrote a whole book—now out of print—about it (*The Official BBEdit Book* from Ziff-Davis Press).

Perhaps BBEdit's greatest strength is that it's wonderful for creating HTML, the language of the World Wide Web.

NOTE I know. I could have included it in the Web chapter. But it's so much more than just an HTML editor I thought it best to put it here, where business-type folks might see it.

It's also the best plain-text editor in the world, bar none.

NOTE What is the difference between a text editor and a word processor? Glad you asked. A *word processor* deals with pages, paragraphs, columns, rulers, fonts, and the like. It can support graphics, multiple columns, footnotes, and other high-end features. A *text editor* does none of the above. It lets you create, massage, format (to some extent), and search plain ASCII text and can often do so better and faster than a word processor.

Let's look at what this free program offers:

◆ Powerful multi-file searching

◆ File size limited only by available memory

◆ No hard limit on number of files open

◆ Easy manipulation of multiple files at once (Hold down the Option key while pulling down the File menu to see the Open Several command.)

◆ Pattern (GREP) searching

◆ Drag-and-drop text-editing

◆ High-performance PowerMac native code

◆ Extensibility using plug-ins

I write all my online columns for *MacCentral* using BBEdit 5 (the commercial version) and also use it to create HTML files for my Web site.

NOTE BBEdit Lite is based on a previous version of BBEdit and isn't as full-featured as the latest release, version 5. The good news is that you'll find a copy of BBEdit 5 Demo—a Save-disabled version of the latest commercial release of BBEdit—on the companion CD. The bad news is that I won't be discussing the 5.0 demo due to space constraints. But if you like BBEdit Lite, it's worth checking out. Just run the Install BBEdit 5.0.2 Demo application.

How to Use It...

Decompress the file BBEdit Lite 4.1.sit, then open the BBEdit Lite 4.1 folder and launch the BBEdit Lite 4.1 program. Or better still, double-click the About BBEdit Lite document.

NOTE It wouldn't hurt to read this document. It tells you a little more about what this wonderful free program can do for you. Hey, why not go whole-hog and read the BBEdit Lite Quickstart.srd document as well? It is very, very good.

BBEdit Lite is pretty much like any text editor. But check out some of its tricks. For example, you can open the Find dialog box, shown in Figure 80.1, by choosing Search ➢ Find or using the shortcut Command+F.

FIGURE 80.1   The BBEdit Lite Find window offers a plethora of helpful options.

![Find dialog box]

| Find |

Search For: ☑ Use Grep ⌘G   Patterns: ▼   [Find ⌘F]
```
kawasaki (not motorcycle)
```
                                                 [Find All]

☐ Start at Top ⌘T   ☐ Selection Only ⌘S   [Replace ⌘R]
☐ Wrap Around ⌘W   ☐ Extend Selection ⌘I   [Replace All]
☐ Backwards ⌘B
                      ☐ Entire Word ⌘E   [Don't Find ⌘D]
Replace With: ☐ Case Sensitive ⌘N
                                                 [Cancel ⌘.]

▽ ☐ Multi-File Search ⌘M   ☑ Batch Find
What: [Folder ▼]   File Type: [All Available ▼]
```
Macintosh HD:
```
                            File Name: [(all file names) ▼]

Folder: [Macintosh HD ▼]
☑ Search Nested Folders   ☐ Skip (...) Folders

You can search backwards, search forwards, search only the selected text, search multiple files on your hard disk simultaneously, use GREP pattern matching, and much more. I daresay the BBEdit Find command is one of the most flexible and powerful I've ever seen.

In addition, BBEdit Lite almost totally keyboard controllable; you seldom need to use the mouse if you prefer not to. I dislike using the mouse, so I like this feature a lot. Table 80.1 shows the keyboard combinations for the available commands.

TABLE 80.1   Keyboard combinations

Key	Modifier	Action
left/right Arrow	none	Move one character left/right
left/right Arrow	Command	Move to beginning/end of line
left/right Arrow	Option	Move one word left/right

TABLE 80.1   Keyboard combinations (Continued)

Key	Modifier	Action
up/down Arrow	none	Move up/down one line in file
up/down Arrow	Command	Move to top/bottom of file
up/down Arrow	Option	Move to previous/next screen page
any of the above	Shift	Make or extend a selection range
Delete	none	Delete selection range or character preceding the insertion point
Delete	Command	Delete all characters back to beginning of line
Delete	Option	Delete all characters back to beginning of word

Another feature I love is the character, word, line, and page counter. Choose Window ➢ Get Info or click the info button—the diamond with an *i* in the middle—as shown in Figure 80.2, to get this information for the currently active document.

FIGURE 80.2   BBEdit's Info feature tells me how many characters, words, lines, and pages I've written.

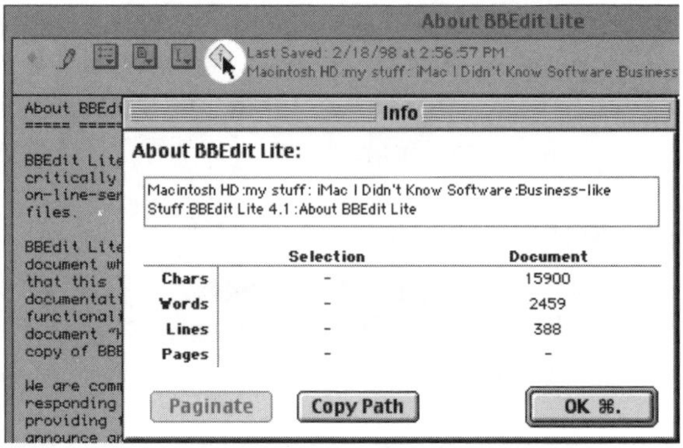

NOTE There's a lot to learn about BBEdit Lite and I strongly recommend you read the Quickstart document, particularly the parts about searching and preferences. You'll never harness the power of this program if you don't read at least those two sections.

My Two Cents...

Hey, the price is right—free—and the whole BBEdit Lite folder uses less than 2 megabytes of hard disk space. You'd be foolish not to keep it around.

NOTE BBEdit Lite is freeware available from Bare Bones Software, Inc. (http://www.barebones.com/).

81 Consultant: Organize Your Life and Much More

Consultant is a to-do list, calendar, contact database, and word processor all in one. I keep my to-do list, my calendar, and my contact database in Consultant. And, best of all, Consultant can sync with my Palm III hand-held device, so my to-do list, calendar, and contact database go with me when I leave the office.

One of Consultant's best features is that it's really smart. So you can type something like "Meet John Smith for lunch tomorrow at noon," and Consultant automatically sets up the appointment on your schedule and links it to John's contact information.

Consultant can also create personalized letters, envelopes, address labels, and much more. And if you currently use another organizer, importing your data is quick and painless.

If you check out only one program on the companion CD, this should be it. It's indispensable.

NOTE News Flash: Power On Software just announced that they have purchased Now Contact, Now Up-To-Date, and Eudora Planner from Qualcomm. Now Contact and Now Up-To-Date were my favorite contact database and calendar/to-do list programs before Mac OS 8.5. When 8.5 came out, the programs broke and Qualcomm never bothered to fix them. Power On has promised to have Mac OS 8.6/9-compatible versions available soon.

Much as I love Consultant, I loved Now Contact and Now Up-To-Date more. So I may be switching back in the near future. In any event, it's nice that Mac users now have some choices in this area. In the meantime, Consultant is a fine program.

How to Use It...

Run the Consultant Installer program to install Consultant, then restart your iMac or iBook. Open the Consultant 2.57 folder and launch the Consultant 2.57 application. When the Register screen appears, click Not Yet to create your trial version. When the Get File dialog box appears, create a new Consultant file by clicking the New button. Click the Yes Primary File button to make this your main Consultant file. Add a password to protect the file if you wish: Click either Add Password or No Password.

Consultant appears with a QuickTip. Read it, and then click Next Tip to read another; click OK when you're finished.

NOTE A QuickTip appears each time you start the program. QuickTips are an excellent way to painlessly learn more about Consultant's powerful features. You can turn them off by clicking the Show at Startup checkbox, but I don't recommend doing so until you've seen them all at least once.

The default view is the Day view. But Consultant is nothing if not flexible. To see another view of your calendar, choose Calendar ➤ Multiday or use the shortcut Command+H, and a multiday view of your calendar will appear.

N O T E   Consultant also has month, week, year, list, and other views. Explore them all in the Calendar menu at your leisure.

Let's create a contact record.

1. Choose Contacts ➤ New Contact or use the shortcut Command+5.

2. Fill in all the fields—name, address, phone, etc.

3. Close the window.

N O T E   One of Consultant's neat features is that you never have to save your file. Consultant continually saves your file automatically.

Now, let's create an appointment (make sure you're using the Multiday view when you begin):

1. Use the arrow keys to navigate to the appropriate date, then click and drag across the time slot you want to reserve. A new Activity window appears.

2. Type a name for this appointment in the New Entry field.

3. Choose a category for this appointment from the pop-up menu.

N O T E   For now, you can choose only the Standard category. You can create your own categories later by choosing Special ➤ Define Categories.

4. Choose a priority for this appointment from the pop-up menu.

5. Click the alarm clock icon to set an alarm that will alert you of this appointment whether or not Consultant is running.

When you're finished, your calendar should resemble the one in Figure 81.1:

FIGURE 81.1   **A two-hour lunch appointment on Wednesday, July 28 with Guy Kawasaki**

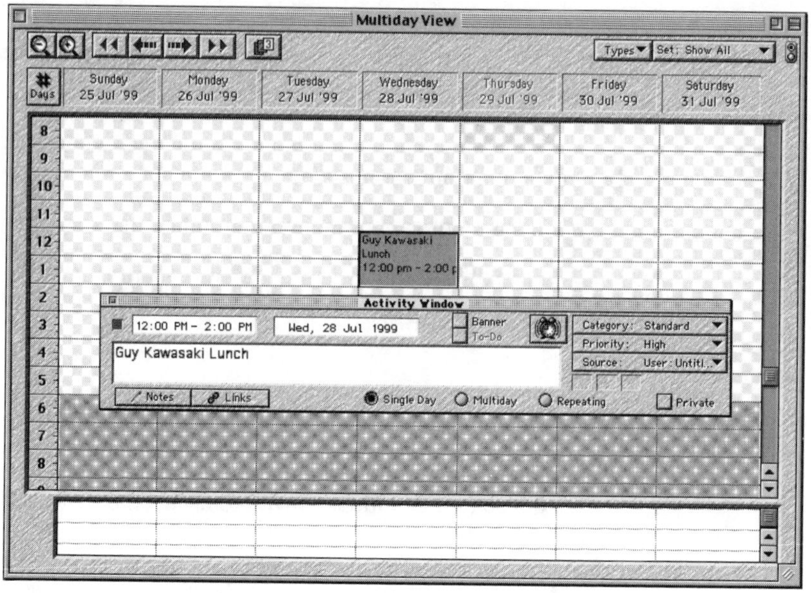

6. Close the Activity window.

To delete an appointment, click it once, then choose Edit ➢ Delete or use the keyboard shortcut Command+D.

Here's another, cooler way to create an appointment:

1. Choose Calendar ➢ Translate, or use the shortcut Command+T.

2. Type **Lunch tomorrow with (name of the contact you just created) at noon**.

3. Click Translate.

A new Activity window appears, with everything configured correctly—the day, time, and name of the appointment. And if you click the Links button at the bottom of the window, you'll see that this appointment has automatically been linked to the proper contact record. Double-click the link to see the contact record.

That's just the tip of the iceberg. I'm going to point out a few other neat features briefly, then show you how to find everything you need to know to use Consultant effectively.

Among the "don't miss" features are the new icons Consultant installs in your menu bar, shown in Figure 81.2.

FIGURE 81.2   These are the Consultant Calendar/To-Do and Contact icons, installed automatically when you installed Consultant; click the icons to display the menus.

Today's to-do items and appointments appear in the clock (Calendar/To-Do) menu; contacts you've marked as Favorite appear in the telephone (Contact) menu. These menus are quite handy during the course of the day when Consultant isn't running.

Another "don't miss" feature is the templates. You can merge contact information from your database into documents such as address labels, fax cover pages, memos, and letters. Find out how by choosing File ➤ Text Template, then choosing an item from one of the myriad submenus, as shown in Figure 81.3.

Finally, Consultant is jam-packed with helpful help. Hold the cursor over any button, like Gantt, at the top of the screen. The name of the button pops up (Gantt View), and an explanation of the button appears at the bottom of the screen. Consultant's RealHelp works with almost everything in the program. It's very cool.

Another way to get help with Consultant is to choose Help ➤ Consultant Help. This brings up Consultant's extensive online help system.

I would also advise you to download the Consultant manual in Adobe Acrobat PDF format from `http://www.chronosnet.com/download/index.html`.

FIGURE 81.3 Templates? Consultant has your templates right here!

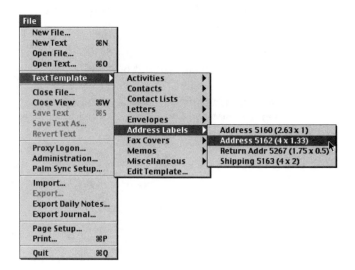

NOTE There's no way I can show you even a small percentage of what this powerful program can do in the space I have allotted. So you're on your own now. The manual is quite helpful.

My Two Cents...

I've already said it. Consultant is an incredible program for anyone who must manage time and/or people. Try it. You'll like it.

NOTE Consultant 2.57 is commercial software available from Chronos (http://www.chronosnet.com) and at the time of this printing costs—without the manual and without Palm Synchronization—approximately $39.95.

82 Idea Keeper: The Idea Processor

Idea Keeper is a free-form information storage and retrieval tool. You can use it to enter and store data in almost any way that suits your needs. You can use it as a diary, personal organizer, outliner, to-do-list manager, URL manager, word processor, note-taking program, etc.

Idea Keeper allows you to keep multiple sets (called topics) of notes (a note is an idea) in which you can format text and insert pictures, links to other files, other notes, sounds, dynamic check boxes, and alarms (notes you can set to go off at any time you want). If you type phone numbers into your ideas, Idea Keeper can recognize and dial them if you have a modem attached.

It's a neat program if you like this sort of thing.

How to Use It...

Run the Install Idea Keeper application. Open the Idea Keeper *f* folder and launch the Idea Keeper PPC application.

To create an idea (a note), choose File ➢ New Idea or use the shortcut Command+N. Give it a name and click OK. A new idea window appears. Type some text, then close the window.

Now choose File ➢ Windows ➢ Open Organizer Window. The organizer window for your ideas and topics appears. You should see that the topic is "Welcome to Idea Keeper" and that there are two ideas, yours and the one that came with the program, "Welcome to Idea Keeper."

Click the checkbox for your idea to reopen its idea window. An idea window is capable of holding all kinds of things in addition to text. You can drag files from the Finder onto an idea window. If you click the file's icon in your idea window, the file launches. You can create a link to another idea by choosing Insert ➢ Idea Link. You can stamp the date and time by choosing Insert ➢ Date & Time or using the shortcut Command+Option+Y.

To insert a URL, choose Insert ➢ URL or use the shortcut Command+ Option+U. The URL becomes "live" and launches your Web browser when you click it. Figure 82.1 shows all of the above.

FIGURE 82.1   An idea link, a file link, a time and date stamp, and a live URL in my idea window

The best feature of all is a fast Find command that finds text in any of your ideas, shown in Figure 82.2. Choose Edit ➤ Find ➤ Find or use the shortcut Command+F.

FIGURE 82.2   Find anything in any idea window fast with Idea Keeper's swift Find command.

> **NOTE**   Other useful Find commands, also found in the Edit menu's Find submenu, include Find Again (Command+G), Replace and Find Again (Command+Shift+G), and Search Amazon.Com (Command+Shift+F).

This is a deep and complex program with many very cool capabilities that I'm unable to delve into here due to space considerations. So much cool software; so few pages! But you should definitely check out some of Idea Keeper's other features, such as alarms, outlining, and stand-alone documents. The Idea

Keeper Documentation that comes with the program is comprehensive and complete; you'd be well served to read it from cover to cover.

NOTE Idea Keeper has extensive balloon help. Turn it on by choosing Help ➤ Show Balloons, then move the cursor over any object in Idea Keeper to see the help message. It's so slick you'll wish every program used balloon help so well.

My Two Cents...

Idea Keeper is a comprehensive, useful program for socking away bits of information. I think many of you will find that it suits the way you work and can take the place of several other programs. There's a lot to it, so be sure to read the manual and use balloon help.

NOTE Idea Keeper is shareware available from Glenn Berntson of Software from Plum Island (`http://ww.softplum.com`) and at the time of this printing costs approximately $30.

83 ReminderPro: So You Never Forget Anything Again!

ReminderPro is a program that, well, reminds you of stuff. It allows you to schedule reminders, the launching of applications, the opening of documents, and reminders sent to pagers.

Your reminders can alert you with an on-screen window and/or a sound. The program uses reminder templates—it comes with ones for bill payment, birthday, and meetings—and you can easily create your own.

NOTE You can find a lot of these same features in Consultant, but if you're looking for a program only to create reminders, this is it.

How to Use It...

Decompress the file ReminderPro 3.6.sit. Then follow these steps:

1. Open the Application folder. Move the ReminderPro file to a convenient place on your hard disk. This is the ReminderPro application.

2. Open the System Extension folder, and copy the ReminderPro INIT file from this folder into the System folder. Your iMac or iBook will ask if it's OK to put it in the Extensions folder. It is.

3. Open the Control Strip Module folder, and copy the ReminderPro CSM file from this folder into the System folder. Your iMac or iBook will ask if it's OK to put it in the Control Strip Modules folder. It is.

4. Restart your Macintosh.

Launch the ReminderPro application. Then fill in your name and organization name. Click OK.

There are four ways to schedule a new reminder:

◆ Choose Schedule ➢ A Reminder or use the shortcut Command+1.

◆ Choose any template from the Schedule menu.

◆ Open the Reminder List (Miscellaneous ➢ Reminder List or use the shortcut Command+R) and click the New Reminder button in the top-left corner of the window.

◆ Choose Quick Reminder or any template from the ReminderPro control strip module, as shown in Figure 83.1.

FIGURE 83.1 The ReminderPro control strip module lets you quickly create a new reminder no matter what program you're currently using.

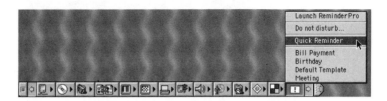

To see ReminderPro in action, use one of the above techniques to create a reminder now. Name it **test reminder** in the Reminder Title field. Type **test reminder** in the Reminder Message field. Schedule it for two minutes from now by clicking the pop-up Minute menu at the bottom of the reminder window. Choose a reminder sound from the pop-up menu if you like. Don't change the Repeating, Reminder Group, and Advance Reminder items for now. Your reminder window should now look like Figure 83.2. Finally, click Add, then click Quit ReminderPro, and wait two minutes.

FIGURE 83.2 My test reminder. Yours should look the same.

In two minutes, a reminder should appear on your screen, just like in Figure 83.3.

FIGURE 83.3 The resulting reminder message

Reminders appear regardless of what program you're using and even if ReminderPro isn't running. That's pretty much the story on ReminderPro.

N O T E Since there's not much documentation, the best way to get to know ReminderPro is to use its built-in help system. Choose Help ➢ ReminderPro Help to use it.

My Two Cents...

Since I use Consultant for lots of other things and it includes alarms, I have little need for ReminderPro. Still, if all you want is an alarm program, this one is cheaper and easier to use than Consultant.

N O T E ReminderPro 3.6 is shareware available from Manoj Patwardhan (mp@kagi.com) and at the time of this printing costs approximately $18.

84 Tex-Edit Plus: More Than a Mere Text Editor

Tex-Edit Plus is an AppleScriptable, styled-text editor that fills the gap between Apple's bare-bones SimpleText and a full-featured word processor. Similar in scope to BBEdit Lite, it is particularly useful for formatting text that is transmitted over the Internet.

With Tex-Edit Plus you can:

◆ Quickly create, edit, and print styled-text documents of any size (limited by RAM).

◆ View and print TeachText or SimpleText read-only (readme) documents.

◆ Easily create TeachText/SimpleText read-only documents, including embedded pictures.

◆ View and print color PICT files, such as those produced by draw programs or Apple's built-in screen snapshot utility.

◆ Copy a selection from a PICT file and crop the image for use in another document.

◆ View, edit, and print text documents created by virtually any word processor or computer.

◆ Reformat downloaded e-mail or text, correcting word-wrap problems and removing extraneous, non-Mac characters.

◆ Prepare text for upload to the Internet, so that people with Wintel or UNIX systems can view the document as it was intended to be viewed.

◆ Instantly quote a brief passage from received e-mail, allowing the sender to remember their original message.

◆ Read any text document aloud, if you have Apple's Speech Manager extension. (You can listen to a SimpleText read-only file, for example, as the text and pictures scroll by!)

◆ Quickly optimize a document for printing, replacing generic, type-writer-era characters with professional-looking, typographically correct text. This feature includes my favorite command name ever—Stupify—which is used to change curly "typographer's" quotation marks and apostrophes (" " and ' ') into straight "typewriter-style" quotation marks (" " and ' ').

◆ Create simple hypertext documents.

◆ Insert attention-getting sound annotations to spice up ordinary inter-office mail.

◆ And more…

Sure it's a lot like the freeware BBEdit Lite, but hey, choice is good. Tex-Edit Plus does a lot of things that BBEdit Lite does, but its interface is completely different. And it does some things—like prepare text for use in e-mail and/or the Internet—somewhat better.

How to Use It…

Decompress the file TexEdit+ 2.5.6.sit, then launch the Tex-Edit Plus application. A blank, untitled window appears. Since Tex-Edit Plus is primarily a text editor, you can do all the things you usually do when editing text.

Tex-Edit Plus makes full use of Apple's extended keyboard including the Forward Delete, Home, End, Page Up, Page Down, and Cursor keys. The F1 through F4 keys invoke the standard Undo, Cut, Copy, and Paste commands.

Tex-Edit Plus has tons of keyboard shortcuts, as shown in Table 84.1.

TABLE 84.1   Keyboard shortcuts

Key	Modifier	Action
left/right Arrow	none	Move one character left/right
left/right Arrow	Option	Move one word left/right
left/right Arrow	Command	Move to beginning/end of line
up/down Arrow	none	Move one line up or down

TABLE 84.1   Keyboard shortcuts (Continued)

Key	Modifier	Action
up/down Arrow	Option	Move to beginning/end of page
up/down Arrow	Command	Move to beginning/end of document
Page Up	Option	Move to the top of the previous screenful of text
Page Down	Option	Move to the bottom of the next screenful of text
Shortcuts for extending the selection:		
Arrow	Shift	Extend the selection
left/right Arrow	Shift+Option	Extend the selection one word at a time
left/right Arrow	Shift+Command	Extend the selection to the beginning/end of the line
up/down Arrow	Shift+Option	Extend the selection to the beginning/end of the page
up/down Arrow	Shift+Command	Extend the selection to the beginning/end of the document
Page Up	Shift+Option	Extend the selection to the top of the previous screenful of text
Page Down	Shift+Option	Extend the selection to the bottom of the next screenful of text
Even more keyboard shortcuts:		
Delete	Option	Delete the previous word
Forward Delete	Option	Delete the next word
Enter/Return	none	Activate the default (outlined) button in dialogs
Escape/Command+period	none	Activate the Cancel button in dialogs

> **NOTE** Command+period will also stop all sound playback, stop all speech, and stop most time-consuming operations. Command+up/down arrow will cycle through panels in the Preferences and Help dialogs. All other pushbuttons have Command+key equivalents based on the first letter in the name of the button. (For example, Command+D activates the Don't Save button in the Save Changes? dialog.)

Tex-Edit Plus is also great for cleaning up text received from PC/Windows users. Do you ever get e-mail or copies of Web pages from Windows users? If so, the text they create often contains strange characters and/or weird little boxes where characters should be, as shown in Figure 84.1.

FIGURE 84.1   **Text that originated on a Windows PC often contains little boxes (linefeed characters) and strange line breaks (invisible carriage returns), as shown on the left.**

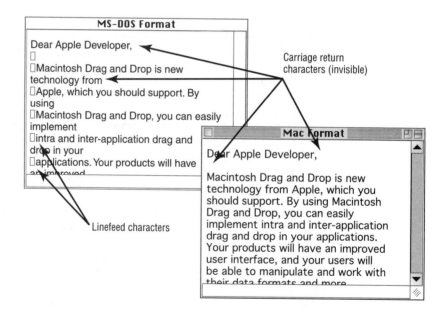

If that happens to you, drop the text into Tex-Edit Plus and use Special ➤ Modify (Command+M) to open the Modify dialog box. The Modify dialog box is Tex-Edit's most complex and powerful feature, as shown in Figure 84.2.

FIGURE 84.2 The mighty Modify dialog box with its myriad options

Modify Document

☐ Replace multiple space characters with: [Single Space ⬍]
☐ Replace each tab with [5] [⬍] space characters.
☐ Strip control characters. (ignore formfeed, return, tab)
☐ Strip high ASCII characters. (ASCII 128–255)
☐ Normalize sentence spacing.
☐ Strip leading spaces.
☐ Strip trailing spaces.
☐ Strip diacritical marks.

Quotes: [Ignore ⬍]
Ligatrs: [Ignore ⬍]
Ellipses: [Ignore ⬍]
Dashes: [Ignore ⬍]

Line Endings
[Ignore Line Endings ⬍]
Min line length: [40] [⬍]
Max line length: [60] [⬍]

[Reset] [Cancel] [OK]

It allows you to globally change (Tex-Edit's author calls this "munge") special characters in the text. If you wish to modify only a portion of the document, select the text of interest and choose Modify Selection. If you don't like the resulting modifications, be sure to choose Undo before doing anything else. Tex-Edit Plus remembers the settings in the Modify dialog box between sessions.

To convert a downloaded document to editable Mac format, first try the Strip CR/LF command. If this causes all the paragraphs to run together, choose Undo and try Replace Multiple Space Characters With Nothing along with Strip Leading Spaces, Strip Trailing Spaces, and Strip CR/LF. If a lot of nonsense characters are still visible, then try Strip Control Characters and Strip High ASCII Characters.

It takes some experimentation, but Tex-Edit Plus can fix almost any kind of problem text. Try it. You'll like it.

NOTE Be sure to read the Welcome to Tex-Edit! document carefully. It's the closest thing to a manual you're going to get. It contains lots of good stuff, so don't ignore it.

My Two Cents...

If you like to edit text, or you often receive text from PC/Windows users that needs cleaning up, Tex-Edit Plus is a great program. Give it a try. I use it often to "un-munge" files I get from my less-enlightened PC-using friends.

NOTE Tex-Edit Plus 2.5.6 is shareware available from Tom Bender (www.nearside.com/trans-tex/) and at the time of this printing costs approximately $15.

Games and Game Demos

Everyone knows the iMac is a wonderful gaming machine. And I'd be remiss if I didn't offer you at least a few new games to check out. So here are eight of my favorites—games from all genres: arcade, card, action, adventure, and more. Six of them are shareware; the other two are demo versions of two of my favorite commercial games. All are tons of fun.

Shall we?

85

3D Klondike: Solitaire with a Sense of Humor

As you probably know, Microsoft Windows includes a solitaire card game. And while your iMac or iBook did come with Nanosaur (take that, Windows users!), they don't include a solitaire game. But never fear—3D Klondike is here. 3D Klondike is similar to Windows' free solitaire game, but it's shareware and, unlike the Windows version, has quite a sense of humor. As you'll soon see.

How to Use It...

Decompress the 3D Klondike v.1.0a.sit file, then launch the 3D Klondike v.1.0a application.

Klondike is a standard solitaire game—the cards are arranged into seven build columns (middle) and one draw pile (left). At the top of the window are spaces for the four aces. A typical game is shown in Figure 85.1.

The goal is to arrange the cards in the build piles in descending order from king down, in alternating suit color. In other words, you can place any red queen on any black king, and any black jack on any red queen, and so on. You can move only kings to an empty build column.

FIGURE 85.1 Klondike's 3D board shows the seven build columns, four spaces for aces, and the draw pile.

Whenever you come upon an ace, you can place it above the build columns. Then you place cards of the same suit upon the ace in ascending order. In other words, if you place the ace of spades, the only card that can go on top of it is the two of spades, then the three of spades, and so on.

To play, choose File ➢ New Game or use the shortcut Command+N. You move a card by clicking it and dragging. It will "stick" if you drag it to an appropriate location. Make any moves you can now.

Next, click the draw pile to draw three cards. You can play the topmost card on a build column or an ace if you find an appropriate spot for it.

If you place the topmost card, you can then place the next card (now the topmost) the same way. Click the pile to draw three more cards when you have no moves for the topmost card. Repeat until you either win or lose the game.

You can also cheat if you so desire, but the program will usually razz you if you try. Since I'm sure some of you are honest, I won't list the cheats here.

(If you're bound and determined to cheat, check out Help ➤ Rules, Tips, and Cheats, or use the shortcut Command+H.)

That's about it for game play. But, as I said before, this is a program with a sense of humor. To see what I mean, do any of the following:

◆ Click any of the faces or heads on the screen including (but not limited to) Steve Jobs and Bill Gates to hear a (usually) funny recorded comment.

◆ Choose File ➤ Boss Coming, or use the shortcut Command+B, to bring up a screen that may keep you out of hot water should you get caught playing this game during business hours.

◆ Choose Hey! ➤ Anyone Want… Pie? to see Bill G. get one right in the kisser. (Did anyone notice that Bill was pied in Figure 85.1?)

◆ Hold down the Option key and pull down the File menu to see the Boost Morale command, which generates a game you *should* be able to win.

◆ Choose Apple menu ➤ A Midsummer Night's Dream for a quick dose of the bard.

Finally, if you win a game, by hook or by crook (either fairly or by cheating), you see a goofy little cartoon (reproduced in Figure 85.2 for those who stink at solitaire but wouldn't think of cheating).

FIGURE 85.2 What you'll see if you win a game!

Of course you can always choose Settings ➤ Turn Off the Jokes! if you get sick of 3D Klondike's oft-puerile attempts at humor.

NOTE If you like 3D Klondike, check out Freeverse Software's other shareware game titles: Burning Monkey Solitaire, Hearts Deluxe, Spades Deluxe, Classic Cribbage, Classic GinRummy, Enigma, CrossCards, The Eclipse, X-Words Deluxe, Blaze of Glory, Deathground, Atlas, and Toys.

My Two Cents...

Hey, it's solitaire, just like the Windows guys have, only funnier. If you're a solitaire fan, you'll love it.

NOTE 3D Klondike 1.0a is shareware available from Freeverse Software (http://www.freeverse.com/) and at the time of this printing costs approximately $15.

86 Alan's Euchre: Like Bridge with a Computerized Partner and Opponents

Alan's Euchre is a card game that's played with a deck of 24 cards (9 through ace in each suit). Euchre is a bit like Bridge, played with four people: two teams of two each, with partners sitting across from one another. In Alan's Euchre, the computer manages your partner and both of your opponents.

How to Use It...

Decompress the file Alan's Euchre 1.1.1 (PPC).sit, open the Alan's Euchre 1.1.1 (PPC) folder, and launch the Alan's Euchre 1.1.1 (PPC) application. Click OK to dismiss the nag screen.

Choose File ➢ New Game to begin. The computer will deal a new hand of Euchre, as shown in Figure 86.1.

The object of Euchre is to be the first team to score 10 points. The game consists of hands of five cards per player. A hand consists of three events: bidding for trump, the play, and scoring. The team who wins three or more out of five tricks earns points.

NOTE You can find the complete rules of Euchre in the Read Me & Release Notes file or in Alan's Euchre's online help (choose Help ➢ Alan's Euchre Help).

FIGURE 86.1 This hand of Euchre is ready to play.

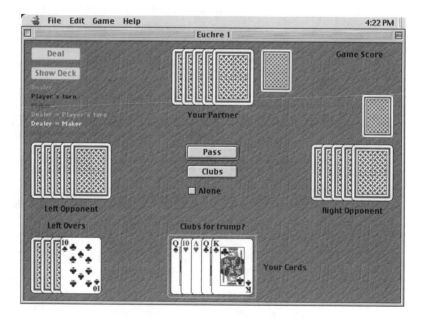

NOTE If you don't see the colored writing on the left side of the window—Dealer, Player's Turn, Maker, and such—choose Game ➢ Draw Key or use the shortcut Command+K to make it appear.

Once you're familiar with the rules, you'll need to know how to interpret the screen (from the Read Me & Release Notes file):

Borders around players cards:

- ◆ Green = dealer
- ◆ Blue = player's turn
- ◆ Red = trump caller, a.k.a. maker
- ◆ Yellow = dealer and trump caller
- ◆ Magenta = All of the above: dealer and maker and player's turn

The K key toggles the various items on the game window. You can also set the K key via Preferences and the Game menu. If it's on, your prompts will flash red every five seconds. This is particularly useful when you're learning the game.

When the trump choice, or Deal and Show Deck, buttons are enabled:

- ◆ The Tab key switches the default button.
- ◆ The Return or Enter key activates the default button.
- ◆ The A key toggles the Alone checkbox.

The following shortcuts work only during game play when it's your turn:

The spacebar or 0 (zero) key   If there is only one playable card, it will be played for you. If there is more than one playable card, each of them will be highlighted briefly. You can also trigger this shortcut via the Game menu.

The W or * (star/asterisk) key   Want to know who's winning? Pressing either key highlights the current trick-winning card. You can also trigger this shortcut via the Game menu.

The P key   Want to see the playable cards? Pressing this key highlights the cards in your hand that are playable for the current trick. You can also trigger this shortcut via the Game menu.

The 1, 2, 3, 4, and 5 keys   Plays that numbered card from your hand. It's the same as clicking the card.

My Two Cents...

I don't care much for computer card games. (If you must know, I prefer my twice-a-month poker games with my cigar-smoking, single-malt-swilling buddies for *my* card fix.) But I have to admit, Alan's Euchre is pretty fun once you figure out how to play Euchre.

NOTE Alan's Euchre 1.1.1 is shareware available from Alan Ewalt (`http://home.earthlink.net/~nmewalt/`) and at the time of this printing costs approximately $5.

87 Bubble Trouble: Addictive, Silly, Cartoony Arcade Game

Ambrosia Products `FAQ.text` describes Bubble Trouble thusly:

> Cutthroat fishies are playing hardball in a squabble over some very wet turf. Think of it as splatball for insufferably cute seafaring critters (hey, they need their fun too).

> Bubble Trouble's world is filled with lusciously-drawn cartoony critters who give that cranky crab from The Little Mermaid a run for his money. But money isn't what you'll be running from: an otherwise peaceful fish bowl has been filled with bubbles that are being tossed around in an enthralling game of "Squish the Fish!"

That pretty much sums it up. And, as my kids will attest, it's very addictive.

How to Use It...

Run the Bubble Trouble Installer, then open the Bubble Trouble 1.0.1 *f* folder and launch the Bubble Trouble application. The first time you play, you'll see a dialog box about resolution switching. Click Change.

When the game loads, you'll see Bubble Trouble's main screen.

NOTE If you leave the game idle for long, it goes into demo mode. Click the mouse or press any key to return to the main screen.

The main screen offers these choices:

New Game   Duh. Starts a new game.

Demo   Even though it says "Game Over," the game demo is running in the background. Click anywhere or press any key to get back to the main screen.

Scores   Shows you the high scores screen. Click anywhere or press any key to get back to the main screen.

Preferences   Set your game preferences here.

Credits   Tells you about the game's authors.

Quit   Ends the game.

So let's have at it. To start a new game, click the New Game button on the main screen.

You control Blinky, a young fish floundering in an underwater maze. To escape, you must defend yourself from the dangerous Denizens of the Deep and earn treasure in the process. The game itself is very easy to control. Just watch the demo a few times to learn the basics. You shouldn't have any trouble learning how to play the game. Just dive in at the deep end and see what works!

The default controls for Blinky are the arrow keys and the spacebar. Use the arrow keys to move the fish; use the spacebar to push bubbles into enemy fish, as shown in Figure 87.1.

It's pretty simple but devilishly difficult. One thing you might want to know is how to change the keys that control Blinky. Just click Prefs at the main screen, then click the Keys icon on the left side of the window. Click New

FIGURE 87.1   I just pushed a bubble onto a fish, scoring a whopping 800 points!

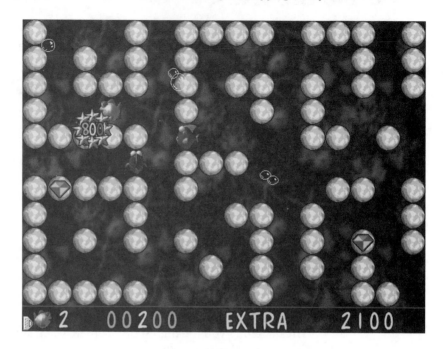

Set, and define the keys for Left, Right, Up, Down, and Push. When you're satisfied, click Save. I like to use the numeric keypad; my preferred key set is shown in Figure 87.2.

FIGURE 87.2   These are the keys I like to use to play Bubble Trouble.

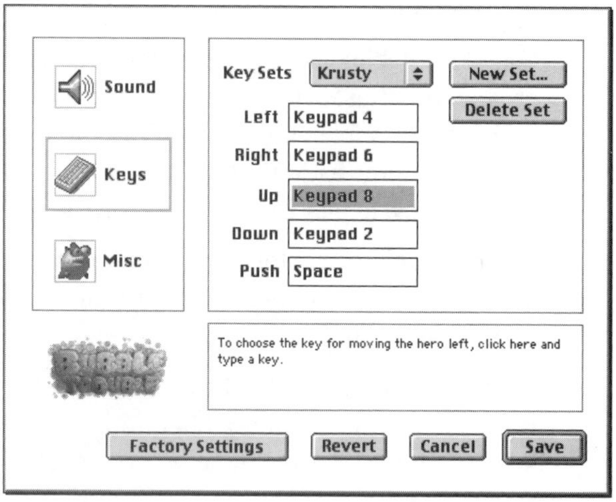

N O T E Check out the Bubble Trouble Web site at http://www.Bubble-Trouble.com/. You can get updates, more music, tips and hints on game play, and much more!

My Two Cents...

What can I say. It's goofy and addictive, and games take only a few minutes (at least at my skill level). Like all addictive games, it has a very high "I'm gonna try that one more time" factor.

It's a lot of fun for your $15.

N O T E Bubble Trouble 1.0.1 is shareware available from Ambrosia Software (http://www.ambrosiasw.com/) and at the time of this printing costs approximately $15.

88 MacChess: You Versus Your iMac

MacChess is (what else?) a chess program for the Mac. I am not much of a chess player, but I'm pretty impressed with how well it plays. It beats me every time.

Oh, and one more good thing about MacChess—it's FREE!

How to Use It...

Decompress the MacChess 5.0.1 EN.sit file, then open the MacChess 5.0.1 EN folder and launch the MacChess 5.0.1 application.

A chessboard appears, along with several other windows, as shown in Figure 88.1.

FIGURE 88.1   MacChess is ready to begin a game.

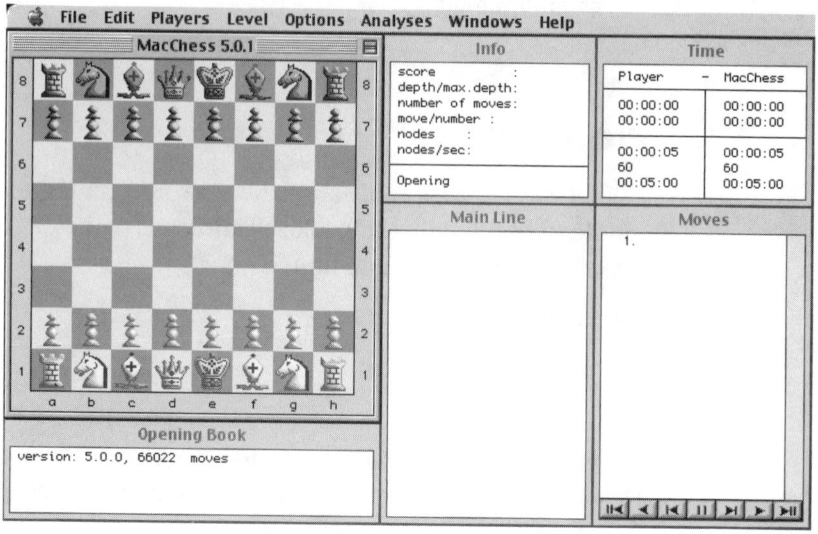

By default, you play the gold pieces at the bottom of the screen, and you go first. To move a piece, click and drag it onto any legal square.

A rudimentary knowledge of chess is helpful but not required.

NOTE If you don't know how to play chess but want to learn, the Learning Chess document describes some helpful Web sites, including a free online chess tutorial at `http://dialspace.dial.pipex.com/town/avenue/xfu49/elementary.htm` and the official, complete rules of chess at `http://193.192.227.142/comms/fidelaws.htm`.

If you're stumped, choose Options ➢ Hint. The game will tell you its best guess for your next move.

NOTE If Options > Hint is gray and unavailable, you'll have to make a move or two on your own before the game will chime in with a hint.

MacChess has a wealth of features. You can adjust almost infinitely how well it will play, and you can start games by giving yourself an advantage if you like. You can also time your moves. You can import PGN (Portable Game Notation) files that show you how games have been played in the past. And much more. I urge you to read the ~ Manual MacChess 5.0 document, which contains information about these useful features.

My Two Cents...

As I said, I'm not really a chess player. Still, MacChess seems strong to me. Unless you're an excellent chess player, I think it'll give you a run for your money.

And you can't beat the price—free.

NOTE MacChess 5.0.1 is freeware available from Wim van Beusekom (beusekom@knoware.nl).

89 Myth II: Soulblighter— Perhaps the Best Mac Game Ever

Myth II is, simply put, my favorite Mac game of all time. It's a real-time battle strategy game where you command troops of mythical creatures— giant Trows, fast and fearless Berzerkers, pig-like Mauls, Molotov-cocktail tossing Dwarves, fireball-shooting Warlocks, and much more. I like to tell people that playing Myth II is strategic, kind of like playing Chess with bomb-throwing Dwarves instead of pawns.

It's great in single-player mode and even better when you play with other living creatures via Bungie.net, the free game-matching service you get with the full version.

The demo on your CD offers but a taste of the endless carnage that is Myth II: Soulblighter. It includes a tutorial, two levels from the single-player campaign, and one network map.

The full version includes:

◆ 25 single-player levels with animated cut-scenes, narration, and an original musical score

◆ Over 20 unit types for you to command

◆ 20 network maps

◆ Campaign editors, Fear and Loathing, that let you create your own maps

◆ Free access to bungie.net, the free Internet gaming service where you can play cooperatively or compete for worldwide ranking. (You must have your own Internet connection to use bungie.net.)

How to Use It...

Run the Myth II 1.2.1 Demo program to install Myth II. Then open the Myth II Demo folder and launch the Myth II Demo application. A dialog box will ask you about switching resolutions. Click the Don't Show This Dialog Again on Startup checkbox, then click OK. The Playable Demo screen appears. Click anywhere, and the Myth II main screen appears.

The first thing to do is check out the tutorial. Click Tutorial on the main screen and read the Mission Objectives when they appear.

NOTE It's a good idea to click the Level tab in the Mission Objectives window and read all the tips for the mission.

A voice-driven tutorial will show you how the Myth II interface works. You'll learn how to move the camera around and how to manage your troops. You'll learn how to blow up stuff using your Dwarves (Figure 89.1) and how to burn things using your Archers or Warlocks.

FIGURE 89.1   My Dwarf has thrown a flaming explosive bottle at the dummies; in just a second they'll blow up in an extremely violent fashion.

It takes a while to get the hang of the game, but don't give up. Go through the tutorial a couple of times if you have to.

When you've mastered the tutorial, click the New Game button to begin the first single-player level.

Rather than describe the game further, let me give you some strategy tips based upon years of Myth-playing experience:

◆ Identify the biggest threats first, then eliminate them. Always try to kill the most dangerous enemies—Warlocks, Dwarves, and Archers—first.

◆ Use Ctrl+click to attack with Warlocks and Dwarves. (Click your dude, then Ctrl+click the ground where you think the enemy will be in a second or two.)

◆ Use formations. In any battle of equal-strength armies, the one that uses formations best will almost always win. Formations 1, 2, 3, 5, 6, and 0 are, in my opinion, the most useful. The others come in handy occasionally but not often.

◆ Never leave your range units (Archers, Warlocks, and Dwarves) unprotected. Fast enemy units such as Ghols can often sneak up and kill them before they can attack. Keep some melee units (Berzerkers, Mauls, Myrkadia, etc.) nearby to defend them.

◆ Master the use of presets. You can select a group of players and assign it a preset by pressing Command and holding down any number key from 1 through 0. It's good to keep each type of troops in a preset, so Archers may be preset 1, Berzerkers preset 2, Warlocks preset 3, and so on. To select a preset group of troops, type Command+1.

◆ High ground provides a distinct advantage for units that shoot (Archers, Warlocks, and Dwarves). If you are on high ground, your arrows, bombs, and fireballs will go farther and you will receive less damage from enemy shots.

◆ Keep your Dwarves spread out. If you bunch up your Dwarves, trust me, someone will come along and kill them all at once. It takes only one well-placed bomb or fireball to wipe out half a dozen Dwarves if they're too close together.

◆ Don't be ashamed to retreat. If a battle is going badly, pull back and regroup. If you charge into a battle you have no hope of winning, your troops will be wiped out and the game will end. Pull back, regroup, and maybe you can regain the advantage.

My Two Cents...

I love this game. After almost a year, I still try to play at least one game a day. I can't think of another game, ever, that I found as enjoyable.

N O T E Myth II: Soulblighter 1.2.1 on the companion CD is a commercial demo. The full version is available from Bungie Software (http://www.bungie.com) and at the time of this printing costs approximately $25. If you buy the full version, look for me on Bungie.Net as "Wookiee."

90 Pac the Man: It's PacMan for the Mac!

Some of you older readers may remember the PacMan arcade game. Pac the Man, in the words of its creator, "is a simple but nice PacMan clone."

There's not much more to say. It looks and plays like PacMan, but with more annoying music. Oh, and it's free.

How to Use It...

Decompress the `PacTheMan.sit` file, open the PactheMan4.0.1e folder, and launch the Pac the Man application. Choose File ➢ New or use the shortcut Command+N to begin a new game.

The default keys are the arrow keys on the keyboard. The object is to complete each level by eating all the little yellow dots. While doing so, you must avoid the other creatures. Figure 90.1 shows you a game in progress.

FIGURE 90.1   I'm the little, round mouth thing with no eyes; the monsters are the other creatures, with eyes.

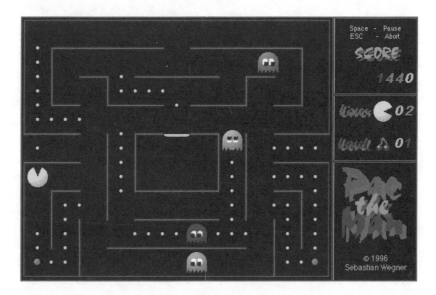

Eating fruit and other objects gives you bonus points. Eating one of the big green dots makes the other creatures vulnerable. When they're vulnerable, they turn blue; when they're blue, you can eat them. When they begin to flash, they're about to turn mean again.

That's about it.

N O T E As with Bubble Trouble, I found it easier to play with the keyboard controls set to the keypad, as shown in Figure 90.2, rather than the arrow keys. You might want to try it that way. To do so, choose Options ➢ Configure Input Device, or use the shortcut Command+I.

FIGURE 90.2 Try using the numeric keyboard keys instead of the tiny arrow keys.

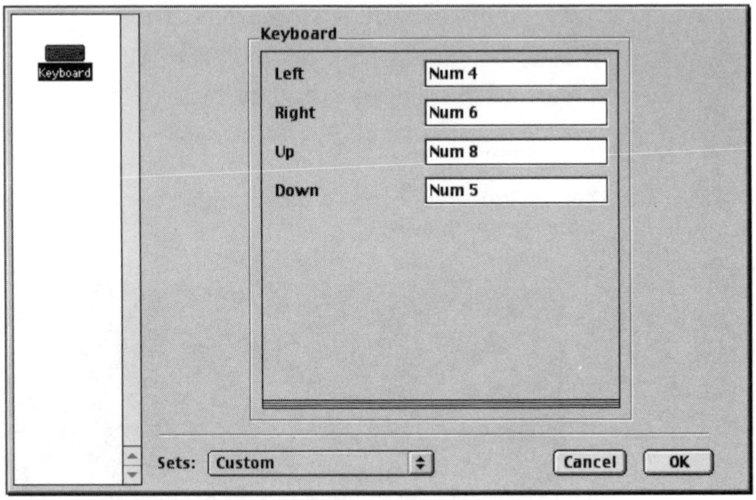

N O T E If you find the music annoying, you can turn it (and the sound effects and/or the background pattern) on and off in the Options menu.

My Two Cents...

What can I say? Either you like Pac the Man or you don't. My kids adored it. They had me e-mail them a copy when they were in Florida visiting Grandma and Grandpa, who have an iMac. It's cute, you can't beat the price, and you can turn the sound off if it annoys you. What more could you ask from a self-admitted PacMan clone?

N O T E Pac the Man 4.0.1e is freeware available from Sebastian Wegner (`http://home.t-online.de/home/mcsebi/index.html`).

91 Slithereens

Slithereens is another game from Ambrosia Software. (Remember Bubble Trouble a few pages ago?)

I hate to keep relying on their catalog, but they write such excellent, concise descriptions of their games that I find it hard to resist. Here's what the Ambrosia product catalog has to say about Slithereens:

> Set in the backyard of the evil Dr. Funkengruven, Slithereens is an adventure that will satisfy your appetite for action. You are Luther, a peaceful snake who was surgically sassified and imbued with a hunger for snakemeat. Unfortunately, there are hundreds of other snakes like you, each wanting the same thing: to munch on you!

It's very cute and lots of fun to play.

N O T E I would like to point out that Ambrosia makes about a dozen other great programs, including many other awesome games such as Apeiron, Avara, Barrack, and Harry the Handsome Executive, plus utilities like the awesome screen-capture utility I used to create all the screen shots for this book, Snapz Pro. Visit their Web site at `http://www.ambrosiasw.com/`.

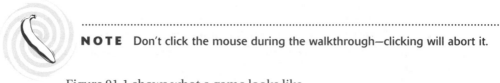

How to Use It...

Run the Slithereens Installer, then open the Slithereens 1.0.0 *f* folder and launch the Slithereens application. A dialog box will offer to change your monitor's resolution. Click Change. The main Slithereens screen will appear.

Click Help to open the Slithereens walkthrough. Since there is no documentation, this is the best way to learn the game.

NOTE   Don't click the mouse during the walkthrough—clicking will abort it.

Figure 91.1 shows what a game looks like.

FIGURE 91.1   **I'm the short snake at the bottom right, fighting for my very life!**

That's about it. Click New 1 Player Game to start playing. The default keys are the darn arrow keys again. But this time you can easily choose the numeric keypad. Click Preferences on the main screen, then click Configure Controls, and choose Number Pad from the pop-up Sets menu (it says "Custom" in Figure 91.2).

FIGURE 91.2   I still say the numeric keypad is better for gaming!

Keyboard	
Player 1 Up	Num 8
Player 1 Down	Num 2
Player 1 Left	Num 4
Player 1 Right	Num 6
Player 2 Up	W
Player 2 Down	S
Player 2 Left	A
Player 2 Right	D

Sets: Custom   Cancel   OK

(Keyboard, Apple USB Mouse)

One interesting feature is that you can play two-player games from a single keyboard. You configure the second player's keys the same way you configured the Number Pad a second ago.

My Two Cents...

Slithereens is pretty darn addictive. It has a huge dose of that "I'm gonna just try this one more time" ingredient that makes a game good. And it doesn't hurt that the graphics and sounds are first rate.

I think you'll enjoy it.

N O T E   Slithereens 1.0.0 is shareware available from Ambrosia Software (http://www.ambrosiasw.com/) and at the time of this printing costs approximately $20.

92 Tomb Raider II

Tomb Raider is one of the most popular game series of all time. Created by Core Design and published on the PC and PlayStation by Eidos Interactive, it was brought to the Mac by Aspyr Media, and it rocks.

For the last time, and only because their purple prose is better than anything I could hash together, here's how their Web site describes the game:

> The award-winning Tomb Raider II is the second chapter in the continuing saga of Lara Croft. Join Lara in her quest for The Dagger of Xian, reputed to posses the power of the dragon. But beware, Lara is not the only one in search of the dagger!

> Drive, swim, climb and conquer Lara's way across the eastern hemisphere and beyond. The adventure begins at The Great Wall of China, but it's not long before Lara is racing snowmobiles in Tibet and speeding her way through the canals of Venice. Swing from chandeliers, uncover a sunken ship, and scale walls in exotic locations.

The demo includes portions of the first level of the full game. The full version of Tomb Raider II has these features:

- ◆ Fifteen-plus levels, from Venice to China, from a sunken ocean liner to Tibetan monasteries!

- ◆ More weapons, including Uzis, a grenade launcher, a harpoon gun, and an M16 rifle!

- ◆ High-quality cinematic cut-scenes using Apple's latest QuickTime technology!

- ◆ A training course and Lara's mansion to train in and explore!

- ◆ Nasty enemies to try to stop Lara's quest: warrior monks, Yetis, jaguars, great white sharks, rabid dobermans, and more!

If you like twitch adventure games, you're gonna love Lara.

How to Use It...

Decompress the `Tomb Raider II Demo.sit` file, open the Tomb Raider II Demo folder, and launch the Tomb Raider II Demo application. The first time the game starts up, it will attempt to detect the right settings for your iMac or iBook for best performance. Click OK when you see the alert box.

NOTE If you later want to change the graphics/sound/joystick settings, simply double-click the Tomb Raider II Setup application in the Tomb Raider II Demo folder.

A game starts immediately. The object is to explore each level (there's only one in the demo), find a magical key to open the magical door, then move on to the next level. Oh, and make sure nothing kills you.

Here's how to use the control keys:

Esc Inventory (Change weapon, use medkit, etc.)

Arrow keys Move Lara

Spacebar Draw weapon

Ctrl Shoot weapon (if drawn), grab (if no weapon drawn)

Command Jump/swim (Can be combined with arrow keys for flips, etc.)

Shift Creep/walk (Keeps you from walking off the edge of cliffs, etc.)

Use the mouse to change the camera angle or view.

NOTE To save your game, press Esc, then arrow down.

That's pretty much it. The best way to learn is to just play for a while. Sure you'll die. Many times. But pretty soon you'll get the hang of it. Not long after that, I predict, you'll buy the full version of the game.

Be sure to save your game often!

My Two Cents...

Tomb Raider II is a beautiful and challenging game—you'll have lots of fun solving this first level.

NOTE   Tomb Raider II on the companion CD is a commercial demo. The full version is available from Aspyr Media (`http://www.aspyr.com`) and at the time of this printing costs approximately $45.

More Cool Stuff

This chapter is the repository for all the programs that didn't fit comfortably into one of the previous six chapters. These programs are the oddballs, the misfits, the weird, and the wonderful.

But I wouldn't have thought for a moment of not including one of them. Each is unique and interesting in its own way.

Without further ado…

93 Bartender's Friend: Drink Database with a Twist

Bartender's Friend is a database of drinks. Tell it what ingredients you have, and it gives you an instant answer to the question "What can I mix?" You can also create a list of your favorite drinks, add a comment to any recipe, sort the lists alphabetically or randomly, and browse all the drinks in the program.

How to Use It…

Decompress the `bartenders friend.sit` file, then open the Bartender's Friend 2.0 folder and launch the Bartender's Friend 2.0 application. Click Continue, then click Not Yet.

Some horrible music plays for a second, then you'll see the main screen, shown in Figure 93.1.

NOTE Bartender's Friend is cursed with some awful theme music and sound effects. You can turn off both in the Sound menu.

In the screen shown in Figure 93.1, I typed the word *beach* into the List Beverages That Have ____ in Their Name field and clicked Show Me. As you can

FIGURE 93.1 Bartender's Friend's main screen—ugly but functional, eh?

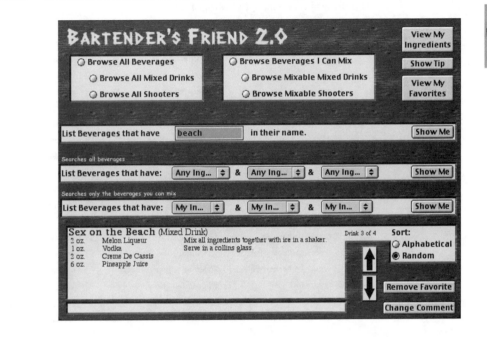

see at the bottom of the window, the program found four drinks, including the one shown, Sex on the Beach. Click the large black arrows to go to the next and previous recipes.

You can also search for recipes that match your criteria by using the pop-up menus.

Click Browse All Beverages in the upper-left corner to browse through the program's 100 included recipes—17 shooters and 83 mixed drinks.

You can tell the program what liquors and mixers you have by clicking View My Ingredients. Figure 93.2 shows the list of possible alcoholic ingredients.

Click the checkbox for each type of liquor you have, then choose the View Non Alcoholic Ingredients button to click the checkboxes for mixers and such. Now you can use the Browse Beverages I Can Mix feature.

My Two Cents...

I usually drink my whiskey neat, and I tended bar in college, so this program isn't of much use to me. It may be useful to you, though, so I included it in spite of its ugliness and bad taste in sounds.

FIGURE 93.2 Once you click the checkboxes for the ingredients you have on hand, you can use the Browse Beverages I Can Mix feature.

View Non Alcoholic Ingredients	☐ Dark Rum	☐ Peppermint Schnapps
	☐ Galliano	☐ Root Beer Schnapps
	☐ Gin	☑ Scotch
☐ Amaretto	☐ Gold Rum	☐ Sloe Gin
☐ Apple Brandy	☐ Gold Schlager	☐ Southern Comfort
☐ Apricot Brandy	☐ Gold Tequila	☐ Spiced Rum (Captain Morgan)
☐ Beer	☐ Grand Marnier	☐ Strawberry Liqueur
☐ Blue Curacao	☐ Green Creme De Menthe	☐ Sweet Vermouth
☐ Brandy	☐ Grenadine	☐ Tequila
☐ Butter Scotch Schnapps	☐ Irish Cream (Bailey's)	☐ Triple Sec
☐ Cherry Brandy	☐ Jack Daniel's	☐ Vermouth
☐ Cinnamon Schnapps	☐ Jim Beam	☑ Vodka
☐ Creme De Banana	☐ Kahlua	☐ Whiskey
☐ Creme De Cacao (Dark)	☐ Malibu	☐ White Creme De Menthe
☐ Creme De Cacao (White)	☐ Melon Liquer (Midori)	☐ White Rum (Bacardi)
☐ Creme De Cassis	☐ Orange Curacao	☐ Wine
☐ Curacao	☐ Peach Schnapps	**Finished**

NOTE Bartender's Friend 2.0 is shareware available from Anthony Zimmerman (http://www.netos.com/anthonyz/bartender/default.html) and at the time of this printing costs approximately $10.

94 Relax: Sit Back and Listen to the Birdies

Relax plays a relaxing sound of a babbling forest stream in the background as you work at your iMac or iBook.

How to Use It...

Run the Install Relax 2.1 application, then open the Relax 2.1 folder and launch the Relax 2.1 application. When the Welcome screen appears, click Demo.

That's it. You can choose File ➤ Preferences and change the volume of the sound.

N O T E   Until you register the software by purchasing it, it runs in a demo mode that has only one sound "environment." If you purchase a copy, you will receive a serial number that unlocks the software and lets you play other sound "environments."

My Two Cents...

Relax is said to be soothing and relaxing. I found it distracting and annoying. To each his/her own.

N O T E   Install Relax 2.1 is shareware available from Software Perspectives (`http://www.sperspect.com`) and at the time of this printing costs approximately $15.

95 Uli's Moose: The Stupidest Mac Trick of All Time Is BACK!

In 1990, in the preface to my now-out-of-print epic, *Stupid Mac Tricks*, I wrote these words:

> If you're wondering why a serious, dedicated, and well-known Macintosh journalist such as myself would embark on such a wacky project, all I can say in my defense is, "The Moose made me do it."

I was referring, of course, to the Talking Moose. Ten years ago, the Talking Moose was the hottest shareware program around. I based a book on it. Baseline Publishing released several commercial programs based on it. Everyone knew the Moose.

Then Mac OS 7 came along. And the Moose stopped working. His author, Steve Halls, was busy becoming a doctor, and his publisher went broke.

And now, through the hard work of M. Uli Kusterer, the Moose is back!

What is Uli's Moose? Glad you asked. Uli's Moose is the 1999 reincarnation of the Talking Moose, released with the permission and cooperation of the original author, Steve Halls. It now works with Mac OS 8 and above, and it's as much fun as ever.

So what does it do? Once installed, from time to time, one of two selectable moose will pop up on your screen and say something stupid, witty, or utterly useless. But you have to see it to understand its charm. Install it. Give it a try.

It really is a Stupid Mac Trick in the nicest sense of the phrase.

How to Use It...

Decompress the `Moose205b.sit` file, then open the folder called The Incredible Elk. Now follow these instructions from the Installation file in the The Incredible Elk folder:

> Drop the "Uli's Moose" extension onto your system folder's icon. The Finder will prompt you that it needs to reside in the 'Extensions' folder. Approve of that. Then take the "Moose" folder that was next to the Moose extension and put it directly into your system folder. Finally, put the 'Moose Panel' application anywhere you find it comfortable, I usually drop it into the system folder's "Control Panels" folder. Restart. The Talking Moose will say "Hello" to you. Be sure to say "Hello" back to the Moose. Until the Moose gets to know you better it is a wise idea to be as polite as possible to him. Offended Mooses sometimes give off a strong musky odor, which is to be avoided at all costs!

Ha! Even the documentation is funny!

NOTE You absolutely must read the `Moose History` file, found in the Docs folder. It's hilarious.

Once you restart your iMac or iBook, the Moose will appear periodically, like this (Figure 95.1).

FIGURE 95.1 Once installed, Uli's Moose pops up and speaks every so often.

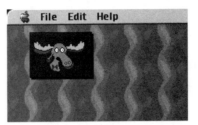

To change the Moose's settings, open the Moose Panel application, as shown in Figure 95.2.

FIGURE 95.2 Adjust the Moose's appearances in the **Moose Panel**.

You can modify the following settings:

Speak How Often Sets the length between the Moose's appearances.

Time for Other Apps Controls how much of your computer's processing power the Moose uses. Leave it alone.

Blink Frequency Controls how often the Moose blinks.

Eyes Follow Mouse   These settings do just what you'd expect.

Repeat   Controls which keys make the Moose repeat his last message. The default is Command+Ctrl+Esc.

Moose Animation   Lets you choose a different Moose.

Click the Test Speak button to make the Moose appear and speak immediately.

My Two Cents...

I know it's dorky and you'll soon grow sick of it, but I HAD to include it here for old time's sake. I hope you like it.

NOTE Uli's Moose 2.0.5b is freeware available from M. Uli Kusterer (http://www.weblayout.com/witness).

96 UpdateAgent Online: Keep Your Mac OS Software Up To Date

UpdateAgent Online Edition is the easiest way to update all the System software—Apple-provided control panels, extensions, applications, and utilities—on your iMac or iBook.

Apple frequently releases updates to the software that came with your iMac or iBook. These updates often offer additional features and/or stability. It is usually a good idea to use the latest versions of Mac OS System software components.

This program scans your hard disk, then compares what you have with a database of the latest releases. If any of your software is out of date, you will have the opportunity to download the updates.

How to Use It...

Decompress the UpdateAgent Online.sit file, open the UpdateAgent Online folder, and launch the PPC application. The main window appears, as shown in Figure 96.1.

FIGURE 96.1 UpdateAgent Online, ready to rock and roll

Now, before you do anything else, make an Internet connection as you usually do. Once you're connected to the Internet, click the Demo button. Now follow these steps:

1. Select your hard drive from the pop-up menu, then click Start to begin scanning your hard drive. This may take a few minutes.

2. When the UpdateAgent Results window opens, deselect any updates you don't want and then press Get, as shown in Figure 96.2.

NOTE Click the little triangle next to the word Details, then click any item to see its description.

3. The Get Files window displays the status of retrieving the files. The updates are downloaded to the New Insider Updates folder located in the root folder of your startup disk.

4. Install the updates.

FIGURE 96.2 UpdateAgent Online's Results window shows the files on my hard disk that are in need of updating.

NOTE You can select Edit ➤ Preferences ➤ General to customize Update-Agent's download folder, automatic schedule, automatic expansion, and sounds.

The free check-up version included on the companion CD updates your Mac OS software only. The upgrade versions can also update hundreds of third-party programs.

The UpdateAgent CD Edition contains 1.3GB of the latest updates and can update your computers over your network. One set is $89.95, and four issues—one delivered every three months—is only $249.95.

The Standard Edition updates all the software on one Macintosh for an entire year for only $49.95. You may update as often as you'd like.

The Limited Edition updates all the software on one Macintosh one time for only $12.95. Get this version if you have only a small amount of software or if your programs don't change often.

My Two Cents...

It's always a good idea to use the latest, greatest software from Apple. This program makes it painless to find out what is out of date on your hard disk. I recommend it.

NOTE UpdateAgent Online is commercial software available from Insider Software (`http://www.insidersoftware.com`) and at the time of this printing the Standard Edition costs approximately $50.

97 USB Overdrive: Use Any USB Device!

This is kind of an unusual program, one that won't be of interest to all of you. But it's a killer thing to have. USB Overdrive lets you use mice, trackballs, joysticks, and gamepads from any manufacturer with your iMac or iBook—even devices not specifically made for the Mac. If it connects via USB, chances are that USB Overdrive can control it. You can configure devices either globally or on an application-specific basis. USB Overdrive understands all kinds of wheels, buttons, switches, and controls and supports scrolling, keyboard emulation, launching, and complex macros, as well as all the usual actions like clicking, control-clicking, and so forth.

Best of all, USB Overdrive can easily handle several USB devices at once. The author claims to have two mice, one trackball, two joysticks, and one gamepad connected to the same iMac—each of them from a different manufacturer.

If you have USB devices or plan to buy any, you're going to love this little gem.

How to Use It...

Decompress the usb-overdrive-11.sit file, open the USB Overdrive 1.1 folder, and run the USB Overdrive 1.1 Installer. After your iMac or iBook restarts, open the USB Overdrive control panel. Wait a few seconds, then click Register Later.

The USB Overdrive control panel appears, as shown in Figure 97.1.

FIGURE 97.1 **The USB Overdrive control panel**

Unfortunately, I can't tell you much about how to configure it, as I don't have a single USB device here to play with. You can find out more by clicking the About button in the USB Overdrive control panel.

My Two Cents...

I hear it works great. If I ever get my hands on a non-Apple USB device, I will certainly give it a shot.

NOTE USB Overdrive 1.1 is shareware available from Alessandro Levi Montalcini (http://www.usboverdrive.com) and at the time of this printing costs approximately $20.

98 It's a Beep Sound Randomizer—YO!

YO! is a beep sound randomizer. YO! enables you to have multiple sound files randomly play as your Mac's alert sound, also known as the system beep.

The version included here is a demo that can use only three sound files at a time. When you register and pay the $20, you get these additional features:

♦ Up to 1,000 sounds randomized as your alert sound

♦ The ability to import `.SND`, `.WAV`, `.AIFF`, `.AU`, and other sound formats

♦ The ability to record your own sounds into your Sounds list

♦ Drag-and-drop support for sound importing and folder selection

♦ Removal of the registration reminder

How to Use It...

Run the YO! v1.0 Installer, then after restarting, open the YO! Console control panel, shown in Figure 98.1.

With YO! installed, your beep sound will rotate among the first three sounds in the list.

Double-click any of the beep sound names to hear that sound. Click the arrows beneath the Volume and Priority columns to change the volume or priority for a sound. Close the control panel, and your beep sounds will be automatically randomized among the top three.

My Two Cents...

I don't care much for beep sounds, so I uninstalled it promptly. Many people tell me they like it, though, so it's included for your pleasure. Enjoy.

FIGURE 98.1 You configure your random beeps in the YO! Console control panel.

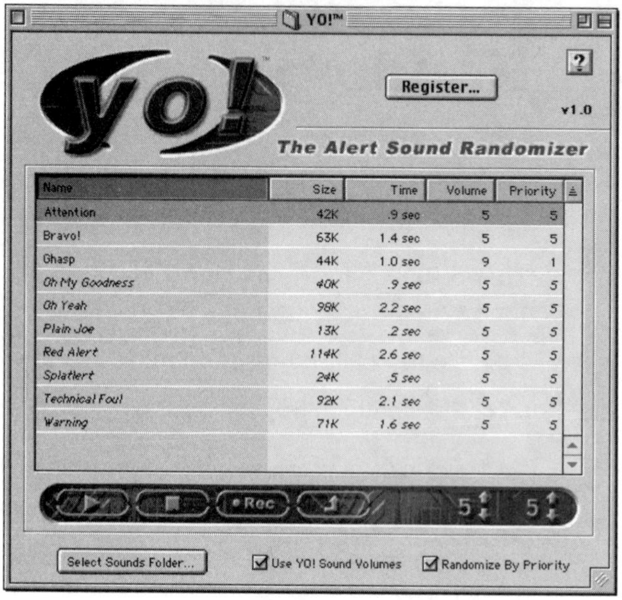

NOTE YO! 1.0 is shareware available from Clixsounds (`http://www`
`.clixsounds.com`) and at the time of this printing costs approximately $20.

INDEX

Note to the Reader: Page numbers in **bold** indicate the principal discussion of a topic or the definition of a term. Page numbers in *italic* indicate illustrations.

Numbers

3D-Klondike game, 326–329, *327, 328*
3.5 connectors, 113, 117
56K modems, 128

A

About This Computer Easter eggs, 159
ACTION Files utility, 215–217, *216*, 233
ACTION GoMac utility, 212–215, *213, 215*
ADB (Apple Desktop Bus) ports, 114, 136–137
adding
    current date to letterhead, 6
    to Favorites on America Online, 25
    graphics
        to letterhead, 5–6, *5*
        to Web pages, 68–69, *69*
    RAM (Random Access Memory), 134
Address Book utility, 300–303, *301*
Adobe PageMill software, **64–71**. *See also* Internet features
    adding graphics to Web pages, 68–69, *69*
    creating links, 70, *70*
    creating Web pages, **65–68**, *66, 67*
    defined, **64**, *65*
    downloading, 64
    Help, 71
    viewing HTML code, 68
ADSL (Asymmetric Digital Subscriber Line) modems, 129–130, 131
advertisements on America Online, turning off, 22–23, *23*
Agent Audio utility, 280–283, *281*
Aladdin DropStuff utility, 218–220
Aladdin StuffIt Expander, 220–222, 266
Alan's Euchre game, 329–332, *330*
alerts
    creating alert sounds, **33–34**
    spoken alert messages, 145–146
    YO! beep sound randomizer, 361–362, *362*
aliases
    in Apple menu, 197
    Apple menu alias on Desktop, 198
    creating, **199**
    defined, **195**
    Favorites feature, 200

AltaVista search engine, 25
AlwaysONline utility, 288–290, *289*
Ambrosia Software
    Bubble Trouble game, 332–335, *334*
    Slithereens game, 343–345, *344, 345*
    Web site, 335, 345
America Online (AOL), **22–27**, **288–290**
    adding to Favorites, 25
    AlwaysONline utility, 288–290, *289*
    Apple support groups, 192
    creating shortcuts to areas, 25
    Find on AOL feature, 24–25, *24*
    Find It on the Web feature, 25
    Help features and technical support, 26–27
    versus Internet service providers (ISPs), 22
    Mac OS Resource Center, 25–26
    message boards, 26
    publishing Web sites on, 72–73
    setting Parental Controls, 23–24
    toll-free phone numbers, 27
    turning off advertisements and unsolicited e-mails, 22–23, *23*
Apple Desktop Bus (ADB) ports, 114, 136–137
Apple menu, **195–198**
    Apple menu alias on Desktop, 198
    customizing, 195–197, *196*
    Favorites feature, 200
    Kaleidoscope Schemes submenu, 274
    Recent Applications and Recent Documents features, 198, *198*
    using aliases in, 197
Apple Technical Information Library (TIL), 49–50, 192
AppleWorks, **2–15**. *See also* software
    cards, **13–15**
        converting to black-and-white, 14–15, *14*
        creating, **13**
        Deb's Birthday Card Template, 13
    certificates, **10–13**
        Bob's Certificate Template, 10–11
        creating with Mail Merge feature, **10–12**, *12*
        customizing, 12–13
        templates for, 10–12
    versus ClarisWorks, 2
    coloring books, **7–10**
        coloring pictures on-screen, 9

converting Drawing documents to Painting documents, 9
creating coloring book pages, **7–8**, *8*, *9*
Deb's Coloring Book Template, 7–8, 14–15
saving graphics in PICT format, 10
creating icons, **167–168**, *167*
graphics
creating JPEG files, 74–75
opening graphics files, 68, 74
headers, 4
letterhead, **3–7**
adding current date, 6
adding graphics, 5–6, *5*
Bob's Letterhead Template, 6
customizing, 3–5, *4*
Deb's Letterhead Template, 3
finding, 5
Mail Merge feature and, 6–7
moving text, 6
opening AppleWorks Stationery folder, 5
saving, 5
section markers, 4
stationery, **3**
templates
Bob's Certificate Template, 10–11
Bob's Letterhead Template, 6
for certificates, 10–12
Deb's Birthday Card Template, 13
Deb's Coloring Book Template, 7–8, 14–15
Deb's Letterhead Template, 3
defined, **3**
appointment calendars. *See* Consultant program; ReminderPro
ASCII files, 92
Ask Jeeves search engine, 25
Aspyr Media Web site, 348
Asymmetrical Digital Subscriber Line (ADSL) modems, 129–130, 131
@Soft Web site, 285
attachments. *See also* e-mail
attaching graphics files to e-mail, 77
exchanging files with PCs via e-mail attachments, 91–93
auctions on the Internet, 53
audio CD music. *See also* sound
playing, 170
playing without the CD, 171
audio ports, 110, 111–113, *112*, 117
awards. *See* certificates

B

background pictures. *See* Desktop
backing up, **17**, **125–127**, **200–205**
to backup storage Web sites, 127, 204–205

to CD-R (CD-Recordable) and CD-RW (CD-Rewritable) drives, 126
creating and rotating backup sets, 204
Dantz Certified Internet Backup Site (IBS), 204–205
Dantz Retrospect Express software, 126–127, 202
Drag'nBack utility, 239–240
DriveSavers service, 201
hardware for, 201–202
importance of, 175, 200–201
installing software and, 209
Quicken data files, 17
to SuperDisk drives, 125–126
what to backup, 202–203
to Zip drives, 126
Baker Street Assistant, 59
Balloon Help Easter eggs, 160, *160*
banking online with Quicken, 18
Bare Bones Software Web site, 307
Bartender's Friend database, 350–352, *351*, *352*
battle strategy game, 337–340, *339*
BBEdit Lite utility, 303–307, *305*, *306*
beep sounds
creating, **33–34**
spoken alert messages, 145–146
YO! beep sound randomizer, 361–362, *362*
Bender, Tom, 324
Berntson, Glenn, 315
Beusekom, Wim von, 337
bill paying with Quicken, 18
birthday cards. *See* cards
Blockbuster Video stores, 148
Blom, Alco, 298
Bob's Certificate Template, 10–11
Bob's Letterhead Template, 6
book shopping on the Internet, 52
bookmark files on book's CD-ROM, 47
book's CD-ROM. *See* CD-ROM (book's)
BottomDollar Web site, 54–55
Bridge game, 329–332, *330*
Brightness settings in Monitors & Sound control panel, 155
Brown, Tom, 266
Bubble Trouble game, 332–335, *334*
Bungie Software Web site, 340
business utilities, **300–324**. *See also* Consultant program; Quicken software
Address Book, 300–303, *301*
BBEdit Lite, 303–307, *305*, *306*
Idea Keeper, 313–315, *314*
ReminderPro, 315–318, *317*, *318*
Tex-Edit Plus, 319–324, *322*, *323*
buying. *See* shopping on the Internet

C

cable modems, 130–131
calendar programs. *See* Consultant program;
    ReminderPro
calling technical support, 191–192, 194
cameras. *See* digital cameras; photographs
cards, **13–15**. *See also* AppleWorks
    converting to black-and-white, 14–15, *14*
    creating, **13**
    Deb's Birthday Card Template, 13
Cassidy & Greene Web site, 229
categories in Quicken, 88
CatFinder utility, 222–224
CD music. *See also* sound
    playing, 170
    playing without the CD, 171
CD quality sound, 32
CD shopping on the Internet, 52
CD-ROM (book's), **208–362**. *See also* freeware; software
    bookmark files, 47
    business utilities, **300–324**
        Address Book, 300–303, *301*
        BBEdit Lite, 303–307, *305, 306*
        Idea Keeper, 313–315, *314*
        ReminderPro, 315–318, *317, 318*
        Tex-Edit Plus, 319–324, *322, 323*
    Conflict Catcher utility, 182–186, *183*, 226–229, *228*
    games, **326–348**
        3D-Klondike, 326–329, *327, 328*
        Alan's Euchre, 329–332, *330*
        Bubble Trouble, 332–335, *334*
        MacChess, 335–337, *336*
        Myth II, 337–340, *339*
        Pac the Man, 341–343, *341, 342*
        Slithereens, 343–345, *344, 345*
        Tomb Raider II, 346–348
    GraphicConverter software, **68, 75–77, 268–271**
        cost of, 271
        creating JPEG files, 75–77, *76*
        cropping graphics, 269–270, *270*
        Help, 271
        opening graphics files, 68
        supported file formats, 268–269
        Web site, 271
    graphics software and graphics
        GraphicConverter, 68, 75–77, *76*, 268–271, *270*
        Icon Tools, 271–273, *272*
        Kaleidoscope, 273–276, *275*
        Planet Earth animated graphic, 276–278, *277*
    icons, 167, 169
    Internet utilities, **288–298**
        AlwaysONline, 288–290, *289*
        Download Deputy, 290–292, *291*
        ircle, 292–294, *293*

        Tex-Edit Plus, 319–324, *322, 323*
        textSOAP, 295–296, *296*
        URL Manager Pro, 297–298
    miscellaneous programs, **350–362**
        Bartender's Friend database, 350–352, *351, 352*
        Relax utility, 352–353
        Uli's Moose, 353–356, *355*
        UpdateAgent Online, 356–359, *357, 358*
        USB Overdrive, 359–360, *360*
        YO! beep sound randomizer, 361–362, *362*
    paying for shareware, 209–210
    sound utilities, **280–286, 352–353, 361–362**
        Agent Audio, 280–283, *281*
        MacAMP Lite, 283–285, *284*
        Relax, 352–353
        SoundMachine, 285–286
        YO! beep sound randomizer, 361–362, *362*
    Stuffit archives, 208–209
    utilities, **212–266**
        ACTION Files, 215–217, *216*, 233
        ACTION GoMac, 212–215, *213, 215*
        Aladdin DropStuff, 218–220
        Aladdin StuffIt Expander, 220–222, 266
        CatFinder, 222–224
        CMTools, 224–226, *225*
        Conflict Catcher, 182–186, *183*, 226–229, *228*
        CopyPaste, 229–232, *230, 231*
        Default Folder, 232–234, *234*
        defined, **212**
        Desktop Resetter, 235–236
        Disk First Aid, 188–190, *189*
        DiskTracker, 236–239, *237, 238*
        Drag'nBack, 239–240
        EZNote, 241–243, *242*
        File Buddy, 243–248, *245, 246, 247*
        FinderPop, 248–250, *248, 249*
        HelpLess, 250–252
        QuicKeys, 252–254
        Snitch, 255–257, *255, 256*
        TechTool, 259–262, *260*
        T-Minus Ten, 257–259
        TypeIt4Me, 262–265, *263*
        ZipIt, 265–266
    viruses and, 208
CD-ROM drive performance enhancement, 150–152, *151*
CD-ROM recorders
    backing up to, 126
    exchanging files with Macintosh computers via, 121
    for Macintosh computers, 115, 136
CE Software Web site, 254
certificates, **10–13**. *See also* AppleWorks
    Bob's Certificate Template, 10–11
    creating with Mail Merge feature, **10–12**, *12*
    customizing, 12–13
    templates for, 10–12

Certified Internet Backup Site (IBS), 204–205
cheat codes in Nanosaur game, 29–30
chess game, 335–337, *336*
children. *See* EdView Internet Safety Kit; games
Chronos Software Web site, 312
ClarisWorks, 2, 106
cleaning mouse, 190–191
clipboards, CopyPaste utility, 229–232, *230*, *231*
clipping services, 44–45
Clixsounds
    Agent Audio utility, 280–283, *281*
    Web site, 283, 362
    YO! beep sound randomizer, 361–362, *362*
CMTools utility, 224–226, *225*
color
    color options for start pages, 43
    coloring pictures on-screen, 9
    converting cards to black-and-white, 14–15, *14*
    in Monitors & Sound control panel
        Color Depth settings, 152–153
        ColorSync settings, 155–156, *156*
coloring books, **7–10**. *See also* AppleWorks
    coloring pictures on-screen, 9
    converting Drawing documents to Painting
        documents, 9
    creating coloring book pages, **7–8**, *8*, *9*
    Deb's Coloring Book Template, 7–8, 14–15
    saving graphics in PICT format, 10
companion CD-ROM. *See* CD-ROM (book's)
comparison shopping services (ShopBots), 54–55
computer book shopping on the Internet, 52
ComputerWare stores, 51
conflicts
    Conflict Catcher utility, 182–186, *183*, 226–229, *228*
    between extensions and control panels, 179–181
connecting USB devices, 114–115
connectors. *See also* ports
    3.5 connectors, 113, 117
    miniplug connectors, 112–113, *112*
Connectrix software. *See* Virtual Game Station; Virtual
    PC
Consultant program, **95–104**, **307–312**. *See also*
    business utilities
    cost of, 96, 312
    creating, **99–102**, **309–310**
        appointments or tasks manually, 101–102,
            309–310, *310*
        appointments or tasks with Translate feature,
            99–101, *100*, 310
        contact entries, 99, 309
    defined, **95**, **307–308**
    deleting appointments, 310
    demo on book's CD-ROM, 95, 307–312
    Help, 96–97, *96*, 98, 311

importing data, 98
installing, 97, 308
linking appointments and contacts, 310
password-protecting files, 97
QuickTip feature, 98, 308
Speech feature, 102–103
starting, 97–98
synchronizing with Palm organizers, 103
templates, 311, *312*
viewing schedules or contacts without starting
    Consultant, 103, *103*, 311, *311*
Web site, 312
word processor, 103
contact managers. *See* Consultant program;
    ReminderPro
content of start pages, 42
context menus. *See also* menus
    CMTools utility and, 224–226, *225*
    FinderPop utility and, 248–250, *248*, *249*
Contrast settings in Monitors & Sound control panel,
    155
control panels. *See also* extensions
    Conflict Catcher utility, 182–186, *183*, 226–229, *228*
    control panel Easter eggs, 159–160
    Default Folder utility, 232–234, *234*
    extension/control panel conflicts, 179–181
    FinderPop utility, 248–250, *248*, *249*
    HelpLess utility, 250–252
    Monitors & Sound control panel, **152–156**
        Color Depth settings, 152–153
        ColorSync settings, 155–156, *156*
        Contrast and Brightness settings, 155
        Geometry settings, 155
        Resolution settings, 153–155, *153*, *154*
    reinstalling, 185
    Snitch utility, 255–257, *255*, *256*
    Speech control panel settings, 141, 142–143, 145–146
converting
    cards to black-and-white, 14–15, *14*
    Drawing documents to Painting documents, 9
copying icons between files, 168–169, *169*
CopyPaste utility, 229–232, *230*, *231*
cost
    of 3D-Klondike game, 329
    of ACTION Files utility, 217
    of ACTION GoMac utility, 215
    of Address Book utility, 303
    of Agent Audio utility, 283
    of Aladdin DropStuff utility, 220
    of Alan's Euchre game, 332
    of AlwaysONline utility, 290
    of Bartender's Friend database, 352
    of Bubble Trouble game, 335
    of CatFinder utility, 224

of Conflict Catcher, 229
of Consultant program, 96, 312
of CopyPaste utility, 232
of Default Folder utility, 234
of Desktop Resetter utility, 236
of DiskTracker utility, 239
of Download Deputy utility, 292
of Drag'nBack utility, 240
of EZNote utility, 243
of File Buddy utility, 248
of GraphicConverter utility, 271
of HelpLess utility, 252
of Icon Tools utility, 273
of Idea Keeper utility, 315
of ircle utility, 294
of Kaleidoscope utility, 276
of MacAMP Lite utility, 285
of Myth II game, 340
of Planet Earth animated graphic, 278
of QuicKeys utility, 254
of Relax utility, 353
of ReminderPro utility, 318
of Slithereens game, 345
of Snitch utility, 257
of SoundMachine utility, 286
of Tex-Edit Plus, 324
of textSOAP utility, 296
of T-Minus Ten utility, 259
of Tomb Raider II game, 348
of TypeIt4Me utility, 265
of UpdateAgent Online utility, 359
of URL Manager Pro utility, 298
of USB Overdrive utility, 360
of ZipIt utility, 266
crashes, **59**, **175–181**. *See also* troubleshooting
    extension/control panel conflicts, 179–181
    restarting after, 177–178, *178*
    Restore in Place command, 178–179
    Sherlock program and, 59
    troubleshooting, 175–177
creating
    aliases, 199
    appointments or tasks in Consultant, **99–102**
        manually, 101–102
        with Translate feature, 99–101, *100*
    backup sets, 204
    beep or alert sounds, 33–34
    business accounts in Quicken, 87, *87*
    cards, 13
    certificates, 10–12, *12*
    coloring book pages, 7–8, *8*, *9*
    in Consultant, **99–102**, **309–310**
        appointments or tasks manually, 101–102,
            309–310, *310*

appointments or tasks with Translate feature,
    99–101, *100*, 310
    contact entries, 99, 309
Desktop background pictures, 163
icons, 167–168, *167*
JPEG files
    with AppleWorks, 74–75
    with GraphicConverter, 75–77, *76*
Kaleidoscope schemes, 274–276
Quicken data files, 17
shortcuts to areas on America Online, 25
Web pages, 65–68, *66*, *67*
Web site links, 70, *70*
credit cards
    Quicken credit card, 21
    and shopping on the Internet, 54
Credit Report feature in Quicken, 21
cropping graphics, 269–270, *270*
current date in letterhead, 6
customizing
    Apple menu, 195–197, *196*
    certificates, 12–13
    letterhead, 3–5, *4*
    start pages, **41–46**
        color options, 43
        content, 42
        Excite page, 41, *41*
        layout, 42–43
        news section, 43–45, *44*
        NewsTracker Clipping Service, 44–45
        selecting start page, 46
        stock portfolio section, 45–46, *45*
CyberCable Web site, 226
Cyberian Outpost Web site, 51, 52

D

D'Amato, Nick, 236
Dantz Certified Internet Backup Site (IBS), 204–205
Dantz Retrospect Express backup software, 126–127,
    202
dates, current date in letterhead, 6
Deb's Birthday Card Template, 13
Deb's Coloring Book Template, 7–8, 14–15
Deb's Letterhead Template, 3
Default Folder utility, 232–234, *234*
Delete key, HelpLess utility and, 250–252
deleting appointments in Consultant, 310
demos. *See* CD-ROM (book's)
Desktop
    aliases on, 199, *199*
    Apple menu alias on, 198
    background pictures, **161–166**
        creating or finding, 163

installing on Mac OS 8.1, 165–166, *165*
installing on Mac OS 8.5 or 8.6, 164–165, *164*
overview of, 161, *162*
Desktop Resetter utility, 235–236
rebuilding Desktop files, 187–188
Detail room in Kai's Photo Soap SE, 37
determining Mac OS version, 55
device drivers, **115**
digital cameras. *See also* photographs
Logitech QuickCam cameras, 124
overview of, 121–122
versus scanners, 123
Digital Subscriber Line (DSL) modems, 129–130, 131
disabling. *See* turning off
disconnecting USB devices, 114–115
Disk Copy program, 150–152, *151*
Disk First Aid utility, 188–190, *189*
disks. *See* floppy disks; hard disk drives; Jaz drives;
SuperDisk drives; Zip drives
DiskTracker utility, 236–239, *237*, *238*
documentation. *See* Help
Download.com Web site, 209
Download Deputy utility, 290–292, *291*
downloading
Adobe PageMill software, 64
Baker Street Assistant, 59
Conflict Catcher, 229
Consultant documentation, 311
EdView Internet Safety Kit, 61
Kaleidoscope schemes, 274
Nanosaur game, 30
plug-ins for Sherlock program, 58–59
QuickTime software, 171
speech recognition software, 140–141
Drag'nBack utility, 239–240
Drawing documents, converting to Painting
documents, 9
drink database, 350–352, *351*, *352*
drivers, **115**
DriveSavers service, 201
DropStuff utility, 218–220
DSL (Digital Subscriber Line) modems, 129–130, 131

E

Earth animated graphic, 276–278, *277*
Easter eggs, **158–161**
About This Computer Easter eggs, 159
Balloon Help Easter eggs, 160, *160*
control panel Easter eggs, 159–160
defined, **158**
finding Macintosh Easter eggs, 161
Script Editor Easter egg, 161
eBay Web site, 53

EdView Internet Safety Kit (EISK), **60–63**. *See also*
Internet features
defined, **60–61**, *60*
downloading, 61
installing, 61–62
limitations of, 63
Smart Zone, 60, *60*, 62–63, *63*
viewing sites outside the Smart Zone, 62–63, *63*
eggs. *See* Easter eggs
EISK. *See* EdView Internet Safety Kit
electronic bill paying with Quicken, 18
e-mail
e-mailing graphics, **74–77**
attaching graphics files to e-mail, 77
creating JPEG files with AppleWorks, 74–75
creating JPEG files with GraphicConverter,
75–77, *76*
exchanging files
with Macintosh computers via e-mail, 119–120
with PCs via e-mail messages or attachments,
91–93
turning off unsolicited e-mails on America Online,
22–23, *23*
Emergency Handbook, 175
Emergency Records Organizer in Quicken, 18–20, *19*
emulation programs, **104–107, 146–149**
advantages of, 104–106, *105*
defined, **147**
Emulation Net Web site, 147, 149
finding, 147, 149
joysticks, game pads and, 148
Pete's Computer and Video Game Emulation Page,
149
shareware and freeware emulators, 149
SoftWindows versus Virtual PC, 106–107
SoftWindows and Virtual PC Web sites, 104
Virtual Game Station, 147–148
Windows games and, 105
enhancing CD-ROM drive performance with Disk Copy
program, 150–152, *151*
entering contact information in Consultant, 99, 309
Enterprise Software Web site, 240
environment sounds program, 352–353
Ethernet networks
Ethernet ports, 111, 115–116, *116*
exchanging files with Macintosh computers via,
118–119, 120
Ettore, Riccardo, 265
Euchre game, 329–332, *330*
Ewalt, Alan, 332
exchanging
Consultant data with Palm organizers, 103
files with Macintosh computers, **118–121**
via CD-ROM recorders, 121

via e-mail, 119–120
via Ethernet, 118–119, 120
via Zip, Jaz, SuperDisk, or Orb drives, 120
files with PCs, **90–95**
compatible file formats, 92
via disk, 93–95, *94*
via e-mail messages or attachments, 91–93
Excite Search shopping service, 54–55
Excite start page, 41, *41*
extended miniplug connectors, 112, *112*
extensions. *See also* control panels
Conflict Catcher utility, 182–186, *183*, 226–229, *228*
extension/control panel conflicts, 179–181
Extensions Manager, 81–82, *82*
HelpLess utility, 250–252
reinstalling, 185
external microphones, 31, 113
EZNote utility, 241–243, *242*

F

Favorites
on America Online, 25
in Apple menu, 200
FAXstf program, **80–84**
advantages and disadvantages, 81
defined, **80**
installing, 81–82, *82*
QuickNote feature, 84
receiving faxes, 84, *84*
sending faxes, 83–84
setting up, 82–83
56K modems, 128
File menu Get Info command, 255–257, *255*, *256*
files. *See also* folders
ACTION Files utility, 215–217, *216*, 233
Download Deputy utility, 290–292, *291*
exchanging with Macintosh computers, **118–121**
via CD-ROM recorders, 121
via e-mail, 119–120
via Ethernet, 118–119, 120
via Zip, Jaz, SuperDisk, or Orb drives, 120
exchanging with PCs, **90–95**
compatible file formats, 92
via disk, 93–95, *94*
via e-mail messages or attachments, 91–93
File Buddy utility, 243–248, *245*, *246*, *247*
file formats
graphics formats supported by
GraphicConverter, 268–269
sound formats supported by MacAMP Lite, 283
icons, **166–169**
on book's CD-ROM, 167, 169
copying between files, 168–169, *169*

creating, **167–168**, *167*
defined, **166**
Icon Tools utility, 271–273, *272*
installing on files, 168
Web sites for, 169
JPEG files, **74–77**
creating with AppleWorks, 74–75
creating with GraphicConverter, 75–77, *76*
Microsoft Office 98 files, 92
password-protecting Consultant files, 97
PICT format, 10
rebuilding Desktop files, 187–188
RTF files, 92
text or ASCII files, 92
TIFF files, 74, 92
financial software. *See* Quicken software
FinderPop utility, 248–250, *248*, *249*
finding
on America Online
Find on AOL feature, 24–25, *24*
Find It on the Web feature, 25
Desktop background pictures, 163
emulation programs, 147, 149
letterhead, 5
Macintosh Easter eggs, 161
the microphone, 31
ports, 110–111
with Sherlock program, **55–59**
Baker Street Assistant, 59
crashes or freezes, 59
defined, **55–56**
downloading plug-ins for, 58–59
searching documents, 56
Web searches, 56–59, *57*
tax deductions in Quicken, 21
floppy disks. *See also* hard disk drives; Jaz drives;
SuperDisk drives; Zip drives
exchanging files with PCs via, 93–95, *94*
for Macintosh computers, 115
folders. *See also* files
AppleWorks Stationery folder, 5
Default Folder utility, 232–234, *234*
Speakable Items folder, 141, 143, *144*
formatting hard disk drives, 189–190
Free Credit Report feature in Quicken, 21
Freeverse Software Web site, 329
freeware. *See also* CD-ROM (book's); software
Aladdin StuffIt Expander, 220–222, 266
BBEdit Lite utility, 303–307, *305*, *306*
CMTools utility, 224–226, *225*
FinderPop utility, 248–250, *248*, *249*
freeware emulation programs, 149
MacChess game, 335–337, *336*

Pac the Man game, 341–343, *341, 342*
TechTool utility, 259–262, *260*
Uli's Moose, 353–356, *355*
freezes. *See* troubleshooting

G

game pads, 148
games
    on book's CD-ROM, **326–348**
        3D-Klondike, 326–329, *327, 328*
        Alan's Euchre, 329–332, *330*
        Bubble Trouble, 332–335, *334*
        MacChess, 335–337, *336*
        Myth II, 337–340, *339*
        Pac the Man, 341–343, *341, 342*
        Slithereens, 343–345, *344, 345*
        Tomb Raider II, 346–348
    Nanosaur, **27–30**
        cheat codes, 29–30
        defined, **27–28**
        downloading, 30
        keyboard shortcuts, 28–29
        playing tips, 29
    PC emulators and, 105
    Virtual Game Station software, 147–148
Geometry settings in Monitors & Sound control panel,
    155
Get Info command, 255–257, *255, 256*
GoMac utility, 212–215, *213, 215*
graphics, **34–37**, **74–77**, **121–124**
    adding
        to letterhead, 5–6, *5*
        to Web pages, 68–69, *69*
    attaching graphics files to e-mail, 77
    Desktop background pictures, **161–166**
        creating or finding, 163
        installing on Mac OS 8.1, 165–166, *165*
        installing on Mac OS 8.5 or 8.6, 164–165, *164*
        overview of, 161, *162*
    digital cameras
        Logitech QuickCam cameras, 124
        overview of, 121–122
        versus scanners, 123
        software, 124
    GraphicConverter software, **68**, **75–77**, **268–271**
        cost of, 271
        creating JPEG files, 75–77, *76*
        cropping graphics, 269–270, *270*
        Help, 271
        opening graphics files, 68
        supported file formats, 268–269
        Web site, 271

graphics libraries
    clip art libraries, 8
    selecting graphics from, 5–6
icons, **166–169**
    on book's CD-ROM, 167, 169
    copying between files, 168–169, *169*
    creating, **167–168**, *167*
    defined, **166**
    Icon Tools utility, 271–273, *272*
    installing on files, 168
    Web sites for, 169
JPEG files, **74–77**
    creating with AppleWorks, 74–75
    creating with GraphicConverter, 75–77, *76*
Kai's Photo Soap SE, **34–37**
    defined, **34**
    Detail room, 37
    Help system, 36, *36*
    interface, 34–35, *35*
    learning to use, 35–36
    quitting, 35
    rooms, 35–37
    starting, 34–35, *35*
opening graphics files, 68, 74
PC-compatible file formats, 92
saving in PICT format, 10
scanners
    versus digital cameras, 123
    Macintosh scanners, 136
    overview of, 122–123
    software, 124
and software on book's CD-ROM, **268–278**
    GraphicConverter software, 68, 75–77, *76,*
        268–271, *270*
    Icon Tools, 271–273, *272*
    Kaleidoscope utility, 273–276, *275*
    Planet Earth animated graphic, 276–278, *277*
graphs in Quicken, 21

H

hard disk drives. *See also* backing up; floppy disks; Jaz
    drives; SuperDisk drives; Zip drives
    disconnecting, 115
    Disk First Aid utility, 188–190, *189*
    DiskTracker utility, 236–239, *237, 238*
    DriveSavers service, 201
    initializing, 189–190
    for Macintosh computers, 136
    Orb drives, 120
Hardman, Peter, 252

hardware. *See also* modems; ports; printers; software
  for backing up, 201–202
  using Macintosh hardware with iMacs and iBooks, 135–137
  Web sites, 50–52, 135, 137
Harris, Laurence, 248
headers in AppleWorks, 4
headphone ports, 111, 117, *117*
Help
  for Adobe PageMill, 71
  for America Online, 26–27
  Balloon Help Easter eggs, 160, *160*
  for Consultant, 96–97, *96*, 98, 311
  for GraphicConverter, 271
  for Kai's Photo Soap SE, 36, *36*
  for ports, 111
  for Quicken, 16–17
  for ReminderPro, 318
HelpLess utility, 250–252
hidden surprises. *See* Easter eggs
Holder, John V., 243
Home Inventory feature in Quicken, 21
HotBot search engine, 25
hotkeys. *See* keyboard shortcuts
hot-swapping USB devices, 114–115
HTML. *See* Adobe PageMill
hung computers. *See* troubleshooting

I

iBook computers. *See also* Macintosh computers; PCs
  connecting headphones, 117
  dos and don'ts, 186–187
  microphones for, 31
  rebuilding Desktop files, 187–188
  restarting, 177–178, *178*
  as Web servers, 71–72, 73
IBS (Internet Backup Site), 204–205
icons, **166–169**. *See also* graphics
  on book's CD-ROM, 167, 169
  copying between files, 168–169, *169*
  creating, **167–168**, *167*
  defined, **166**
  Icon Tools utility, 271–273, *272*
  installing on files, 168
  Web sites for, 169
Idea Keeper utility, 313–315, *314*
iMac computers. *See also* Macintosh computers; PCs
  dos and don'ts, 186–187
  iMac Channel Web site, 48
  iMac Web sites, 47–48
  iMacInTouch Web site, 47
  rebuilding Desktop files, 187–188
  restarting, 177–178, *178*
  as Web servers, 71–72, 73

importing data into Consultant, 98
information managers. *See* Consultant program; ReminderPro
initializing hard disk drives, 189–190
Insider Software Web site, 359
Install Relax utility, 352–353
installing
  backing up and, 209
  Consultant, 97, 308
  Desktop background pictures
    on Mac OS 8.1, 165–166, *165*
    on Mac OS 8.5 or 8.6, 164–165, *164*
  EdView Internet Safety Kit, 61–62
  FAXstf, 81–82, *82*
  icons on files, 168
Internal Modem (telephone line) ports, 111, 116, *116*
Internet Backup Site (IBS), 204–205
Internet features, **41–77**. *See also* Web sites
  Adobe PageMill software, **64–71**
    adding graphics, 68–69, *69*
    creating links, 70, *70*
    creating Web pages, **65–68**, *66*, *67*
    defined, **64**, *65*
    downloading, 64
    Help, 71
    viewing HTML code, 68
  customizing start pages, **41–46**
    color options, 43
    content, 42
    Excite page, 41, *41*
    layout, 42–43
    news section, 43–45, *44*
    NewsTracker Clipping Service, 44–45
    selecting start page, 46
    stock portfolio section, 45–46, *45*
  EdView Internet Safety Kit (EISK), **60–63**
    defined, **60–61**, *60*
    downloading, 61
    installing, 61–62
    limitations of, 63
    Smart Zone, 60, *60*
    viewing sites outside the Smart Zone, 62–63, *63*
  e-mailing graphics, **74–77**
    attaching graphics files to e-mail, 77
    creating JPEG files with AppleWorks, 74–75
    creating JPEG files with GraphicConverter, 75–77, *76*
  Sherlock search program, **55–59**
    Baker Street Assistant, 59
    crashes or freezes, 59
    defined, **55–56**
    downloading plug-ins for, 58–59
    searching documents, 56
    Web searches, 56–59, *57*

shopping sites, **50–55**
  books, 52
  CDs, 52
  comparison shopping services (ShopBots), 54–55
  computer books, 52
  credit cards and, 54
  Cyberian Outpost, 51, 52
  eBay, 53
  Lands End, 53
  Macintosh auctions, 53
  Macintosh hardware and software, 50–52
  music, 52
  online auctions, 53
  overview of, 50–51
  security and safety issues, 53–54
  Sharper Image, 53
Web publishing, **71–73**
  on America Online or Internet service providers, 72–73
  iMacs and iBooks as Web servers, 71–72, 73
Internet search engines, 25
Internet service providers (ISPs)
  versus America Online, 22
  publishing Web sites on, 72–73
Internet utilities, **288–298**. *See also* CD-ROM (book's)
  AlwaysONline, 288–290, *289*
  Download Deputy, 290–292, *291*
  ircle, 292–294, *293*
  Tex-Edit Plus, 319–324, *322, 323*
  textSOAP, 295–296, *296*
  URL Manager Pro, 297–298
Inventory feature in Quicken, 21
investment tracking feature in Quicken, 21
investments
  stock portfolio section of start pages, 45–46, *45*
  Stock Portfolio Tracking feature in Quicken, 21
ircle utility, 292–294, *293*
ISDN modems, 128–129, 131
ISPs. *See* Internet service providers

J

Jaz drives. *See also* floppy disks; hard disk drives
  exchanging files with Macintosh computers via, 120
  exchanging files with PCs via, 93–95, *94*
  for Macintosh computers, 136
Jim Smith Web site, 303
joke speech recognition demo, 141–142, *142*
Jones, Mitch, 257
joysticks, 148
JPEG files, **74–77**. *See also* graphics
  creating with AppleWorks, 74–75
  creating with GraphicConverter, 75–77, *76*

K

Kai's Photo Soap SE, **34–37**. *See also* graphs; photographs
  defined, **34**
  Detail room, 37
  Help system, 36, *36*
  interface, 34–35, *35*
  learning to use, 35–36
  quitting, 35
  rooms, 35–37
  starting, 34–35, *35*
Kaleidoscope utility, 273–276, *275*
Kennedy, Rod, 286
keyboard shortcuts
  in Alan's Euchre game, 331
  in BBEdit, 305–306
  in Nanosaur game, 28–29
  QuicKeys utility, 252–254
  in Tex-Edit Plus, 320–322
  T-Minus Ten utility, 257–259
  in Tomb Raider II, 347
keyboards
  HelpLess utility, 250–252
  for Macintosh computers, 136
  replacing, 115
  USB keyboards, 115
KidPix, using AppleWorks graphics in, 10
kids. *See* EdView Internet Safety Kit; games
Klondike game, 326–329, *327, 328*
Krenek, Mark, 259
Kusterer, M. Uli, 356

L

Lands End Web site, 53
Landweber, Greg, 276
layout of start pages, 42–43
learning Kai's Photo Soap SE, 35–36
legacy hardware
  other Macintosh hardware, 136–137
  printers, 135–136
Lemke Software, 271
letterhead, **3–7**. *See also* AppleWorks
  adding current date, 6
  adding graphics, 5–6, *5*
  Bob's Letterhead Template, 6
  customizing, 3–5, *4*
  Deb's Letterhead Template, 3
  finding, 5
  Mail Merge feature and, 6–7
  moving text, 6
  opening AppleWorks Stationery folder, 5
  saving, 5
libraries. *See* graphics

links in Web pages, 70, *70*
Logitech QuickCam cameras, 124
Lunar Software Web site, 278

M

Mac OS Resource Center on America Online, 25–26
MacAMP Lite utility, 283–285, *284*
MacChess game, 335–337, *336*
Macintosh computers. *See also* iBook computers; iMac
    computers; Microsoft Windows; PCs
    determining Mac OS version, 55
    Easter eggs, 161
    exchanging files with, **118–121**
        via CD-ROM recorders, 121
        via e-mail, 119–120
        via Ethernet, 118–119, 120
        via Zip, Jaz, SuperDisk, or Orb drives, 120
    hardware and software Web sites, 49, 50–52
    information Web sites, 48–50
    modems for, 136
    online auctions for, 53
    printers for, 135–136
    QuicKeys utility, 252–254
    retail stores, 51
    scanners for, 136
    SCSI, Printer, Modem, or ADB (Apple Desktop Bus)
        ports, 136–137
    USB devices and, 115
    using hardware for, 115, 135–137
    Web sites about Macintosh devices, 135, 137
Mail Merge feature
    creating certificates, 10–12, *12*
    creating mail merge documents, 6–7
manually creating appointments or tasks in
    Consultant, 101–102
memory (RAM), **131–134**
    advantages of adding, 134
    defined, **132**, *132*
    virtual memory, 133–134
menus
    Apple menu, **195–198**
        Apple menu alias on Desktop, 198
        customizing, 195–197, *196*
        Favorites feature, 200
        Kaleidoscope Schemes submenu, 274
        Recent Applications and Recent Documents
            features, 198, *198*
        using aliases in, 197
    context menus
        CMTools utility and, 224–226, *225*
        FinderPop utility and, 248–250, *248*, *249*
    File menu Get Info command, 255–257, *255*, *256*
message boards on America Online, 26

Micromat Web site, 262
microphones. *See also* sound; speech features
    external microphones, 31, 113
    microphone ports, 110, 111–113, *112*
    PlainTalk microphones, 112, 144
    and sound recording, 31
    speech recognition software and, 140, 144
Microsoft Office 98 files, 92
Microsoft Outlook Express, 93
Microsoft Windows. *See also* Macintosh computers;
    PCs
    emulation programs, **104–107**, **146–149**
        advantages of, 104–106, *105*
        defined, **147**
        Emulation Net Web site, 147, 149
        finding, 147, 149
        joysticks, game pads and, 148
        Pete's Computer and Video Game Emulation
            Page, 149
        shareware and freeware emulators, 149
        SoftWindows versus Virtual PC, 106–107
        SoftWindows and Virtual PC Web sites, 104
        Virtual Game Station, 147–148
        Windows games and, 105
    USB devices and, 115
Miller, Julian, 232
MindSpring Web site, 224
miniplug connectors, 112–113, *112*
mixed drink database, 350–352, *351*, *352*
modems, **128–131**. *See also* hardware
    56K modems, 128
    ADSL/DSL (Asymmetric Digital Subscriber Line)
        modems, 129–130, 131
    cable modems, 130–131
    Internal Modem (telephone line) ports, 111, 116, *116*
    ISDN modems, 128–129, 131
    Macintosh modems, 136
    Modem ports, 114, 136–137
    selecting, 131
    telephone jack splitters, 116
Monitors & Sound control panel, **152–156**. *See also*
    control panels
    Color Depth settings, 152–153
    ColorSync settings, 155–156, *156*
    Contrast and Brightness settings, 155
    Geometry settings, 155
    Resolution settings, 153–155, *153*, *154*
Montalcini, Alessandro Levi, 273, 360
Moose program, 353–356, *355*
mouse
    cleaning, 190–191
    for Macintosh computers, 136
    replacing, 115
moving text on letterhead, 6

multimedia. *See* graphics; sound
music, **52, 170–172**. *See also* sound
    music shopping on the Internet, 52
    playing audio CD music without the CD, 171
    playing audio CDs, 170
    playing with RealAudio or QuickTime software,
        171–172
Musse, Eric de la, 226
Myth II game, 337–340, *339*

N

Nanosaur game, **27–30**. *See also* games
    cheat codes, 29–30
    defined, **27–28**
    downloading, 30
    keyboard shortcuts, 28–29
    playing tips, 29
news section of start pages, 43–45, *44*
NewsTracker Clipping Service, 44–45
Nifty Neato Web site, 257

O

O'Connor, Turlough, 250
online auctions, 53
online banking and bill paying with Quicken, 18
online technical support, 192–193
Open dialog box
    ACTION Files utility and, 215–217, *216*, 233
    Default Folder utility and, 232–234, *234*
opening
    AppleWorks Stationery folder, 5
    graphics files, 68
optimizing CD-ROM drives, 150–152, *151*
Orb drives, 120
organizers. *See* Consultant program; ReminderPro
Outlook Express, 93

P

Pac the Man game, 341–343, *341, 342*
PageMill. *See* Adobe PageMill
Painting documents, converting Drawing documents to, 9
Palm organizers
    Macintosh computers and, 136
    synchronizing Consultant with, 103
Parental Controls on America Online, 23–24
password-protecting Consultant files, 97
Patwardhan, Manoj, 318
paying bills with Quicken, 18
paying for shareware, 209–210
PCs. *See also* Macintosh computers; Microsoft Windows
    emulation programs, **104–107, 146–149**
        advantages of, 104–106, *105*
        defined, **147**

        Emulation Net Web site, 147, 149
        finding, 147, 149
        joysticks and game pads, 148
        Pete's Computer and Video Game Emulation
            Page, 149
        shareware and freeware emulators, 149
        SoftWindows versus Virtual PC, 106–107
        SoftWindows and Virtual PC Web sites, 104
        Virtual Game Station, 147–148
        Windows games and, 105
    exchanging files with, **90–95**
        compatible file formats, 92
        via disk, 93–95, *94*
        via e-mail messages or attachments, 91–93
performance enhancement for CD-ROM drives,
    150–152, *151*
personal finances. *See* Quicken software
personal information managers. *See* Consultant
    program; ReminderPro
Pete's Computer and Video Game Emulation Page, 149
phones
    Internal Modem (telephone line) ports, 111, 116, *116*
    telephone jack splitters, 116
    toll-free numbers for America Online Help, 27
photographs, **34–37, 121–124**. *See also* graphics
    digital cameras
        Logitech QuickCam cameras, 124
        overview of, 121–122
        versus scanners, 123
        software, 124
    Kai's Photo Soap SE, **34–37**
        defined, **34**
        Detail room, 37
        Help system, 36, *36*
        interface, 34–35, *35*
        learning to use, 35–36
        quitting, 35
        rooms, 35–37
        starting, 34–35, *35*
    scanners
        versus digital cameras, 123
        Macintosh scanners, 136
        overview of, 122–123
        software, 124
PICT format, 10
PIMs. *See* Consultant program; ReminderPro
Pirri, Mark N., 239
PlainTalk microphones, 112, 144
Planet Earth animated graphic, 276–278, *277*
playing. *See also* sound
    audio CD music without the CD, 171
    audio CDs, 170
    music with RealAudio or QuickTime software,
        171–172

PlayStation emulator, 147–148
plug-ins for Sherlock program, 58–59
Plum Island Software Web site, 315
Portfolio Tracking feature in Quicken, 21
ports, **110–117**. *See also* connectors
    ADB (Apple Desktop Bus) ports, 114, 136–137
    audio ports, 110, 111–113, *112*, 117
    defined, **110**
    Ethernet ports, 111, 115–116, *116*
    finding, 110–111
    headphone ports, 111, 117, *117*
    Help, 111
    Internal Modem (telephone line) ports, 111, 116, *116*
    Modem ports, 114, 136–137
    Printer ports, 114, 136–137
    SCSI ports, 114, 136–137
    USB (Universal Serial Bus) ports
        defined, **111**, **114–115**, *114*
        hot-swapping USB devices, 114–115
        microphones and, 112
        USB Overdrive utility, 359–360, *360*
        USB printers, 135–136
posting messages to AOL message boards, 26
Power On Software
    ACTION Files utility, 215–217, *216*, 233
    ACTION GoMac utility, 212–215, *213*, *215*
    new software, 308
    Web site, 215, 217
PricePulse shopping service, 55
printers
    Printer ports, 114, 136–137
    using Macintosh printers, 135–136
printing System Profile information, 193–194
problems. *See* troubleshooting
publishing Web sites, **71–73**
    on America Online or Internet service providers,
       72–73
    iMacs and iBooks as Web servers, 71–72, 73
purchasing. *See* shopping on the Internet

Q

QuickCam cameras, 124
Quicken software, **15–21**, **85–90**. *See also* business
    utilities
    backing up data files, 17
    creating data files, 17
    Emergency Records Organizer, 18–20, *19*
    Free Credit Report feature, 21
    Help features, 16–17
    Home Inventory feature, 21
    MacInTax and, 86
    online banking and bill paying, 18
    overview of, 15–16

Quicken credit card, 21
QuickEntry program, 20
reports and graphs, 21
small business applications, **85–90**
    categories, 88
    creating business accounts, 87, *87*
    overview of, 85–86
    QuickReport feature, 89
    reports, 88, 89–90, *89*, *90*
    when to use Quicken, 86–87
    Stock Portfolio Tracking feature, 21
    Tax Deduction Finder, 21
QuicKeys utility, 252–254
QuickNote feature in FAXstf, 84
QuickTime software, 171–172
QuickTip feature in Consultant, 98, 308
quitting Kai's Photo Soap SE, 35

R

RAM. *See* memory
Rampell Software Web site, 290
reading documents aloud with SimpleText software, 146
RealAudio software, 171–172
rebuilding Desktop files, 187–188
receiving faxes, 84, *84*
Recent Applications and Recent Documents features in
    Apple menu, 198, *198*
recordable CD-ROMs
    backing up to, 126
    exchanging files with Macintosh computers via, 121
    for Macintosh computers, 115, 136
recording sounds, 31–33
Redpoint Software Web site, 252
reformatting hard disk drives, 189–190
Relax utility, 352–353
ReminderPro utility, 315–318, *317*, *318*
reports in Quicken, 21, 88, 89–90, *89*, *90*
resolution
    Desktop background pictures and, 163
    Resolution settings in Monitors & Sound control
       panel, 153–155, *153*, *154*
restarting iMacs and iBooks, 177–178, *178*
Restore in Place command, 178–179
retail stores for Macintosh hardware and software, 51
Retrospect Express backup software, 126–127, 202
Ric Ford's iMacInTouch site, 47
Riccisoft Web site, 273
Rich Text Format (RTF) files, 92
rooms in Kai's Photo Soap SE, 35–37
Rose, Arlo, 276
rotating backup sets, 204
RTF files, 92
running Disk First Aid, 188–190, *189*

S

safety of shopping on the Internet, 53–54
St. Clair Software Web site, 234
Save dialog box
 ACTION Files utility and, 215–217, *216*, 233
 Default Folder utility and, 232–234, *234*
saving
 graphics in PICT format, 10
 letterhead, 5
scanners. *See also* photographs
 versus digital cameras, 123
 Macintosh scanners, 136
 overview of, 122–123
 software, 124
scheduling software. *See* Consultant program;
 ReminderPro
screen resolution
 Desktop background pictures and, 163
 Resolution settings in Monitors & Sound control
  panel, 153–155, *153*, *154*
Script Editor Easter egg, 161
Script Software Web site, 232
SCSI ports, 114, 136–137
search engines, 25
searching. *See* finding
section markers in AppleWorks, 4
security of shopping on the Internet, 53–54
selecting
 modems, 131
 start pages, 46
sending faxes, 83–84
servers, iMacs and iBooks as Web servers, 71–72, 73
setting America Online Parental Controls, 23–24
setting up FAXstf, 82–83
shareware. *See also* CD-ROM (book's)
 paying for, 209–210
 shareware emulation programs, 149
sharing
 files with Macintosh computers, **118–121**
  via CD-ROM recorders, 121
  via e-mail, 119–120
  via Ethernet, 118–119, 120
  via Zip, Jaz, SuperDisk, or Orb drives, 120
 files with PCs, **90–95**
  compatible file formats, 92
  via disk, 93–95, *94*
  via e-mail messages or attachments, 91–93
Sharper Image Web site, 53
Sherlock search program, **55–59**. *See also* finding;
 Internet features
 Baker Street Assistant, 59
 crashes or freezes, 59
 defined, **55–56**

downloading plug-ins for, 58–59
searching documents, 56
Web searches, 56–59, *57*
shopping on the Internet, **50–55**
 books, 52
 CDs, 52
 comparison shopping services (ShopBots), 54–55
 computer books, 52
 credit cards and, 54
 Cyberian Outpost, 51, 52
 eBay, 53
 Lands End, 53
 Macintosh auctions, 53
 Macintosh hardware and software, 50–52
 music, 52
 online auctions, 53
 overview of, 50–51
 security and safety issues, 53–54
 Sharper Image, 53
shortcut keys. *See* keyboard shortcuts
shortcuts to areas on America Online, 25
Silesa Software Web site, 292
SimpleText software, 146
SkyTag Software Web site, 248
Slithereens game, 343–345, *344*, *345*
small business software. *See* business utilities; Quicken
 software
Smart Zone in EdView Internet Safety Kit, 60, *60*,
 62–63, *63*
Smith, Jim, 303
Snitch utility, 255–257, *255*, *256*
Soap software. *See* Kai's Photo Soap SE
software. *See also* AppleWorks; CD-ROM (book's);
 control panels; extensions; freeware
 Adobe PageMill software, **64–71**
  adding graphics to Web pages, 68–69, *69*
  creating links, 70, *70*
  creating Web pages, **65–68**, *66*, *67*
  defined, **64**, *65*
  downloading, 64
  Help, 71
  viewing HTML code, 68
 Dantz Retrospect Express backup software,
  126–127, 202
 Disk Copy program, 150–152, *151*
 EdView Internet Safety Kit (EISK), **60–63**
  defined, **60–61**, *60*
  downloading, 61
  installing, 61–62
  limitations of, 63
  Smart Zone, 60, *60*, 62–63, *63*
  viewing sites outside the Smart Zone, 62–63, *63*
 emulation programs, **104–107**, **146–149**
  advantages of, 104–106, *105*

defined, **147**
Emulation Net Web site, 147, 149
finding, 147, 149
joysticks and game pads, 148
Pete's Computer and Video Game Emulation
Page, 149
SoftWindows versus Virtual PC, 106–107
SoftWindows and Virtual PC Web sites, 104
Virtual Game Station, 147–148
Windows games and, 105
FAXstf program, **80–84**
advantages and disadvantages, 81
defined, **80**
installing, 81–82, *82*
QuickNote feature, 84
receiving faxes, 84, *84*
sending faxes, 83–84
setting up, 82–83
Kai's Photo Soap SE, **34–37**
defined, **34**
Detail room, 37
Help system, 36, *36*
interface, 34–35, *35*
learning to use, 35–36
quitting, 35
rooms, 35–37
starting, 34–35, *35*
KidPix, 10
Nanosaur game, **27–30**
cheat codes, 29–30
defined, **27–28**
downloading, 30
keyboard shortcuts, 28–29
playing tips, 29
QuickTime software, 171–172
RealAudio software, 171–172
for scanners and digital cameras, 124
Sherlock search program, **55–59**
Baker Street Assistant, 59
crashes or freezes, 59
defined, **55–56**
downloading plug-ins for, 58–59
searching documents, 56
Web searches, 56–59, *57*
SimpleText software, 146
software Web sites, 49, 50–52
speech recognition software, **140–144**
downloading, 140–141
microphones and, 140, 144
Speakable Items folder, 141, 143, *144*
Speech control panel settings, 141, 142–143
"Tell me a joke" demo, 141–142, *142*
using, 143–144, *144*
updating, 49, 356–359, *357, 358*

Software from Plum Island Web site, 315
Software Perspectives Web site, 353
SoftWindows program, **104–107**. *See also* emulation
programs
advantages of, 104–106, *105*
games and, 105
versus Virtual PC, 106–107
Web site, 104
solitaire game, 326–329, *327, 328*
Sony PlayStation emulator, 147–148
sound, **30–34**, **280–286**
audio ports, 110, 111–113, *112*, 117
CD quality sound, 32
creating beep or alert sounds, 33–34
finding the microphone, 31
microphones
external microphones, 31, 113
microphone ports, 110, 111–113, *112*
PlainTalk microphones, 112, 144
and sound recording, 31
speech recognition software and, 140, 144
music, **52**, **170–172**
music shopping on the Internet, 52
playing audio CD music without the CD, 171
playing audio CDs, 170
playing with RealAudio or QuickTime software,
171–172
recording sounds, 31–33
Sound Input and Sound Output ports, 110, 111–113,
112
utilities on book's CD-ROM, **280–286**, **352–353**,
361–362
Agent Audio, 280–283, *281*
MacAMP Lite, 283–285, *284*
Relax, 352–353
SoundMachine, 285–286
YO! beep sound randomizer, 361–362, *362*
Speakable Items folder, 141, 143, *144*
speaker ports, 110, 111–113, *112*
speech features. *See also* microphones
in Consultant, 102–103
reading documents aloud with SimpleText software,
146
Speech control panel settings, 141, 142–143,
145–146
spoken alert messages, 145–146
speech recognition software, **140–144**
downloading, 140–141
microphones and, 140, 144
Speakable Items folder, 141, 143, *144*
Speech control panel settings, 141, 142–143
"Tell me a joke" demo, 141–142, *142*
using, 143–144, *144*

speeding up CD-ROM drives with Disk Copy program, 150–152, *151*
splitters for telephone jacks, 116
spoken alert messages, 145–146
start pages, **41–46**. *See also* Internet features
    color options, 43
    customizing content, 42
    customizing layout, 42–43
    Excite page, 41, *41*
    news section, 43–45, *44*
    NewsTracker Clipping Service, 44–45
    selecting, 46
    stock portfolio section, 45–46, *45*
starting
    Consultant, 97–98
    Kai's Photo Soap SE, 34–35, *35*
startup conflicts, 179–181
stationery in AppleWorks, **3**
stereo miniplug connectors, 112, *112*
stocks
    stock portfolio section of start pages, 45–46, *45*
    Stock Portfolio Tracking feature in Quicken, 21
stores for Macintosh hardware and software, 51
strategy game, 337–340, *339*
StuffIt Expander, 220–222, 266
SuperDisk drives. *See also* floppy disks; hard disk drives
    backing up to, 125–126
    exchanging files with Macintosh computers via, 120
    exchanging files with PCs via, 93–95, *94*
    for Macintosh computers, 115
surprises. *See* Easter eggs
synchronizing Consultant with Palm organizers, 103
system crashes. *See* troubleshooting
System Profile information, 193–194

T

talking to your iMac or iBook. *See* speech recognition software
tape drives, for Macintosh computers, 136
tasks. *See* Consultant program; ReminderPro
Tax Deduction Finder in Quicken, 21
tax software, 86
technical support. *See also* troubleshooting
    for America Online, 26–27
    for iMacs and iBooks, **191–194**
        calling, 191–192, 194
        online support, 192–193
        printing System Profile information, 193–194
        Technical Information Library (TIL), 49–50, 192
TechTool utility, 259–262, *260*
telephones
    Internal Modem (telephone line) ports, 111, 116, *116*
    telephone jack splitters, 116
    toll-free numbers for America Online Help, 27

"Tell me a joke" demo, 141–142, *142*
templates. *See also* AppleWorks
    Bob's Certificate Template, 10–11
    Bob's Letterhead Template, 6
    for certificates, 10–12
    in Consultant, 311, *312*
    Deb's Birthday Card Template, 13
    Deb's Coloring Book Template, 7–8, 14–15
    Deb's Letterhead Template, 3
    defined, **3**
text files, 92
text utilities. *See also* AppleWorks; word processors
    BBEdit Lite, 303–307, *305, 306*
    Idea Keeper, 313–315, *314*
    Tex-Edit Plus, 319–324, *322, 323*
    textSOAP utility, 295–296, *296*
    word processors versus text editors, 303
3D-Klondike game, 326–329, *327, 328*
3.5 connectors, 113, 117
TIFF files, 74, 92
Tijdgat, Onno, 294
TIL (Technical Information Library), 49–50, 192
T-Minus Ten utility, 257–259
To Do lists. *See* Consultant program; ReminderPro
toll-free phone numbers for America Online Help, 27
Tomb Raider II game, 346–348
trackballs, 115
Translate feature in Consultant, 99–101, *100*
troubleshooting, 59, **174–186**. *See also* technical support and backing up, 175
    with Conflict Catcher utility, 182–186, *183*, 226–229, *228*
    crashes, freezes, and hung computers, **59, 175–181**
        extension/control panel conflicts and, 179–181
        restarting after, 177–178, *178*
        Restore in Place command, 178–179
        Sherlock program and, 59
        troubleshooting, 175–177
    overview of, 174–175
    restarting iMacs and iBooks, 177–178, *178*
    with Restore in Place command, 178–179
    startup conflicts, 179–181
    Troubleshooting or Emergency Handbook, 175
Turner, Keith, 224
turning off America Online advertisements and unsolicited e-mails, 22–23, *23*
TypeIt4Me utility, 262–265, *263*

U

Uli's Moose program, 353–356, *355*
University of Wisconsin-Madison Space Science and Engineering Center Web site, 277
Unmarked Software Web site, 296

unsolicited e-mails on America Online, 22–23, *23*
updating software
    UpdateAgent Online utility, 356–359, *357*, *358*
    VersionTracker Online and MacUpdate utilities, 49
URL Manager Pro utility, 297–298
USB (Universal Serial Bus) ports. *See also* ports
    defined, **111**, **114–115**, *114*
    hot-swapping USB devices, 114–115
    microphones and, 112
    USB Overdrive utility, 359–360, *360*
    USB printers, 135–136
utilities, **212–266**, **350–362**. *See also* CD-ROM (book's)
    ACTION Files, 215–217, *216*, 233
    ACTION GoMac, 212–215, *213*, *215*
    Aladdin DropStuff, 218–220
    Aladdin StuffIt Expander, 220–222, 266
    Bartender's Friend database, 350–352, *351*, *352*
    CatFinder, 222–224
    CMTools, 224–226, *225*
    Conflict Catcher, 182–186, *183*, 226–229, *228*
    CopyPaste, 229–232, *230*, *231*
    Default Folder, 232–234, *234*
    defined, **212**
    Desktop Resetter, 235–236
    Disk First Aid, 188–190, *189*
    DiskTracker, 236–239, *237*, *238*
    Drag'nBack, 239–240
    EZNote, 241–243, *242*
    File Buddy, 243–248, *245*, *246*, *247*
    FinderPop, 248–250, *248*, *249*
    HelpLess, 250–252
    QuicKeys, 252–254
    Relax utility, 352–353
    Snitch, 255–257, *255*, *256*
    TechTool, 259–262, *260*
    T-Minus Ten, 257–259
    TypeIt4Me, 262–265, *263*
    Uli's Moose, 353–356, *355*
    UpdateAgent Online, 356–359, *357*, *358*
    USB Overdrive, 359–360, *360*
    YO! beep sound randomizer, 361–362, *362*
    ZipIt, 265–266

V

version of Mac OS, determining, 55
VersionTracker Online Web site, 49
viewing
    HTML code in Adobe PageMill software, 68
    schedules or contacts without starting Consultant,
        103, *103*, 311, *311*
    Web sites outside EdView Internet Safety Kit Smart
        Zone, 62–63, *63*
Virtual Game Station software, 147–148

virtual memory, 133–134
Virtual PC program, **104–107**. *See also* emulation
    programs
    advantages of, 104–106, *105*
    games and, 105
    versus SoftWindows, 106–107
    Web site, 104
viruses, 208
voice recognition software. *See* speech recognition
    software
volume control for headphones, 117

W

Web pages. *See* Adobe PageMill software
Web servers, iMacs and iBooks as, 71–72, 73
Web sites, **46–50**. *See also* Internet features
    ACTION Files, 217
    ACTION GoMac, 215
    Aladdin DropStuff, 220
    Aladdin StuffIt Expander, 222
    Alan's Euchre, 332
    Ambrosia Software, 335, 345
    America Online Find It on the Web feature, 25
    Apple Technical Information Library (TIL), 49–50,
        192
    for Apple technical support, 192–193
    Aspyr Media, 348
    @Soft, 285
    backup storage sites, 127, 204–205
    Bare Bones Software, 307
    bookmark files on book's CD-ROM, 47
    Bubble Trouble game, 335
    Bungie Software, 340
    Cassidy & Greene, 229
    CatFinder, 224
    CE Software, 254
    chess sites, 336
    Chronos Software, 312
    Clixsounds, 283, 362
    CMTools, 226
    Conflict Catcher, 229
    Consultant program, 312
    CopyPaste, 232
    CyberCable, 226
    Cyberian Outpost, 51, 52
    Desktop Resetter, 236
    Download.com, 209
    eBay, 53
    Emulation Net site, 147, 149
    Enterprise Software, 240
    EZNote, 243
    FinderPop, 250
    Freeverse Software, 329

GraphicConverter software, 271
hardware sites, 50–52, 135, 137
iMac Channel, 48
iMac sites, 47–48
Insider Software, 359
ircle utility, 294
Jim Smith, 303
joysticks and game pads, 148
Kaleidoscope utility, 276
Lands End, 53
Logitech, 124
Lunar Software, 278
about Macintosh devices, 135, 137
Macintosh hardware and software sites, 49, 50–52
Macintosh icons, 169
Macintosh information sites, 48–50
Micromat, 262
MindSpring, 224
Nanosaur game, 30
Nifty Neato, 257
PlayStation games, 148
Power On Software, 215, 217
publishing, **71–73**
    on America Online or Internet service providers, 72–73
    iMacs and iBooks as Web servers, 71–72, 73
Rampell Software, 290
Redpoint Software, 252
Ric Ford's iMacInTouch site, 47
Riccisoft, 273
St. Clair Software, 234
Script Software, 232
search engines, 25
Sharper Image, 53
Sherlock searches, 56–59, *57*

Silesa Software, 292
SkyTag Software, 248
Software from Plum Island, 315
Software Perspectives, 353
software sites, 49, 50–52
SoftWindows, 104
University of Wisconsin-Madison Space Science and Engineering Center, 277
Unmarked Software, 296
URL Manager Pro, 298
USB Overdrive, 360
VersionTracker Online, 49
Virtual Game Station, 148
Virtual PC, 104
WebRing sites, 48
Wegner, Sebastian, 343
Windows. *See* Microsoft Windows
word processors. *See also* text utilities
    in Consultant, 103
    versus text editors, 303

Y

Yahoo! Shopping service, 55
YO! beep sound randomizer, 361–362, *362*

Z

Zimmerman, Anthony, 352
Zip drives. *See also* floppy disks; hard disk drives
    backing up to, 126
    exchanging files with Macintosh computers via, 120
    exchanging files with PCs via, 93–95, *94*
    for Macintosh computers, 115, 136
ZipIt utility, 265–266